Praise for *Missing Sarah*

Shortlisted for the 2003 Governor General's Literary Award
for Non-Fiction
Winner of the 2004 VanCity Prize for best book
pertaining to women's issues by a B.C. author
Winner of the 2004 George Ryga Award
for social awareness in B.C. publishing
Honourable mention for the 2004 Vancouver Book Award

"A compelling read ... *Missing Sarah* is an honest appraisal of what
went wrong. It unfolds ... with richness and finely crafted detail.
Settle in, turn off the phone and have a box of tissues beside you,
because this book deserves to be read in one sitting."

—*National Post*

"She brings her sister to life ... Never is it as brutal as the subtext, but
its hammerlike impact is never diminished. And, through it, Sarah
speaks directly to the reader."

—*The Globe and Mail*

"A compassionate but chilling story..."

—*Montreal Mirror*

"A powerful book ... [It] documents with painstaking care Sarah's
gradual descent into a life of drug addiction and street prostitution."

—*The Vancouver Sun*

"A stirring memoir ... poignant..."

—*Winnipeg Free Press*

"More than just a personal reminiscence, *Missing Sarah* earnestly examines the whole issue of the sex trade and its workers … riveting reading."

—*Edmonton Journal*

"A gripping memoir…"

—Canadian Press

"*Missing Sarah* is haunting … I hate to cry, and cry I did, reading *Missing Sarah* … Thank you, Maggie de Vries, for bringing this story to light. For making the news headlines from far across the country a little more real. For writing this book and introducing us to Sarah."

—*The Intelligencer* (Belleville, ON)

"A powerful evocation … compelling … hauntingly honest…"

—*GLV*

"Sensitive, soul-searching, heart-wrenching … *Missing Sarah* demands our attention."

—*Daily News* (Kamloops, BC)

"This is a sad and tough story. It puts a face, a family face, on the sex worker, and it calls for different treatment of those involved in the trade."

—*Red Deer Advocate*

PENGUIN

MISSING SARAH

MAGGIE DE VRIES is a writer, editor, teacher and the award winning author of four children's books, including *Chance and the Butterfly*, a B.C. Book Prize Honour Book and OLA Best Bet; *How Sleep Found Tabitha*; *Once Upon a Golden Apple*, which she co-wrote with Jean Little; and, most recently, *Tale of a Great White Fish, A Sturgeon Story*, which won the 2007 SPCA Henry Bergh Children's Book Award and the Christie Harris Illustrated Children's Literature Prize. De Vries remains a regular commentator on the Pickton tragedy and travels the country giving talks about issues affecting women in sex work. She lives in Vancouver.

Also by Maggie de Vries

Chance and the Butterfly

How Sleep Found Tabitha

Once Upon a Golden Apple

MISSING SARAH

a memoir of loss

MAGGIE DE VRIES

A portion of the author's royalties from the sales of *Missing Sarah*
will be donated to PACE Society (Prostitution, Alternatives, Couseling and Education),
an outreach organization in Vancouver's Downtown Eastside

PENGUIN

an imprint of Penguin Canada Books Inc., a Penguin Random House Company

Published by the Penguin Group
Penguin Canada Books Inc., 320 Front Street West, Suite 1400, Toronto, Ontario M5V 3B6, Canada

Penguin Group (USA) LLC, 375 Hudson Street, New York, New York 10014, U.S.A.
Penguin Books Ltd, 80 Strand, London WC2R 0RL, England
Penguin Ireland, 25 St Stephen's Green, Dublin 2, Ireland (a division of Penguin Books Ltd)
Penguin Group (Australia), 707 Collins Street, Melbourne, Victoria 3008, Australia
(a division of Pearson Australia Group Pty Ltd)
Penguin Books India Pvt Ltd, 11 Community Centre, Panchsheel Park, New Delhi – 110 017, India
Penguin Group (NZ), 67 Apollo Drive, Rosedale, Auckland 0632, New Zealand
(a division of Pearson New Zealand Ltd)
Penguin Books (South Africa) (Pty) Ltd, 24 Sturdee Avenue, Rosebank, Johannesburg 2196, South Africa

Penguin Books Ltd, Registered Offices: 80 Strand, London WC2R 0RL, England

First published in Penguin Canada hardcover by Penguin Canada Books Inc., 2003
Published in Penguin Canada paperback by Penguin Canada Books Inc., 2004
Published in this edition, 2008

7 8 9 10 (OPM)

Copyright © Maggie de Vries, 2003, 2008

Editor: Cynthia Good

All art and photographs in the book are courtesy of Maggie de Vries, except for page vii (by perission of
Daniel Gautreau) and the final photograph in the insert (by permission of Graid Hodge/*The Vancouver Sun*).

Manufactured in the U.S.A.

ISBN: 978-0-14-317044-0

Library and Archives Canada Cataloguing in Publication data available upon request.

Visit the Penguin Canada website at **www.penguin.ca**

Special and corporate bulk purchase rates available;
please see **www.penguin.ca/corporatesales** or call 1-800-810-3104.

To sex workers everywhere,
in memory of Sarah Jean de Vries

If you could look inside my mind,
Would you like the woman you find?
Would you understand me?
Would you want to love me?

Look deep into my windows,
Past the mass hysteria of confusion.
Look deeper, look farther.
Now look, look harder,
Past the illusion, past the disillusion,
Past the hurt, anger and self-retribution.
If you can, what do you see?

Don't look if you don't care
For you won't ever find me there.
Like a child, beaten and raped,
I'll run and hide for my safety's sake.

True love, true hate, I know what they are
My defences are weak,
My wishful thinking leaves me wounded,
Down on my knees, begging, pleading.

Please, God, one, just one of them must really care for me.

—Sarah de Vries

CONTENTS

AUTHOR'S NOTE

WHILE I'VE USED REAL NAMES throughout the text, I've decided, for a variety of reasons, to give six people pseudonyms. Asterisks mark the first instance where their respective names appear—Anne in Chapter Two, Nick and Angela in Chapter Four, Charlie and Miranda in Chapter Six and Shauna in Chapter Nine.

PROLOGUE

M<small>Y SISTER SARAH</small> is one of Vancouver's missing women, but she isn't missing any more.

On Tuesday, August 6, 2002, after I finished teaching my children's literature class at the University of British Columbia, I dropped by my friend Kathryn's house. We drove down to a golf course on the river. In that peaceful, green setting, we ate grilled ham and cheese sandwiches and fat, spicy Mojo fries, with no idea that police officers were hanging around in my neighbourhood, waiting. I dropped Kathryn off and drove home. First thing, as always, I picked up the phone. There were six messages. The last one was the important one.

Constable Audrey Williams needed to talk to me today, she said. She left her pager number and her cell phone number. Dread washed over me, mixed with some kind of twisted hope. Was this *the* call? I called back. She was nearby, she and another constable. Could they drop by?

A second's silence, and then, "Yes," I replied. They were coming to tell me that they had found Sarah. I knew that. Five minutes, the constable said. In a daze, I reshelved a few of the children's books I had brought home from the university, talking myself into I wasn't sure what. What if they were coming for some other reason? Then I would have to climb back out of the dread and go on waiting.

I did not have to make that climb. "We've found Sarah's DNA at the farm," Constable Williams said as soon as she walked through my door.

Some sort of emotion shot through me, a numbness, a ringing in my head, but I had two virtual strangers in my apartment. I was hardly going to swoon or fall upon them weeping and gnashing my teeth. We sat in the living room and they shared more information. Sarah's DNA had been found on the property. It was not blood DNA. No charges would be laid in Sarah's case unless more evidence was found. Still, here they were, two police officers, bearers of bad tidings. The presence of Sarah's DNA at the Dominion Avenue site in Port Coquitlam—after seven murder charges and four cases of DNA without charges, eleven of the missing women already having been linked with that piece of property—confirmed what I already knew. Four years and four months earlier, in the wee hours of April 14, 1998, someone picked Sarah up on the corner of Princess Avenue and Hastings Street and drove her out to a farm in Port Coquitlam, an eastern suburb of Vancouver. There she was murdered.

Perhaps in the months and years to come the police will find more evidence—Sarah's blood or remains; perhaps they will lay charges. For me, though, the discovery of Sarah's DNA at that location is enough. I am no longer waiting for the phone to ring. I am no longer seeing a police cruiser in the neighbourhood and wondering if the officers are coming to talk to me. I am not wondering if maybe, just maybe, Sarah is out there, somewhere, alive. I am not driving along a country road and thinking, What if she's buried in that field or in those woods? I am face to face with the truth.

In the spring of 2002, soon after the search began, a reporter phoned me to inquire if the police had asked my family about Sarah's dental records. She mentioned an article in *The Province* earlier that week that talked about an expert at Simon Fraser University who can get reliable DNA from teeth.

Oh, I thought, they've got teeth.

I have had a number of such revelations during conversations with members of the press, the police, or while reading, watching or listening to the news. Oh, I think each time. And I wish that I could go and vomit. I wish that I could purge all that information and what it means. Bits of my guts should come flying out my mouth. Bleeding stigmata should appear on my skin. But none of that happens.

The horror of imagining that my sister's teeth are in a lab somewhere, which leads to the horror of imagining where they were before and how they got there, is marked only by a prickling in the back of my throat as I write these words. The reality comes in the ink flowing onto the page in the solitude of the crowded Swartz Bay/Tsawwassen ferry where I am writing this.

I am writing this book to make it real for myself, to gather all that has passed in the last four years and pin it to the page. I am getting to know Sarah better now that she is dead than I did when she was alive.

I am also writing this book to make it real for you, the reader. Many Vancouver women are missing. At least fifteen of them have been murdered. They are gone, but I want all of us to know them, to know what and who we have lost. If we can start to leave the gritty image of the sex worker behind and begin to see real people, real women, to look them in the eye and smile at them and want to know who they really are, I think that we can begin to make our world a better place for them and for us, for everyone.

For now, I will tell Sarah's story. She helps me to do that through her journals, which she kept for many years. Periodically throughout this book, she speaks for herself. *I'll try to begin,* she wrote in December 1995. *Just try to remember this is not a story with a plot. This is me, my thoughts, emotions, opinions, and just plain "Sarah" and situations I've found myself in.* Throughout her journals, she addresses a readership. When she wrote, she imagined readers.

She imagined you.

one

CHILDHOOD

S ARAH WAS AN ADORABLE ELEVEN-MONTH-OLD BABY when she came to us. She was the fourth and last child in our family. I'm the eldest, born in 1961. Peter is second, born in 1963. Mark is third, born in 1967 and adopted in 1968. And Sarah was last, born on May 12, 1969, and adopted in April 1970. Her birth mother had named her Sherry, but my parents changed her name to Sarah, a family name that sounds similar to Sherry. While Mark's birth mother was Dutch and Mark is blond and blue-eyed just like my Dutch father and my brother Peter, Sarah's parents were of mixed race—black, Aboriginal and Mexican Indian as well as white. To all appearances, Mark had been born into our family. Not so, Sarah.

Mum had always thought that she would like to have two biological children and then adopt. She discussed it with Dad and he agreed. Adoption seemed a responsible act, a way of opening up our family to others without adding to the earth's population. So the adoption process was begun.

Sarah came to our home for several visits before she moved in permanently. She had been in a foster home for a few weeks, and before that had lived with her birth mother on weekends and another family during the week when her mother was working. When Sarah was ten months old, her birth mother decided that she could no longer care for her and placed her for adoption. The woman who babysat her loved her dearly and asked to adopt her, but at that time the fact that she knew Sarah's birth mother was an insurmountable obstacle to the people at Child Welfare. Today, when adoptions in which the adoptive family maintains contact with the birth family are encouraged, that family connection would have been an advantage.

Mum and Dad first saw Sarah when they went to visit her in her foster home. Mum remembers Sarah being very sober that day, looking her prospective parents over carefully, almost as if she knew that these people might turn out to be important in her life. Given the amount of change that she had already experienced, it may well be that she had learned to consider newcomers with care. Sarah's first visit to our house was more cheerful. Mum took her down to the beach and Sarah loved it there. "She just had a ball," Mum says. "I would make little towers of driftwood and she would knock them down with great delight and roll around in the sand and thoroughly enjoy herself."

When you adopted a child in the late sixties or early seventies, the theory was that that child was to be looked upon as the same as a biological child; all ties to the birth family were cut, and the child was to see the adoptive parents as his or her true parents and they would see the child exactly as they would if he or she had been born to them. In the letter finalizing Sarah's adoption, the superintendent of Child Welfare wrote, "She has become for all purposes your child, and you have become her parents as if she had been born to you."

Over the past three decades it has become clear how wrong-headed (although well meaning) such a sentiment is. The love between an adopted child and adoptive parent is as great as that between a child and the birth parent, the bond as strong, but the unique experience of each adopted child needs to be acknowledged, the necessary support provided. It is traumatic for a child, even a child of eleven months, to have her whole world change completely, to be abandoned by everyone she has known. With open adoptions now, in the twenty-first century, such abrupt changes are avoided where possible. The notion that adoptive children miraculously morph into members of their new family also fails to take into account issues of race, ethnicity and culture, as well as the fact that each of us, no matter with whom we live or how little we know about our past, springs from generation after generation of ancestors back to the beginning of time.

We loved Sarah dearly and she loved us. But nothing can erase the fact that she had parents and grandparents and great-grandparents and great-great-grandparents of whom we could tell her almost nothing. We did know that her father was a musician, that her mother liked to skydive, and a little bit about the racial mix of her parents and grandparents. Like Sarah, her father was adopted.

Our family did what we knew how to do to help Sarah adjust, but I don't think that we had any real idea of what it was like for her. She was visibly different from us, and no guidance was given my parents with regard to that difference. Still, we welcomed her with great love. A woman I spoke to recently remembers me positively vibrating with excitement as I told my classmates that a baby girl was coming to live with us. I was so glad to hear that, because I do not remember the event at all—a sad fact.

My mother's older sister, Aunt Jean, remembers me saying, "I've decided not to have any children. They're too much trouble." Around the same time, when I was nine, I said to her, "You know, I like Mark and Sarah all right. I mean, I love them, of course. But it was certainly more peaceful when it was just me and Peter." It seems to me natural that my feelings about adopting a younger brother and sister were mixed, but overall I believe that I was happy to see our family grow.

A few months after Sarah came to us, Aunt Jean, who is the children's writer Jean Little and the one from whom Sarah takes her middle name, wrote a poem for Sarah. She included it in a little blue booklet with photos on every page.

Gift

What can I give you, Sarah,
Now that you are ours . . .
The shine of a snowflake, Sarah . . .
The fragrance of flowers . . .
Rainbows and rivers, Sarah . . .
Hopscotch and swings . . .
Songs that a Sarah sways to
When her mother sings . . .
Books to make friends with, Sarah,
Stories and rhymes . . .
A slide where a small girl, Sarah,
Laughs as she climbs . . .
Good food for you to eat, Sarah,
Enough and to spare . . .
Laughter, Sarah, every day,
To joy in, to share . . .

Tears?
Yes, there will be times, Sarah,
When you must weep
But may sorrow also give you
Courage to keep,
A faith that shall hold and heal you
As long as you live,
A oneness with all who hurt, Sarah,
And a self you can give . . .
Whether you plant a garden
Or paint or write or sew,
The magic of making something, Sarah,
I want you to know.

I give you a sister, Sarah,
To love you, to scold.
Always her hand will be there, Sarah,
For you to hold . . .
And here is a brother, Sarah.
Maybe you should have two.
Brothers are pests—and people
Who stand up for you.
These two need a little sister
To delight in and defend
And you need them—to beware of,
Bedevil and befriend.

Here is a subtler gift, Sarah,
Your place in our clan.
You're "ours" and we all are yours, Sarah,
Child and woman and man.
Whatever you do or don't, Sarah,
You're now within.
Whatever we are or aren't, Sarah,
We are your kin.
Oh, Sarah, you may feel wonder
At sunlight, at birds,
At the strength of your father, Sarah,
At the cadence of words . . .
Puns I'd give you . . . and April
Complete with a skipping rope . . .
And a friend to tell a secret . . .
And tomorrows . . . and hope . . .
And I want you never to feel, Sarah,
The slightest surprise
When you read her love for you, Sarah,
In your mother's eyes . . .

These gifts, though, are yours already.
I give you just my name
. . . And my world has been brighter, Sarah,
Since you came.

Each love gives its own light, Sarah,
Kindled and kept by two.
Some loves flicker and fail, Sarah;
Some shine a whole life through.

We have set ours alight for always.
It has a lovely sheen.
Let this be our gift to each other,
Sarah Jean.

MUM REMEMBERS SARAH settling into our home very readily. "I don't remember it being a struggle at all," she says, and that's how I remember Sarah's early years too. The difficulties came later. Sarah writes about them herself:

APRIL 10, 1996

Adopted by Jan and Pat de Vries at eleven months of age. Maggie the oldest, Peter the second oldest are their biological children by birth. Mark the third oldest was also adopted, and myself, the baby and the literal black sheep of the family. I thought I was no different. I was just too young to acknowledge the world around me carrying on. Too young to see the disapproval and hate, too naive to see it was all aimed towards me. "Pretty Brown," that's what she called me; my mother had a way to make things seem right. My brother Peter told me on more than one occasion that when I was born there was a sun in my mother's stomach, that's why my skin was so chocolatey. I believed it with all my wee heart, feeling very special for the fact that I was the one and only de Vries child chocolatey brown.

When my mother read this, she pointed out that Sarah wrote it "three weeks before she gave birth herself to her second child whom she intended to abandon." She was setting her son up for the same experience that she had had. At the same time, it may have been his imminent birth that got her thinking that day about her own childhood.

Sarah's recollection seems to be that she was made to feel loved and accepted and that her difference was acknowledged in empowering ways. At the same time, she seems to have been aware of that difference early on.

Sarah had turned-in feet when she came to us. She had to wear shoes attached to one another with a metal bar that held her feet turned out. From just before she came to us and for close to a year, Sarah wore that contraption almost twenty-four hours a day. She developed very strong arms and shoulders and a powerful upper body. At one year old, she could climb the slide with that bar on her shoes using the strength of her arms and her knees for balance. Mum reminded me that Dad invented a gizmo like a skateboard that Sarah could lie on to roll around on the living room floor. She could swing sitting up earlier than most kids because she had such strength in her arms. Sarah seemed to accept wearing the bar. She simply got on with things. Still, it must have been a tough thing for a child to go through, especially at the same time that she was being uprooted. I wonder if all those early chin-ups had something to do with Sarah's incredibly erect carriage as an adult. I always envied her the strength and dignity of her posture.

Sarah seemed to adjust to our family. She was bubbly, outgoing, bonded with lots of people, knew her own mind.

When Sarah was two and a half or three, Dad's brother and his wife came for a visit with their baby, Rachel. Aunt Georgi recalls Dad playing a game with Rachel, throwing her into the air and catching her, chanting, "Racheltje Boom, Racheltje Boom" (the *ch* makes a slightly guttural *h* sound). Rachel would giggle and giggle, and Dad would play the game endlessly.

"When is that Racheltje Boom baby going home?" Sarah asked finally, ready to return to being the baby of the family herself.

Most summers we would go to Aunt Jean's cottage in Muskoka, cottage country in Ontario, three hours northeast of Aunt Jean's home in Guelph. We all loved it there. On our first visit to the cottage with Sarah, when she was two and Mark was four, they would march around with round plastic dishpans on their heads, singing, "Hattie, hattie, hattie." They played together a lot. "The other thing that she was so good at," Mum tells me, "was picking wild strawberries. Her little fingers would get in there and she would pick and pick and pick." Those strawberries were tiny and the most delicious things on earth. I'm sure that Sarah was just like me and when she was picking and picking and picking, she was also eating and eating and eating.

At around that time, Aunt Jean took Sarah to the Guelph library. Sarah was wearing a little white sunsuit and had pink bows in her hair, little ponytails. And the librarian said to Aunt Jean, "What is she?"

Aunt Jean said, "What do you mean, what is she? She's a beautiful little girl. That's what she is."

"You know what I mean," the woman said. "What is she?"

"She's a little girl that Jan and Pat have adopted. She's my niece."

"Oh, isn't that wonderful of them?" she said.

Aunt Jean gave up at that point and left. Afterward a friend told her that as soon as she got out of the library, the librarian said, "They should leave them with their own kind."

Sarah didn't hear that part, but she did hear, "What is she?"

Aunt Jean also remembers being down on the beach in Vancouver with Mum and all of us kids. A woman walked up to Mum and said, "She's not very dark, is she. Not really so very dark." She was pushing for information. Why did Mum have three white ones and one dark one? Was there a different father? What was going on? This kind of thing happens many times every day in the lives of children adopted into families of a different race. It happens even more often in people's minds. People look and they wonder and they move on, or they wait for all to be revealed. But the words are spoken out loud often enough that the child comes to know what others are thinking even when nothing is said.

Ironically, that comment—"They should leave them with their own kind"—is voiced frequently today, but for a legitimate reason. "They should not take children away from their own culture and place them in another." Aboriginal groups fight the loss of their children after generations of having their children taken from them willy-nilly.

A family photo from that time tells its own story of Sarah's place among us. In the black-and-white photo, Grandma, Mum and I are lined up in similar poses, showing three generations of women, highlighting the resemblance in our profiles. Sarah is tucked in at the edge, beaming at the photographer. I love the photo, the image of all of us together, four related girls and women. Sarah didn't pose like the rest of us, perhaps in part because she was younger. But I don't think that's the only reason. The rest of us are emphasizing a family resemblance. Sarah could not be part of that.

When Sarah was a little older, Grandma witnessed an exchange between Mark and Sarah that inspired Aunt Jean years later to write her picture book *Jess Was the Brave One*. Mark was crouched down by a rock peering at the gap between the rock and the ground underneath. With a stick he would poke into that gap, levering the rock up just a bit. Then, nervously, he would let it fall. Grandma said that Sarah watched from a distance for a while, then marched up, hefted the rock, looked underneath, said, "There's nothing under there," dropped it and walked away. Perhaps Mark was enjoying imagining what was under that rock, and Sarah thought that was silly and wrecked his game. Maybe she wanted him to play with her instead. Whatever the case, Sarah had a no-nonsense, take-action approach, even as a little girl.

Mum read aloud to all of us when we were little and Dad told us stories and read to us too. Sarah fit right in with her love of stories.

"I remember the four of you being on the bed in the big front room," Mum says. "I was reading *The Hobbit* to Mark and Sarah. You and Peter came tiptoeing in and the next thing all four of you were lying across the bed listening."

Books and stories were a huge part of all our lives growing up. Dad used to tell us stories that went on and on for months or even years, crazy stories that we loved. He told Mark and Sarah about the Dodos from Dodoland. Aunt Jean remembers him getting them to point out Madagascar on the globe. That was Dodoland. Only years later did she realize that the dodo is a real bird that did come from that part of the world.

One day, when Dad had Sarah with him on his bike, he stopped a truck from dumping refuse over a cliff at UBC. He happened to be passing by, saw what was going on and placed the bicycle, child and all, in front of the truck. As a soil scientist, he had a particular interest in saving the beach around the university from erosion and from dumping. The men were angry, but could do nothing in the face of a small child. Sarah was four or five and I imagine her thriving on an adventure like that. I would have been mortified and perhaps a little frightened, but Sarah would not have been afraid. She always admired Dad for his activism. Despite all the trouble that she got into in later years, she carried with her to the end a belief in standing up for what was right, no matter what.

When Sarah was five, Ria, a family friend, had a baby boy. Finally, Sarah had the opportunity to be older, to take care of someone, to treat someone as a little brother without that little brother taking her place in the family. She loved to push Julian in his stroller and would often go on outings with Ria and Julian. It was central to her sense of self, I think, then and always, to feel important to others, needed by them. Her relationship with Julian gave her the chance to express that side of herself.

One of Sarah's favourite people when she was little was a man named Mohni, who was doing a post-doctorate with Dad. He was a warm, loving man and he came from India. He was one person Sarah knew who had brown skin like hers. One day, Peter recalls, when Sarah was four or five, Mohni came to the house with a little pepper plant. The plant went right in the middle of the dinner table. Mohni would reach out, pick a pepper and eat it with his meal. Sarah was fascinated.

Mum and Dad told her never, never to touch those peppers. They explained that the peppers would burn her, but Sarah couldn't resist. She picked a pepper and took a bite. Just as Mum and Dad had warned, it burned her mouth terribly. She started to cry, rubbed her eyes and then burned those too. Mum and Dad were sympathetic, but reminded Sarah that they had told her not to do that. "I felt a lot of sympathy for Sarah over that," Peter says. "But," he goes on, "it was an example of her wanting to try stuff. She wasn't afraid." Experiences like that with the peppers didn't teach her to trust adults' advice and save herself some pain. She went right on following her own lead.

Sarah loved not only to be read to but to read, even before she was able. Mum remembers her once, ever-so-seriously reading a book that was upside down. She was mad when Mum suggested she turn the book the other way up. "Everyone in the family read and she wanted to too. But not to be taught. She liked to *know* like everyone else," Mum says.

I received my first letter from Sarah in June 1976. She was barely seven, still in grade one. I was almost fifteen, in a troubled period of my life, and I was spending a month with Grandma and Aunt Jean in Ontario. "Maggie, I wish you were here," Sarah wrote. "A raccoon came to our house and I gave him a piece of bread and I miss you. So does Mum. So I can't wait until you come back. From Sarah. I love you. The End." Underneath, she had drawn a house with smoke coming out the chimney and a girl standing to one side. A week later, Mum forwarded another letter from Sarah: "Maggie, I got my foot stuck. I miss you. I heard your letter. You said, 'I will send Sarah a postcard.' Love Sarah." Underneath is a picture of a girl with a dog on a leash, signed "Sarah." I wish now that I had the postcard that I sent to her, but of course I only have letters received, not sent.

By that time, Sarah was very conscious of the fact that we were her adoptive family, not her biological family. In a note to me, Mum wrote recently, "Remember when she was young, seven or eight, and would get mad at me, she would say with a pout and a flounce, 'If my real mother were here . . .'"

School had started out well for Sarah at Wesbrook, the preschool all of us had attended and loved. And her early report cards from Queen Elizabeth and Queen Mary elementary schools were largely positive, although she had problems with math skills. She managed reading well and enjoyed art. But there was a dark side to her school experience, even that early on. Here, the 1996 journal entry in which she wrote about Mum calling her Pretty Brown continues:

Elementary school sucked. I guess you could say that I was
one of the loser loners. I had peace of mind when I was alone.
I didn't have to talk or be somebody that I didn't like. In my
elementary school years I went to Queen Mary Elementary at
4th and Trimble. It's a four block walk from my dad's house
now. My parents got divorced a few years before I went to
high school. Anyway, every day I would walk to school. It was
walking home after school that I had a deep inner fear for. Some
kids used to wait for me to start walking home. They would then
push, shove, kick, punch, yell, throw stones and swing sticks at
me. Chasing me half a block from my house. Nigger, coon,
spook, jungle bunny, moon cricket, spear chucker, spade, and
a few more.

I want to say that what she says isn't true. Could she have been going through all that and we didn't know it? She never told any of us that she was being harassed to the extent that she describes, or that she was a victim of violence. She goes on to describe being hit in the head with a rock. But surely that didn't happen then. And surely those hurtful names are an accumulation over years, not ones spilling out of the mouths of the kids of West Point Grey. After all, she writes the passage in 1996, twenty years later. At the same time, I must be careful not to dismiss her words. Whether what she writes is true or not, my resistance to believing springs, I think, from the difference between us. I never heard racist slurs growing up because I'm white. For a child to experience any degree of racism and then go home to a family where no one else shares her experience must be very hard. One of the most difficult things to explain to people is a feeling that you have experienced but they have not. How much more difficult for a child—and a youngest child, at that?

In grade three Sarah came home in agony about a school assignment and confided her troubles to Mum. Mum knew that she wasn't happy in school, but now it was worse because the class was studying family roots and children were asking her prying questions. "She started to cry about being adopted," Mum says. "She didn't know how to explain it. She didn't understand it. And she cried and cried." Mum talked to her about her roots and offered to come to her class to explain to them about being adopted. Sarah agreed immediately; her relief was palpable. So Mum did. She talked to Sarah's class about the whole adoption process, she answered their questions honestly, and she asked them how many lived just with their mums or just with their dads or with somebody else. Quite a few put up their hands. Sarah had thought she was the only "different" person in the world, but many of her classmates were different in some way too. "It was a great relief to her, my going," Mum says. "I should have done a lot more of that." That visit helped Sarah, as Mum says; she found school easier to cope with for the rest of that year. However, while she may have learned that other kids feel different too, her particular experience was unique among her classmates.

Still, Sarah always had a great deal of confidence and pleasure in life. The day after we heard that Sarah's DNA had been found, my husband, Roland, my brother Peter and I went over to Dad's house to look at old family slides with Dad and his wife, Joan. I was afraid that seeing pictures—especially slides because they are so lifelike—of Sarah as a little girl would be heartbreaking. Instead, the experience was joyous. So many happy pictures: skating down at Jericho, swimming and picnicking on the beach, hiking in Lighthouse Park, blowing out candles on birthday cakes—so much activity as a family and so much fun in much of it. In many pictures, Sarah's face makes sense of the expression "dissolved in laughter." All of her is incorporated in her pleasure. Such times are easy to forget when someone you know has been caught in a cycle of prostitution and drug addiction for almost fifteen years and is on the list of the missing for more than five years after that.

IN MAY 1978, when she had just turned nine, Sarah sent Dad and me a letter when we were in Holland visiting my Dutch grandparents. "Dear Maggie and Daddy, How are you and your parents? I miss you both very much. I had a nightmare. It was that you and Maggie were in deep danger. But most of all, I miss you both. I wish you and Maggie and Pake and Beppe happy weeks and days. Here's a picture for you all. Love, Sarah." Her letter touches me now with its worry and generous spirit. Shortly after Dad and I returned from Holland, Mark and Sarah went to Ontario to spend the summer at Aunt Jean's cottage in Muskoka, to get help from Aunt Jean on their math and writing skills. The summer in Ontario seemed to benefit them both. Sarah wrote me a letter:

To Maggie,

I got your letter. It is very nice of you to write to me. . . .
Aunt Gretta has a bird called Peter and she always says, "Sing, Peter, sing, sing, sing, sing." I got bitten, but not very hard. I got little marks on my arm and that is all.

Is Katy all right? How are my guinea pigs? It is so hot, I can't stand it. I think I could get lost here. It would be so easy, I think.

Aunt Jean bought us some goggles. I got white ones and Mark got blue. We both got them because of chlorine.

Love, Sarah.

Neither she nor I knew it at the time she wrote the letter, but we would not live together in the same house for two years—and never again while all four of us were children.

1978 September 12   Lillian Jean O'Dare last seen
1979 March 30   Wendy Louise Allen last seen

two

A FAMILY DIVIDED

THROUGH THE MID-SEVENTIES, tension had been growing between my parents. Sarah was only six or so when our best years as a family were over. She had had the fewest stable years when, in August 1978, my parents separated.

And she had taken the disagreements between Mum and Dad very seriously. I remember holding on to her during one furious argument, comforting her as best I could. Aunt Jean remembers another time when Mum and Dad were in their room yelling. "Sarah was outside their door, crying her heart out. Sobbing and sobbing." I can see Sarah in my mind, standing there crying, not wanting to miss what was being said because of its huge power to affect her life, but not able to bear it. Taking it all on herself. As so many children do, she blamed herself for the problems between her parents.

That August, Mum joined Mark and Sarah in Guelph. The three of them stayed there for a year while Peter and I remained in Vancouver with Dad. That year was tough for both Sarah and Mark—for all of us, in fact, Mum and Dad included. Our family was split in two; Mark and Sarah had changed homes; we four children had become two pairs, thousands of kilometres apart. Mum wrote to me from the cottage six days after she left:

> Mark and Sarah have done really well in their schoolwork and still are doing so. They get obstreperous and silly still sometimes, but Mark in particular seems more mature and relaxed than he did in May. I'm hoping to find an apartment in the Victory School district so the kids can go there to school.
>
> Mark is sitting here beside me and he asks if you would send all his comic books and little cars. Sarah wants her Cher doll and all the Barbie clothes that fit her. . . .
>
> Jean is sitting at the other end of the table and I asked her if she had a message for you. She says, "From one brave person to another, keep on mashing the potatoes."

Aunt Jean had been diagnosed with glaucoma in her one remaining eye that spring. She spent the summer tutoring and caring for her youngest niece and nephew, and then found that they were not going home, that she was needed as a support for half of a divided family. She *was* brave! So was I, although I didn't realize it at the time.

In fact, I stopped "mashing potatoes" over and over again that year, my last year of high school. I whined and complained. I skipped school. I screamed and yelled. I berated my father. I phoned my mother over and over again and laid my pain at her feet. I drank excessively. I experimented with sex, with alcohol and marijuana, with magic mushrooms and LSD. But time passed and I survived. I wonder often why it was that I survived and Sarah did not.

It is an unanswerable question: issues of race and adoption are part of it; Sarah's youth when Mum and Dad started on the road toward divorce is another part; our different personalities must have played a part as well. Sarah was much more of a risk taker than I was. I rebelled, but I was never drawn to Vancouver's downtown world as she seems to have been. Circumstance plays a role as well. I never met anyone who was in a position to introduce me to that world. Sarah did.

Mark and Sarah did go to Victory School as Mum had hoped they would, and I think that it was good in many ways. But it was the school where friends of mine had been the target of racism a few years earlier and where the administration had refused to take action. Sarah, while a student there, was pushed to the ground. Racist slurs were flung at her. She talked about it to Aunt Jean—Aunt Jean who is blind and was once tied to a tree as a child and had rocks thrown at her, Aunt Jean who knows the power of words. She advised Sarah to say in as scornful a voice as she could muster, "Caucasian," to the next child who insulted her. It worked for a while, but of course it did nothing to address the ignorance at the root of the problem.

Aunt Jean believes that it was mainly one boy who bothered Sarah that year. He ripped the felt off the back of her coat. If there were others, he was the ringleader. Aunt Jean talked to Sarah about that. She tried to help Sarah understand the boy's troubles. He was a foster child, apparently, always in the principal's office, having suffered who knows what in his short life. Still, when a child is being tormented by another child, understanding the tormentor is not enough. The torment needs to stop.

Some good things did happen to Sarah that year. She was a patrol girl and that meant a lot to her. Her teacher liked her and she liked her teacher. Aunt Jean remembers Sarah coming home all excited because her teacher had said that her "eyes sparkled like stars." That kind of comment stays with a person!

Aunt Jean remembers two stories that Sarah wrote that year. One was called "The Deserted Playground." On the cover Sarah had drawn a picture of an empty swing.

"My friend, Emily, was out on the playground," the story went. "Now the playground is empty and Emily is in the hospital.

"I went to see her and I said, 'How are you?'

"And she said, 'I have broken every bone in my body.'

"And I said, 'Oh, Emily. How do you feel?'

"And Emily said, 'To die or not to die, that is the question.' And she died."

Aunt Jean was pretty impressed that Emily could still speak with every bone in her body broken. "You know," she said to Sarah, "there are hundreds of bones in the body."

"Yes," Sarah replied. "I know that and they were all broken."

Aunt Jean asked how Emily could talk. "Never mind, Aunt Jean," Sarah said firmly. "All her bones were broken."

After Aunt Jean told me that story, I looked through two fat folders that Dad gave me of Sarah's childhood art and writing, and found another story that Aunt Jean had mentioned. Reading all Sarah's childhood writing, I am struck by how much of it explores death, abandonment, grave danger. Things generally work out better, though, than they do in "The Deserted Playground."

The story that I found has a note from Mum to Dad attached: "Thought you might like this story of Sarah's. She had to write a story that took place in the South American rain forest." The version that I have is untitled. It is dated February 1979, when Sarah was almost ten.

"I was sleeping in an airplane when my dad said, 'Wake up.' My mom and my brother and I woke up. My dad said, 'We have to make a crash landing, so put on your seat belts.'

"We crashed and we were all okay. We started out on foot and ran into a poisonous snake. My dad killed it. I saw a baby lion. I ran to pick it up and I fell into a trap for lions.

"Just then, we heard native people. My dad said, 'Hide!' They did, but I was trapped.

"The native people took me away. The rest of the family followed. When we got to the village, they tied me to a pole and left me there till morning.

"I heard my dad say, 'Mark, go untie your sister.'

"'Okay, Dad,' Mark said.

"I was untied in a minute and we were off. We stopped at a safe place to sleep and eat. We ran into a band of army ants and all my brother could say was, 'Neat-o!' as they passed us.

"I wondered when we would be rescued. I asked my dad.

"He said, 'I don't know, Sarah. I just don't know.'

"Then I heard a noise. We all ran down to the beach and there was a hovercraft. The man said, 'Climb aboard.' We did and we were off."

Aunt Jean comments on the story as she remembers it. "The part that is interesting is that they were native people. But the other part that's even more interesting to me is that she saw Mark as her co-victim and her ally. They were both uprooted and moved to Ontario. If you said to her, 'Come on, Sarah. It's time to go home,' she would say, 'My home is in Vancouver.' 'Are you going home for lunch?' 'My home is in Vancouver.' And she would go on and on until finally it just about drove your mother crazy. Sarah didn't want to be in Ontario."

Dad is there for her in the story, although he sends Mark in for the actual rescue, but Dad is also baffled. "I don't know, Sarah. I just don't know." Clearly, she missed him. She wanted him around but she recognized that the distance between Vancouver and Guelph made it impossible for him to be in her life very much that year.

Also in February 1979, Sarah sent us a card:

Dear Maggie and Peter and Dad,

I am a patrol girl now. I cross people and if they're bad, I can send people to the post till the bell rings. I miss you all very much and I hope you can all come again sometime. Aunt Jean read *Roll of Thunder, Hear My Cry*. A boy in the story was called T.J. T.J got beaten up. He had three broken bones and a broken jaw and blood coming out of his mouth.

I am not happy here at all. My only friend is Andrea Smith. She is nice and kind.

Goodbye now, Maggie and Peter and Dad.

Write back, please.

The book that she refers to, by Mildred Taylor, is all about race, about the violence toward and subjugation of black people at the hands of whites. She would have heard many books read aloud, but that is the one she wanted to tell us about.

Aunt Jean told me about another book that was important to Sarah then, *The Great Gilly Hopkins* by Katherine Paterson. Mum read it aloud at the cottage that year. Sarah listened to much of it with her head on Aunt Jean's chest, her tears soaking through Aunt Jean's shirt. Gilly is a foster child who believes that her mother is going to come for her, that her mother loves her and wants her. "When Sarah really started to cry," Aunt Jean says, "was when the mother came and then wouldn't have anything to do with her. Her real mother came and then wanted to get rid of her. Gilly's whole dream fell apart." They read it right to the end while Sarah wept silently. "The whole front of my shirt was sopping," Aunt Jean says.

Then Sarah sat up, looked at Mum and said, "What would you do if my real mother came and tried to take me away from you?"

Mum said, "I'd kick her in the shins, I'd punch her with my fist and I would run. I would run as fast as I could in the other direction."

And Sarah grinned. "That's good," she said.

Sarah needed to know that Mum would fight for her no matter what and that Mum's love for her was as big as the universe. At the same time she had to make sense over and over again of the fact that somewhere out there was a "real mother" who had given her away. She was free to question and explore the boundaries as long as she knew that Mum was going to hold on to her tight.

In addition to losing her biological family, Sarah must have felt that she had lost Dad and Peter and me that year when she and Mum and Mark lived in Ontario. I suspect that younger children miss older siblings more than vice versa; sad to say, but older siblings are often entirely wrapped up in their own lives. That was certainly true of me that year. I missed Mum desperately, although I was furious with her for leaving. And I was focused on myself and Dad and Peter, the two family members who were with me in Vancouver.

Aunt Jean told me about artwork that Sarah did that year, pictures that she had up in her house for years, one in particular. "I would have loved it no matter who had drawn it," she said. "It was that good." It was a drawing of children skating. One small child was falling. "She had on a little stocking cap and a snowsuit. She had skates on her feet. Her arms stuck straight up in the air and her legs stuck straight up in the air and she was coming down on her bum. It was so full of colour and action. It was so alive. So witty."

THE NEXT SUMMER, 1979, Mum and Mark and Sarah moved back to Vancouver. I had just finished high school and now traded places with them, moving to Guelph to begin a general arts degree. Dad moved into an apartment for a year and Mum moved back into the house we grew up in. Peter and Mark and Sarah lived with her that year. Dad explained his arrangement with them in a letter. "This evening Sarah and I are going out to dinner. I take them one at a time, Mark, Peter, Sarah. I guess we'll go to the White Spot."

The tension between Mum and Dad became much more evident to Mark and Sarah, I think, once Mum was back in Vancouver. Mum and Dad were going through the long, painful process of extricating their lives from one another at the same time that they were trying to make joint decisions about child rearing and where the younger two should live. At the end of October 1979, Mum wrote, "Jan came for supper and that went okay. Then he started fixing Sarah's light for her. She runs around after him like an amorous delighted talkative little shadow, and it is nice for her, but not for me." It's great that it was possible for Dad to come to supper and to help out with things, but I know from my own experience that kids pick up on every scrap of tension between estranged parents. Sarah was especially attuned to it, I think, because she did not feel completely secure in the world.

Over the next three or four years Sarah poured her energy into turning Mum's attention toward Dad and Dad's toward Mum in whatever ways she could. She reported back and forth from one household to the other. It accomplished nothing, of course, other than to make Sarah seem manipulative and to make her feel, I suspect, powerless—which she was.

It also must have been difficult for both Mark and Sarah, changing cities and schools two years in a row. It does seem, though, that Sarah made friends in each place, and picked up on some old friendships when she returned to Vancouver. At the same time, she worried about her friendships. In September 1979, Mum wrote, "Sarah was crying tonight because Nicole won't be her friend and someone put her pencils in the wastebasket." That was the beginning of grade five.

Sarah was back at Queen Mary Elementary School that year. By coincidence, Ria—the family friend whose baby Sarah had been fond of—put me in touch recently with Sarah's grade five teacher, Laurel Johannson, who now lives on Vancouver Island. Laurel remembers Sarah clearly, almost twenty-five years later.

"She had a beautiful smile," Laurel says. "I remember her as being kind of quiet, not overly confident." The class was called a family grouping and spanned grades three to five. Most of the children in that class had been together for more than two years, so it may have been especially hard for Sarah to join them as a new student. "Some of the other kids had strong personalities," Laurel tells me. "I remember Sarah as an average student. I don't remember her as really struggling." She also remembers how much Sarah liked drama, and the photos that Laurel showed me from the year attest to that.

Sarah wrote me several letters that year, some of them typed, some handwritten. They are chatty, full of stories about her pets. For example,

Dear Maggie,

I have a new Barbie doll. She has blonde hair. I pierced her ears with my own earring. I'm going to a Halloween party on October 27. I got A on my math three times in a row. I wrote a story about a girl who could turn into anything she wanted. She ended up marrying a vampire. I am looking forward to seeing you at Christmas. Katy is fine. Mom took Katy to the vet to be cleaned because she had burrs in her

fur from something. I'm fine. Mom's fine. Peter is fine.
Mark is fine. I am going to be a black cat for Halloween. My
room is cleaner than ever before in my little life. I'm taking
swimming lessons and I'm in intermediate. I'm taking gym
lessons. I can fall into a backbend. The teacher calls me
Miss Flexible because of all the bendy things I can do. I will
show you when you come.

Do not forget it, Maggie de Vries.

I love you very much.

Love, your silly sister, Sarah, who is only ten.
xoxoxoxoxxxooxo

I like the name Miss Flexible. She really was. Two years later, Mum
wrote in her journal, "Sarah is playing with some girls who are visiting their grandmother across the street. I saw her go up to them.
They were doing bends and trying to do the splits. She kicked off her
shoes and did the splits across the sidewalk." Later, when Sarah was
not living at home, Mum wrote, "She has started learning break-
dancing, apparently like Michael Jackson, street dancing. Athletic,
robot movement that originated on the streets of New York." And
she was very good at it.

Mum was finishing her nursing degree that year, 1980, and was
uncertain about where she wanted to settle after that. She seriously
considered moving back to Guelph and was tossing ideas around in
her head. Then she asked Mark and Sarah if they would want to stay
in Vancouver without her, "and they happily said yes, they would,
they could write me and visit sometimes. I began to realize that
maybe they could do without me, but I couldn't do without them. I
had a lot of thinking to do." Ultimately, Mum decided to stay in
Vancouver. I don't believe that Mark and Sarah really meant that they
would happily watch Mum move off to Ontario without them. They
did, however, let her know their preference for living in Vancouver in
clear terms.

In February 1980, when Sarah was almost eleven, Mum found out that Sarah and a friend had been shoplifting candy from stores on Tenth Avenue. "Good grief," Mum wrote, "she doesn't seem to take it very seriously. I wonder. Well, maybe she does. I'm sure she won't do it again. But why am I sure? Just because I am." Sarah did do it again, later on, when she was much more miserable. Many kids shoplift when they are ten and eleven. I shoplifted regularly for at least six months when I was fourteen and fifteen. I hated myself for it, but could not stop—until I was caught once and then almost caught a second time. In my case, shoplifting was one of many symptoms of unhappiness. It was a way to get accepted among my peers, and perhaps it was a cry for help as well.

Several months after the shoplifting incident, Sarah wrote a story about her family. "Once upon a time there was a little boy named Mark Andrew de Vries. He lived in a big wood house on First Avenue. Mark has a very nice sister called Maggie or Maggie Saggie and Jellybeans. Mark has another sister who was very nice to him. Her name was Sarah Jean Sherry de Vries. Maggie Margaret de Vries called her Sarsley Parsley. Mark Andrew de Vries had a big brother named Peter Ellard de Vries. Mark had a very nice mother named Pat Patricia Little-de Vries who called Mark Marky. Mark also had a very nice father who would give him pop every day." She gathers all of us around her, and interestingly tells the story through Mark's place in the family instead of her own. I did call her Sarsley Parsley. I had forgotten that. In this piece, Sarah claims her birth name along with the names Mum and Dad gave her. She is gathering together her whole family, her whole history, her whole self.

To my delight, while I was working on this book, I found one letter that I sent to Sarah. It was in a box of Sarah's drawing and school papers in Dad's basement. I wrote it during the middle of my first year of university, at the start of the second term, when I began to apply myself.

Dear Sarah,

Hi!! How's it going? Do you have any snow in Vancouver? We only have a few centimetres here. It's strange, but very nice. I am having a good time here. I'm working hard in school and things like that and just enjoying myself too. I hope you are. How's Dad? How are your guinea pigs? How's Katy and Cocoa and the rabbit?

Missy and Posy are fine except that they still bark all the time. I liked the story you sent Grandma and Aunt Jean. Aunt Gretta liked the animals you made her. And the shell print you gave me sits on my bedside table. Did you get some Dutch licorice?

There are icicles hanging outside my window and dripping as the sun melts them. The road down by Becker's has been pulled up and they're replacing it.

Well, I have studying to do, so I'd better go. I'll see you soon.

Love, Maggie

P.S. I'd love it if you'd send me a picture you've drawn to hang on my wall.

That summer, I moved back to Vancouver to do my second year of university at UBC. Mum bought a house up the hill, fifteen blocks or so away from Dad's. In June, Dad moved back into the house on First and Peter stayed there too. Mum, Mark, Sarah and I lived together in the new house on Twelfth.

Sarah made several comments that year about what Mum had taken and what she had left behind in Dad's house. "Did you ask Mum why she took all the good stuff?" she said to Dad. She wasn't siding with Dad, exactly, just trying to make sense of things and stirring them up at the same time.

So much was lost to all of us. When we lived together on First Avenue, a seagull used to come every day to a stand in the backyard and we would feed him bread. Sometimes he came right onto the balcony. Soon after moving back in, Dad said, "I haven't seen the seagull." Sarah replied, "I think he's dead." A half-empty house, a family split in two. Even the gull seemed to have deserted us.

Mum had finished her degree, and started to work at UBC Extended Care. She worked twelve-hour shifts, sometimes at night, sometimes in the day. We would pass each other on our bicycles as she headed home and I headed out to my classes. It was a juggling act for her, being there for Mark and Sarah and also starting a demanding career.

While all these changes were going on, Dad met the woman he would marry six years later, Joan, who teaches English at Vancouver Community College. She moved in with him in early 1981, shortly before Mark and Sarah began moving back and forth between Mum's house and Dad's. They moved down the hill to Dad's house in January 1981, and stayed there until August, visiting Mum on Wednesday evenings. During one of her stints at Mum's house, Sarah had her twelfth birthday party. Ten girls came for cake and ice cream and a trip to the bowling alley. Mum wrote, "She looks older these days and has grown a lot, I would say." She was finishing grade six and she had a group of friends.

That summer, Mark and Sarah drove with Dad and Joan across Canada to visit Dad's brother and his family in Cape Breton. Sarah was twelve; Mark was fourteen. Mark remembers fighting viciously with Sarah in the back seat of the car. "She didn't want to go," he tells me. Sarah's reluctance was a sign of the advent of adolescence, I think, with the growing unwillingness to participate in family activities. But they had good times on the trip too, Mark says.

Still, through grade seven she enjoyed herself a lot of the time both at Dad's house and at Mum's.

She used to go to work with Joan on professional development days. Sarah would bring books and paper and would draw. Once she wrote a poem. "She liked an audience," Joan says, "and was very pleased when my students looked at her drawings and complimented her on them. She also read her poem to the class. She was well behaved and enjoyed the positive attention." When I was going through the files of Sarah's childhood art, I found many pictures drawn on the back of documents from Vancouver Community College. Sarah enjoyed having another adult woman in a primary role in her life.

Dad and Joan had a black Lab at the time. "Sarah loved dressing up my very patient dog, Licorice," Joan says. "She had a trunk full of dress-up clothes. A T-shirt with Licorice's front legs through the sleeves, a half slip around the dog's middle (Licorice had to be careful about walking on the slip) and a kerchief tied around her head made the dog look like a bedraggled woman." Licorice was very special to Sarah. When Sarah visited Dad's house in later years, seeing the dog was a great joy. Licorice wasn't pained by Sarah's choices, by her lifestyle. The pet was simply delighted to see her.

Mark and Sarah lived with Mum from August 1981 until August 1982. I was away for much of that year, first in Ontario, then in Europe. I spent a few months at a religious community in Switzerland where Dad's sister lives. It was an amazing year for me, travelling throughout Switzerland, France and Holland, often alone, spending time with my Dutch relatives as an adult, practising Dutch and French, and exploring my spiritual side. While I was away, Sarah wrote me five letters. She was twelve at the time.

First, though, Aunt Jean wrote to me while she was on a visit to Vancouver:

> I'm in your room sitting on your bed with my feet on the rug
> I made you and I'm wishing you were here. . . . Sarah is her
> usual messy, happy, grouchy, quiet, noisy, fine self. We are
> planning to go to Victoria tomorrow to see Emily Carr's
> house again and we may take her along. . . . I asked Sarah

what she wanted for Christmas. Here is her answer. 'A colt and a calligraphy set.' Afterwards she added 'earrings and clothes and I've asked Dad for a chemistry set.' No mention of dolls any more. She is growing up. Isn't that lovely, though—a colt and a calligraphy set?

❧

Sarah wrote:

Dear Maggie,

How are you? I am fine. . . . In French I got twenty out of twenty-five on my project. The project is on the family. Ours, of course. Under your picture I put that you are smart, intelligent, nice, friendly. xxoo I miss you very much, but I am glad you are having a good time. Remember Mimi? She has two new kittens, both black, and one day they could not find them. They looked all over for them, but guess what . . .

I went to Victoria for a day and we saw the birds painted on the attic ceiling in the House of All Sorts and we saw the museum.

If you have time, I would like you to think of a Christmas present for yourself and send a letter back and I could buy it for you and send it, but it has to be under five dollars. For me, I would like a small thing like a box of Dutch licorice or earrings.

Mimi found the kittens in a motorcycle helmet hanging on the wall.

Now it's time for me to say ta ta, au revoir, bonjour, see ya later, write soon, bye.

Love, Sarah Jean de Vries

❧

At the side she has written two dozen x's and two dozen o's. "To make up for six months," she wrote beside them. I love the way she builds suspense in this letter by withholding the location of the kittens until the end.

In November 1981, she wrote to me again, reporting on the death of her guinea pig.

Dear Maggie,

How are you? I am fine.

I have some good news and some bad news . . .

My Christmas present may be late because I am making it for you. I only have a little bit done, but I am working hard on it. My bad news is very sad. I know you know how it feels. My Hen Wen is, elle a mort. She died Monday, November the 16, 1981. She was only 3 too. I was horrified to see her still as a doorknob. I found her in the morning. I thought she was sleeping so I touched her on the head and nothing happened, but she was cold and hard so I knew she was dead. I just stood there very unhappy. I had trouble going to school that day.

When I told Mum and Dad, they were sad too. But more good news, we might get a new one to keep Moonshine company.

I hope you are having a dynamite time. I miss you very much and all I want for Christmas is my two front teeth. I'm just joking!!! I just want a 13 page letter telling all the things you have seen, heard, eaten, liked and all the fun you are having, but maybe a tin for earrings or something small. Just wait till you get home. Sybilla will be so excited.

I got all your letters. I knew I had to write you a letter, so here I am at 10:00 sitting in my bed writing to you. I know you think I'm crazy, but I'm not. I just miss you so much. I wish you were here with me, Mark, Mom. I know they all miss you, even Moonshine. Hen Wen would too, but she mort (died). . . .

When you come back, do you want a little party? I could arrange one for you. I'll ask Mom, but first you write and tell me and then I'll ask. Okay? See ya in a couple months. Miss ya a lot. So does everybody else.

Love, Sarah de Vries

Around the same time, Dad wrote to me in Switzerland and told me that he was deliberating about whether or not Mark and Sarah should come to live with him. "Continuity and routine require that they stay there," he wrote. "Mark is doing quite well at his new school. . . . On the other hand, I—we—and that includes Joan and Peter—have a lot to offer, and I think that they benefit tremendously from living with us routinely rather than just visiting us every second weekend and every Wednesday." It was the hardest kind of decision, one to which there is no right or wrong, no tidy way to make the juggling work.

Another letter from Sarah arrived in December:

Dear Maggie,

. . . I have bad news. I'm afraid Moonshine might have to be put to sleep. Because her stomach is swollen and her eye is infected.

I just got my braces tightened and they hurt. I made Mom her Christmas present. I made her Christmas cards. It is my night to make dinner and I am making lamb chops and rice, salad. We had a spelling bee which is a spelling contest in front of the whole school in our groups of blue, yellow, red. Yellow won every single contest we had. Now we are having a dance competition. I mean square dance. . . .

I'm looking forward to March so I can see you again. On my report card I got satisfactory and some C+, B, C. We also got our class picture. There is one here for you. Well, I hope you like it. I have to go make dinner.

Remember, take care and that you have my love to go with you no matter what happens to you and that I miss you and I am worried sick that you might get hurt or something and end up in the hospital. So take care.

Love, Sarah

P.S. I just found Moonshine dead. December 15, Tuesday 1981.

❧

I have the picture with the letter. Sarah is wearing a pink gingham dress with a high, ruffled collar. She is smiling broadly, but perhaps slightly tentatively, through her braces. She is twelve and a half years old.

Sarah did get a calligraphy set that Christmas of 1981, but she did not get a colt:

Dear Maggie,

How are you? I am fine.

When you come back, I want to do lots of things with you to make up for right now. I got a calligraphy set, 4 dollars, this pad of paper with four colours with envelopes to match, a pair of leather boots, a knapsack, and my favourite gift is my new pets, Miss Bianca and Miss Tiggy Winkle. They are gerbils, but I've got lots more things coming from Dad and Joan. I miss you very much. I wish you would come home early.

Love, Sarah

❧

Shortly after Christmas 1981:

Dear Maggie,

How are you? I am fine.

. . . I was thinking when you got back sometime you could take me to the wax museum in Gastown if you want. We all went to a singalong in the cathedral on Granville. . . . My gerbils are fine. They make a lot of noise in the night.

I would like it if you would send me a letter with your picture in it.

Love, Sarah [signed in calligraphy]

January 21, 1982:

Dear Maggie,

How are you? I am fine.

It was snowing in December and stopped on January 2 and it's snowing again.

You know all the murders that happened in August? Well, the man was caught. Robert Clifford Olson. He has life in jail now.

I got 49/50 on my spelling dictation. Thank you very much for the soap and your postcards. I'm writing on one now. . . .

I miss you ever so much. So I keep hoping we can do a lot of things together to make up for all this time. I got a paper route for every Wednesday which pays $2.50. I was hoping we could see movies, go shopping and just talk. Well, goodbye. Miss you.

Love, Sarah

Finding these letters and reading them and then reading them for the purposes of this book has been devastating. Sarah is so alive in them, eager and imaginative and loving. In every letter she suggests things that we could do together, the desire to spend time together, to go places, to talk. And then the passing reference to Clifford Olson.

When I read the letters for the first time, I was desperate to know whether I answered them. Was I giving her the attention she needed? I found a notebook from that trip to Switzerland in which I recorded all the letters I received and sent, and I did in fact reply to each of Sarah's letters, but it still feels to me as if her need and what I was able to give were greatly mismatched.

Sarah was almost thirteen by the time I came back from Switzerland in the spring of 1982. Instead of going to the wax museum in Gastown, she and I went to Victoria for two days and one night to celebrate her thirteenth birthday. We took the bus, stayed at the Empress Hotel, and saw and did everything we could: the wax museum, the Miniature Museum, Underwater World, Beacon Hill Park, afternoon tea at the Empress. It was a special weekend. I worked for UBC Catering for the summer and then left for Montreal at the end of August to do my third year of university at McGill. I did not seem to be able to settle on one university or one city for more than a year at that time. Vancouver kept pulling me home and then, I think, pushing me away again. After the trip to Victoria, I expect that I did not give Sarah as much attention as she wanted. I was twenty-one years old and wrapped up in my own life.

At that time, Sarah was beginning to object to moving back and forth between Mum's and Dad's houses. She wanted to stay at Mum's house for grade eight, which she would start that fall. After some debate, she agreed to live with Dad and Joan and Mark and Peter as planned. So Mark and Sarah moved back in with Dad and Joan, and Sarah started high school at University Hill Secondary School, a small high school on the edge of the UBC campus.

In a letter to me dated October 10, 1982, Mum wrote, "Sarah seems to be doing really well. She went to her first dance at U-Hill. I picked her up after it and she seemed comfortable about the evening. She's going to be a punk rocker for Halloween. I'll have to get her some pink hairspray." But then, in a letter three weeks later, she wrote, "I've just had a call from Jan. Sarah is skipping a few classes and generally being defiant and foul-mouthed and not getting some of her projects done. . . . I do wish she would put some effort into skills development at school because she is so far behind." After a hopeful beginning, it turned out that the transition to high school did not go well for Sarah.

Sometime that year, Aunt Jean was listening to a book on tape that Mum had made for her. At the end of one of the cassettes Mum's voice stopped and Sarah's took over. Sarah had secretly taped an interview with herself. Aunt Jean doesn't have the cassette any more, but she remembers the gist of the interview.

"What is your name?"

"My name is Sarah Jean de Vries."

"What kind of family do you have?"

"Well, I'm adopted."

"How do you feel about that?"

"Not too good."

And she went on and on about how the adults in her life were trying to make her into a slave. "It was all mixed up," Aunt Jean said. But one line stood out: "My parents are divorced because of me."

I don't know why Sarah became more unhappy that fall. She protested against staying at Dad's house. Tensions rose both between her and Dad and between her and Joan. She was unwilling to do certain jobs around the house, or she did them sloppily. Neither Dad nor Joan was prepared to put up with that.

Children of divorced parents where custody is shared always have another option, another home to go to. When I was fourteen and so angry that I could not bear it, I would have gone to the other parent's house if there had been one. The year that I lived with Dad, I would have run to Mum over and over again if she hadn't been thousands of kilometres away. It seems natural—if often misguided—to look for the source of one's unhappiness in one's living situation, rather than within oneself. However, what Sarah eventually discovered was that although she may have found living with Mum easier in some ways, she was not happy there, either.

A letter from Dad dated November 7, 1982, reads: "Mark and Sarah are okay, Mark more okay than Sarah. Sarah is getting into trouble in school. On Monday she is having a meeting with the principal and her advisor, Peggy Beck. On Friday afternoon I had a meeting with Sarah's skills teacher—she has been tested; in math she is at the 4.7 grade level, and in spelling, 5.2 (whatever that means). U-Hill has changed so incredibly much, but in spite of the change it is still the best school around. This weekend I gave Sarah a big pile of extra math—multiplying, dividing, adding and subtracting fractions. She did them willingly. I haven't checked out her work yet. She has been very rude and nasty to her teachers; it is some sort of defence mechanism, I guess. Things have been going rather well this weekend, so perhaps and hopefully she is getting the message . . . Sarah wants to write something, here she goes."

Dear Maggie,

I hope you are having a good time. I wish you were coming out to Vancouver for Christmas. I hope you will write me soon, so you can tell me what you want for Christmas. . . . I don't like U-Hill. The teachers are not very good. I hate my skills teacher. We have lots of fights. We both end up fine afterwards. Remember Anne*? Her parents don't want her any more. She is at a special home for runaways. She has been kicked out of school. She smokes, but she is still the same as always.

Zachary is very big now. His grey and white patches blend very nicely together. Coco found a mouse and it was still alive so I saved it. I took it inside to calm it down, then I took it back outside and it clung to me like it liked me. It probably did. I miss you very much. Mark is having a dropping fit. He drops plates, glasses, watches, silverware etc. One day he broke the silverware cabinet, the one where the glasses go with the front part glass. So right now we have broken glass in the cabinet. I hope you like the birds.

Love, Sarah [two stickers of birds from the Canadian Wildlife Federation]

Always humour and always animals in among the unhappy bits.

In December Dad wrote that Sarah's attitude was improving. Yet, when she saw the white lights on the Christmas tree, she said, "I can't stand white lights, why don't you get coloured lights? White lights are boring. The tree looks stupid." Unkind words, but such unkindness is not unusual, I think, among teenagers. She was being nasty to everyone—to her teachers, to Dad, to Joan, to Peter, to Mark—and no one knew how to cope, how to help her.

Christmas that year was good, though. Mark and Sarah and Peter stayed over at Mum's on Christmas Eve and then went to Dad's mid-morning when Mum had to go to work. Sarah was getting along better with Joan and with Dad. Dad was feeling hopeful.

Anne, the girl that Sarah referred to in her letter, was a close friend of Sarah's. She lived near Dad's house; she was adopted and Aboriginal. She was probably the first girl, the first potential friend, that Sarah met who shared her experience of being different in both those ways, race and adoption. I'm sure they found comfort in one another. But Anne was deeply troubled. I never knew the details of what Anne went through before she was placed in her home near our house, but I think that she had been uprooted more than once and that she may have suffered some form of abuse. Sarah's troubles at that point are more difficult to define, but she was growing more and more unhappy. As they grew older and started high school, possibly even before that, they went places together they should not have gone. It's much easier in high school than in elementary school to slip between the parents' and the school's radar, at least for a time.

A photojournalist, Daniel Gautreau, interviewed Sarah when she was seventeen. Years later and days before I finished revisions on this book, an old friend of mine chanced to run into him in Mexico, and when Daniel came home he discovered that he still had the tape of that seventeen-year-old interview along with some of Sarah's poems. I found myself listening to my teenage sister answering many of the questions that I had wished for years that I could ask her. It was strange to hear her voice, especially after I had been so immersed in her life for so long. She became present for me as I listened, almost as if I could look up and there she would be, and I could answer her.

In that interview she spoke about her first trips downtown, her first experiences of street life. "I had a friend who used to live at home. She brought me down there once or twice and I got to know a few people there. Then, I just left home for there." The friend that she referred to was Anne.

Joan remembers how Sarah changed as she got older. Sarah would go into Joan's things every day and take whatever she wanted—clothes, jewellery, pens, paper. She made no effort to hide them, but would use them and leave them lying around. "I would only realize after I had gone to put on a belt or use a pen and had driven myself crazy trying to find where I could have possibly misplaced it," Joan writes. Dad would talk to Sarah about it. He tried to be patient, but it kept happening. "After weeks of this," writes Joan, "I suggested that I put a lock on my study door and keep all my belongings in that room. Your dad felt that what she was doing was a symptom of her fascination with me, but it was driving me crazy." Joan was surprised to learn later that Sarah was doing the same thing to all of us at Mum's house and that we too had put locks on the doors to our rooms.

At the same time that this stealing was happening, Joan found a joint in Sarah's room. On February 21, 1983, days before she ran away, Sarah was caught shoplifting jewellery from Eaton's. And Sarah was saying things to Dad like, "You are not my real father, Dad. I don't have to live here. I don't have to obey you." She said the same thing to Mark: "I hate you. You are not even my real brother."

I had forgotten about the locks on the doors. I lived in Mum's house from May 1983 until August 1984 while I completed my bachelor of arts degree at UBC. We ended up living in a kind of lockdown. Eventually, all the bedrooms in the house had deadbolts on the doors—all the bedrooms, that is, except for Sarah's. Even now, it doesn't seem to me as if we had much choice. She would go into my room, take whatever she wanted, toiletries, earrings, office supplies, use it however she wanted, often destroying it in the process. And at one time during that period, Anne crawled in through our dog door and stole money, jewellery and car keys from Mum. Those locked doors must have made Sarah feel even more isolated than she had before. And however practically justifiable those locks were, they had a symbolic meaning that could only have made things worse. Interestingly, although Sarah took things from our rooms all the time, she was furious with Anne for stealing from us.

Mum wrote about Sarah's reputation in a letter early in 1983: "I told Sarah what you had heard and that you were worried about her. She should know just how far and how fast rumours travel. You might drop her a note with some suggestions on how to get rid of a bad reputation before it gets entrenched. It would come better from you than from me because you've been there recently. I am right out of the picture as far as Sarah is concerned and she's probably right." While true that I was so much closer to Sarah in age and had been the subject of painful gossip more than once in high school, I was by now already grown up and didn't know how to talk to Sarah about the parts of her life that were troubling her.

In mid-January, my friend Kathryn wrote to me about seeing Sarah at the local pool. She was astonished at how beautiful Sarah was. She saw her again at the local theatre. Mum and Mark and Sarah were there to see *The Man from Snowy River,* a favourite of Mum's to this day. Sarah mentioned the movie in a January letter to me.

Dear Maggie,

I'm glad you wrote to me. I'm sorry this is not official writing paper! I should have written to you <u>a long</u> time ago. You are very welcome. I had a fun time sending you your present. No, I did not make the scarf, although it would have been more special if I had made it for you. I had a great Christmas, but I wish you were here for it. I am really enjoying 1983. I have made a lot of friends at school in grades 8, 9, 10. They are all really nice. School is getting harder by the day. I'm sort of keeping up with my classes, but the essays come so fast. I'm taking social studies, math, French, P.E., drama, soccer. . . .

I saw a really good movie called *Man from Snowy River*. It was really good. Super great. You must go see it. I would love to come out and visit you sometime. I've been to Montreal five times, but not enough to go sightseeing. We have had no snow whatsoever this year or last year, only rain. (blah). Out here everybody is into roller skating, so when you come back we should go swimming and go roller skating. Say hello to Dea and Nancy for me.

All my love, Sarah

With the letter is a pencil drawing of a woman with two long braids down her back, sitting on a tall stool knitting a scarf. She is facing a fire burning in a fireplace and a window with snow falling outside. A spotted cat is curled up on the floor beside her. The woman faces away from the viewer.

PETER WAS AN AVID BASKETBALL PLAYER in his teens and twenties. When he was nineteen, he played a game at his old high school between graduates and the high school team. Sarah came to watch. She was thirteen years old. During the game, Peter twisted his knee. He let out a cry of agony and fell to the ground. Sarah shrieked, "Peter!" and ran out onto the court and dropped to her knees at his side.

"I was embarrassed," Peter says.

"Sarah, I'm okay, go back and sit in the stands," he told her at the time.

Years later, she told him how hurt she had been. She had felt rejected. She had felt his embarrassment and taken it to heart. "That was astonishing to me and still is," Peter says. Until Sarah spoke to him about the event, he had never given it another thought, but it had stuck with Sarah, wounding her.

How many times did that happen? I wonder: Sarah feeling hurt by something to which the rest of us were oblivious. I know the feeling, when a positive or caring emotion gets turned on its head without warning. It is as if the world betrays you in that moment and you are exposed, completely vulnerable. I did that to Sarah once when she was very small—four, I think. I was twelve and, as many twelve-year-old girls are, or were then, I was humiliated by the mere fact of menstruation, let alone the possibility of speaking to anyone about it. Sarah found a used sanitary napkin in the bathroom and thought I was hurt. I remember so clearly her face as she approached me: open, filled with love and concern. I don't remember what she said, but I do remember how I silenced her. "Do you want your face smashed in?" I snarled. Her face filled with hurt and confusion. "No," she replied.

That is perhaps my saddest memory. I can forgive my twelve-year-old self, I think, but only now, after all these years. The words sprang from my mouth, unbidden. I had snarled at both my father and Peter when they tried to say anything to me about menstruation and I was doing the same here, protecting myself, though what I thought I was protecting myself from, I don't know. This time the price was high. It seems to me not unlike Peter's experience on the basketball court, except that Peter was not deliberately unkind.

We never intended to deny Sarah a meaningful role in our family. But perhaps she thought that we did.

1983   June 22   Rebecca Louisa Guno last seen

1984   January 1   Yvonne Marlene Abigosis last seen

1984   January 30   Sherry Lynn Rail last seen

three

RUNNING AWAY

WHEN SARAH WAS IN GRADE EIGHT, just before she turned fourteen, she ran away from Dad's house. I was living in Montreal that year, studying at McGill, and I remember how helpless I felt when Mum called to tell me that Sarah was gone, how hard it was to imagine Sarah out in the world somewhere, out of reach. Sarah was only away for a few days that time, but it felt like forever, even more to Mum and Dad and Joan than it did to me. Sarah phoned Mum several times while she was away, and in the end, she came home—but to Mum's house instead of Dad's. That was when she seemed to start to feel a pull from another world, a world where she felt accepted, where she felt a sense of belonging. She was well into puberty. She was not happy at home, with Dad or with Mum. She was shuttling back and forth between the two houses. Our family was still in turmoil.

It was a hard time.

I have asked myself, often, where she went, whom she met, what was said, how those first steps, the beginnings of her new life, took place. We know she went downtown with Anne, the one who broke into Mum's house, but we don't know much more than that. Several boys and young men in our neighbourhood got into trouble with the police periodically. One of them had been charged with rape. Did he hurt Sarah?

Now, as I meet more and more women who ran away in their teens and ended up working the streets, I am learning that the transition can happen in many ways. Sarah could have taken the bus downtown all by herself, or hitchhiked, and she could have met with ease people—both other kids and adults—who would have helped her learn the ropes. Their motives could have been potential exploitation, or concern, or perhaps they were just kids banding together.

Once, when I was fifteen, I ran away from home. I don't remember what precipitated it, just that I was hurt, angry and desperate. I felt powerless. The only thing that I had the power to do was leave. So I did. I remember that it was dark outside. I ran down the hill, up to Second Avenue and down a lane onto a large property surrounded by woods.

Where could I go after that? My sense of powerlessness grew as I realized that the only place I could go was home. I don't think I was gone for more than half an hour.

Peter, my brother, ran away that same night. He did better than I did. He had the foresight to take his bike and ride to a friend's house, where few questions were asked, where he could stay overnight without a parental call being made to check into the situation. Peter called home in the morning and returned home that day.

When we talked about our experiences, Peter and I agreed that the tie to home was so strong that staying away seemed inconceivable. We knew where we belonged even when we were desperate to belong anywhere else but there. Sarah's tie to home was not as strong as ours, I think. She did come home over and over again for the next six years, until she was nineteen, but always she struggled and always she left.

That January 1983, before she ran away for the first time, Sarah wrote me another letter that she did not finish. Dad forwarded it to me later on, when he found it in her room.

Dear Maggie,

How are you? I am fine.

I heard that I will be staying with you while Dad is in
Holland. I have a humanities exam on metaphors and allitera-
tion, Mennonites, Chinese, Japanese, Doukhobors, narrative,
descriptive, expository writing, fragments and run-ons,
spelling rules, consonants with prefixes and suffixes, migra-
tion, immigrants, immigration, writing a news story with a
lead sentence. I pray I pass. I can't wait till you come out here.
I have Cecil for French. He is really nice. I don't really like
Marcie, James or Lynda. I don't really know why I hate them,
but I do. I went to see *Tootsie*. It is really funny and he really
looks like a lady. In science we had to dissect a cow's eye. It
was interesting, yet gross. At U-Hill everybody tries to be like
a Valley girl. I myself hate it. It sounds so funny, but like the
song. "Valley Girl." Liz, Christine and I were talking and we
started saying, "Freak me with a spoon" and "Gag me green."
It is supposed to be "Gag me with a spoon" and "Freak me
green."

I'm in a drama class at Carnarvon School every Wednesday.
It's really good. It goes for six weeks and teaches you to act the
person or character you have to be with your whole body and
actions and face expressions.

&

She wrote me another letter on February 23, 1983, three days
before she ran away:

Dear Maggie,

I have not written a letter to you for a long time. I feel quite
guilty about it too. I can't wait until May because I will be
able to stay with you. We have a lot of catching up to do. I

can hardly believe that you will be here in two months. Guess what? I might be taking Jazz lessons. I am already taking acting lessons. I'm getting worried about turning fourteen in May. I want to know if you thought it is a good age to be. I'm doing fine in school, but I'm not too sure about math. I'm passing everything else. I've got good news, B+ in French. Probably C– to C+ for science, C– to C+ for P.E., C– to C+ in Hum I, C– to C+ in Fine Arts. We have not got our report cards yet, but when I do I will write and tell what my marks are for grade 8. I saw *Tootsie*. It is a super, great, wonderful movie. You must go see it and tell me what you think of it. Then you must go see *Ghandi*. It is a super wonderful movie too. I saw the play *Taming of the Shrew*. It was done in a play where all the characters in it were punk (puke) but it was really funny. I'm getting to the point where I can't stand Joan any more, but she probably is getting to the point where she can't stand me. Mark and I fight more now too. Peter and I just don't talk unless we are arguing with each other. We are having chili for dinner tonight. Did you hear about the Marilyn Monroe doll that costs $600 dollars up to $2,000? Have you ever heard the song Industrial Disease yet? Well, I have to go now because my class is over.

Love you all the time, so never forget that I love you.

Love, Sarah de Vries

P.S. See you in April, love me (Sarah)

P.P.S. Did you have a good Valentine's Day? You will always be my valentine.

I Love You Ya Ya Ya and with a love like me you know you should be glad.

Love you always Maggie.

Did I answer her letter? Did I tell her what it was like for me to be fourteen? Did I put aside time for her when I came back to Vancouver that April? Now, as I read her letter, I think that maybe it was good that I wasn't in Vancouver through many of those years, because I didn't become one of the people she had trouble with. I was removed from her day-to-day life, so she could have something of a clean slate when she wrote to me. But whatever I did or did not do back then (and I don't remember much), I feel her now, reaching out to me through these letters. And I am unable to reach back to her, unable to change one single thing.

On February 26, 1983, Mum wrote in her journal, "I am sick with dread. Sarah is missing from Jan's house, has been since last night at 11 p.m." Sarah had phoned Mum at midnight, telling her that she was with her friend Anne and Anne's boyfriend, who had a car. Anne had not been seen at her group home in two weeks. Apparently, they had picked Sarah up near Dad's house. Mum woke up over and over again all night to memories of violent, grief-filled dreams. She finished her journal entry with these words: "I don't know what to do."

Sarah continued to run away in the months to come, and Dad often searched for her. "I drove to the West End," he writes, "in my yellow Renault. I walked Davie and Broughton looking for her, yet hoping I would not find her, because . . . then what? Try to catch her? Drag her to the car, kicking and screaming? Take her home? And then what? We felt so totally desperate. Hopeless. Helpless."

Within a few days of running away, Sarah was back living with Mum. Of the weekend when Sarah was gone, Mum later wrote, "It was so very horrible. I will never be the same again." However, once Sarah was home again, but in Mum's house instead of Dad's, she was as happy as she could be, at least for a time. "Sarah acts as though a whole mountain has just been lifted off her back," Mum wrote to me. "She dances around here 'being co-operative' and pleasant and doing as she is asked. I wonder how long it will last. Probably just as long as I greet her with smiles and tell her all the positives and try not to make too many requests and not to turn the ones I do make into condemnations, all of which I am concentrating on. We are being mutually supportive and we are both trying to be consistent about it, which is not usual for either of us. When you come home, we will be such pleasant company, you will scarcely recognize us." But Sarah's happy state would not last until my homecoming.

Dad too wrote to me about the terrible weekend when Sarah was gone, but he said little—only that it was hard. I know that he was deeply saddened by all that took place. In the meantime, I was struggling with my own plans. I wanted to come home, to complete my B.A. at UBC. I did well at McGill but I missed Vancouver, and I think that I felt strange being far away when Sarah was having such a difficult time.

Mum sent me a note and a letter from Sarah. She was looking forward to seeing me, she said, and glad to report that Sarah still seemed happy. She went on to write about concerns that Dad had about my coming back to Vancouver: "The worst thing for you here is probably the depressing business of Jan's and my push-pull stuff—watching the family troubles." Dad, too, wrote that I should think about what was best for me, that it was all right for me to put myself first.

They were both right. It was hard for me to be back in Vancouver, caught up in all the family pain again and seeing close up the difficulties that Sarah was having with all of that and her own growing up. Nevertheless, I'm glad that I came home when I did.

The letter from Sarah that came along with Mum's note is happy. It doesn't convey the yearning of many of her other letters, before or after.

Dear Maggie,

How are you? I am fine.

I hope you have a super trip back here. Mark says that it is really boring if you don't have a lot to do on the bus. I hope to be at the bus terminal to pick you up on the day you come back. Now this is good news. There's a new guy at our school and he is in grade nine. His name is Paul. I like him and he said he likes me. He is really, really nice, funny, and has a super personality. I think he's cute, but I really like him.

Zacky has been a bad cat this year. So far, he ate all the feathers on the mantel, broke a vase, two cups, chewed my shoelaces into tiny tiny bits and scattered dog food all over the kitchen. Now for Sybilla. She tried to attack the mailman and he sprayed her in the face. Coco has been really good so far except for pouncing on little mice and bringing them inside. When you come back, you're going to see a different house, totally different. We have a bigger back porch, really nice front porch. Mom's room looks really good. We have a nice cabinet that Carmel made to hold all our records and stereo and TV. My room is totally different. My desk is built onto the gate around the staircase, my bed is on the ground. I have a matching bedside table and dresser. All my stuffed animals are on my bed. In my window seat I have a hanging plant and a marionette or puppet called Lucy. She is a bird with pink feathers on her head and tail. I have posters all over my room. So far I have read one good book that is called *Dreamspeaker*. It's a super book and you should read it. I'm just going to start *I Never Promised You a Rose Garden*. Now for the third degree.

How are you?

How are your classes going? How is Georgi, Pieter and Rachel? (Oops, forgot Peter Ainsley.) How is the weather doing? Are you getting excited about the trip home? How is your diet going? Remember diet is Die with a "t." But don't die on me please.

I have a joke for you. Why are rhinoceroses' nostrils so big? Give up now do ya? Well . . . because their fingers are so big. Make sure you tell Rachel and Dea that one. I think it's quite funny. Well, I should sign off now. See ya soon.

Lots of love, Sarah

I finished up my third year of university in April 1983 and took the bus back to Vancouver with two friends, who ended up staying at my house for part of the summer. Mum was away at a conference for a while in May, and I was responsible for Sarah. By that time, she was running away again. She would climb out her bedroom window, down onto the little roof over the front stoop, and somehow get down from there. I had no idea what to do when that happened, but one day, one of the friends who was staying with me, Bo, was driving along East Broadway when she saw Sarah enter an old rundown building. She had enough sense not to follow Sarah inside, but stopped, called the police and waited for them to come.

The police did come. They went inside and got Sarah. And they brought her home and left her with Bo. When I got home, Sarah and Bo were faced off in the kitchen, Sarah furious with Bo for having her picked up by the police, Bo determined that Sarah would still be at home and in one piece when I arrived.

Sarah's face was oddly white that day, Bo told me recently.

"What have you got on your face?" Bo asked Sarah.

"Makeup," Sarah said.

"It doesn't look like makeup," Bo replied.

"Well, it is."

"Are you trying to make your face white?"

"Fuck off and leave me alone!"

And that was the end of it. But Bo has reflected on that white makeup over the years and placed it in the context of her experience.

Bo grew up as a Jewish child in a Jewish community on the east side of Vancouver. She started out at Eric Hamber Secondary School, a school that she says was described as one-third, one-third, one-third, meaning one-third Jewish, one-third Asian and South Asian, and one-third white. Then, in grade eleven, she was—as she put it— "spat out into the real world," when she transferred to University Hill Secondary. Eric Hamber and the surrounding community had been "a relatively safe and unreal world," she says, a world in which one could be lulled into believing that a range of cultures could mix comfortably. When Bo first went to U-Hill, she was aware that some-thing was wrong, something was different, but she couldn't figure out what it was.

"I was spinning," she says.

After about a week and a half, it hit her: she had entered the white world, the protestant world—a minority worldwide, but in power terms a majority, and at U-Hill a majority in every sense. Although she's sure that there were a few more in other grades, she remembers only two black kids and one South Asian kid at the school. Five years later, when Sarah was in grade eight, there were a few more black and Asian kids, but not many.

"When I saw Sarah doing what she was doing," Bo says, "I tuned in. I was straightening my hair. She was whitening her face. Sarah was living in a very, very white world."

In the white world of West Point Grey and in her white adoptive family, Sarah's body, with its dark, curly hair, dark eyes and brown skin, was not a comfortable home for her. No, that's not right. West Point Grey was not a comfortable home for her. But she did not have the tools to realize that at the time. Her skin and her hair were differ-ent, so she felt unhappy about them, about her own flesh. I suspect that when she went downtown and met other people, people with a whole range of backgrounds, with their own troubles, their own diffi-culties fitting in, and experienced that bonding that can be especially powerful between troubled teens, she felt for the first time as if she belonged.

I do not like to accept the idea that Sarah felt better dealing with the dangers of the streets than being at home with us. I want to think that bad people were keeping her there, pumping her full of drugs, threatening her if she left, until she was too addicted to escape. At least, that is what I tended to believe. Now, as I talk to women who knew Sarah back then and women who had experiences similar to hers, I am learning that, at least for Sarah, it wasn't like that. We did not understand her experience and she did not know how to help us to understand.

Also while Mum was away and I was responsible for Sarah, she and several other kids broke into the house of a good friend of Sarah's. They used a ladder, apparently, and stole a thousand dollars' worth of goods. The next month, once Mum was back, Sarah broke into the house across the street from Dad's in broad daylight. The people there were family friends whom Sarah knew well and liked. She must have been in a terrible state to do such things, to deliberately hurt people close to her.

That June, Mum left Sarah in Dad's custody for a day while she had to be out of town. Sarah tried to leave Dad's house, so he held on to her to stop her. She had been doing yard work to pay back the neighbours whom she had robbed. When Dad wouldn't let her go, she called 911. The police officer who responded commented that Sarah had run away four times. "More than that," Sarah said.

The break-ins and the call to the police took place after Sarah had moved to Mum's house. Moving in with Mum had been Sarah's stated goal when she ran away in February, yet clearly her problems continued to grow worse even there.

She was hanging around with some very messed-up kids, but she would not have been if she had been happy herself. I suspect that she realized that whatever was wrong was not going to be solved by a change of address and that that realization made things worse for her. She couldn't run away from herself, but she could run away to a place where nobody told her what to do, where she didn't have to deal with the challenges of school, where there were people who seemed just like her, and where she was admired, seen as having something to offer.

Sarah spent much of the summer of 1983 in Ontario, part of the time with Aunt Jean and Grandma and part of the time at a camp that was Seventh-day Adventist. She hated the camp and was angry at Aunt Jean and Grandma through most of her stay. "I think she felt shipped away," Aunt Jean says.

Her first week at camp seemed to go all right, and she spent the following weekend at Aunt Jean's cottage with a friend from camp.

That was the time she wrote in the guest book. She had been to the cottage often over the previous twelve years and it was special to her, as it was to all of us. I'm so glad that we have what she wrote while there in 1983, because I think that she meant it just as deeply as she meant what she wrote years later about the troubles with being adopted into a white family.

July 10, 1983

Dear Aunt Jean,

I really love you a lot and I am so glad to have been adopted into this family. Thanx for buying the property for all your little friends to come and vacation on, like Mark, Sarah, Maggie, Peter and the rest of the crew.

Love ya a lot. Please don't sell the cottage. It's too valuable (sentimental value).

Love ya, Sarah de Vries

P.S. Love Gramma a lot too.

It is hard to believe that the girl who wrote that was the same one who ran away repeatedly, and who was in so many ways unhappy. But she did. And she was.

She went back to camp after that, and somehow things went sour, although she did write several happy letters home to Mum while she was there. When Aunt Jean and Grandma went to get her at the end of her stay, she came out with her duffle bag and shoved it into the car. The only one around was a counsellor who was there to say goodbye to her. Once she was in the car, she looked out the window at him and said, "I'm coming back." He said, "Goodbye, Sarah." And she repeated, "I'll be back. I'll be back next year. I'll be back."

"It was a threat," Aunt Jean says. "I don't know what it was all about. He just stood there, leaning on a railing, and watched us pull out of the parking lot." Aunt Jean could not bring herself to ask Sarah about the exchange. Sarah was in no mood to discuss it. But she was clearly unhappy.

And I wonder, what happened at that camp? And what had happened in the fall of 1982 at school that made Sarah turn against all her teachers? Did things occur that we never knew about? Or were the circumstances that we did know about enough to bring on the depth of misery and the degree of alienation that Sarah experienced?

Within days of returning from camp, Sarah had discovered the street scene in Guelph, a world that Aunt Jean and Grandma had not even known existed in their small city. Sarah seemed to become a different person then. "It was really scary," Aunt Jean says. "She became withdrawn, cold. It was hard to talk to her. She just shut up and wouldn't answer." Aunt Jean suspected that drugs were behind the drastic change in Sarah's behaviour, but I'm not so sure. I think that she was deeply unhappy, and very, very angry. When she hooked in with the street life in Guelph, she had great difficulty communicating with Aunt Jean or Grandma and couldn't seem to break through to the Sarah that they knew.

One night, Aunt Jean found a shirt of Sarah's hacked to pieces in the bathroom. "It looked like a dismembered person," Aunt Jean says. Sarah had turned the shirt into a vest and left the mess behind for someone else to deal with. Sarah's destroying her things and cutting up her clothes used to drive Mum crazy too. But, however messy and thoughtless she may have been, Sarah was not engaging in wanton destruction. She was struggling to create her own style, her own identity.

Another day, Aunt Jean was walking downtown when she heard Sarah yelling, "Aunt Jean, Aunt Jean, up here." She looked all around and finally located Sarah in an upstairs window of a cheap hotel. "I would have been scared to death to go up in there," Aunt Jean says. Sarah was up there yelling at Aunt Jean, doing who knows what. She was not hiding. In fact, she seemed to be eager to alert Aunt Jean to her presence and to let the people she was with know that that was her aunt Jean.

She was able to find the street life in Guelph effortlessly, it seems. I wonder who the people were, what sort of people they were, whether they hurt Sarah in any way. Did she simply feel drawn to them, that they were in some way her kind?

Several days later, Sarah took off again, this time at night. Grandma called the police at 1:00 in the morning. An officer brought Sarah home. Sarah came into the house vibrating with excitement, trying to share what she had experienced. She had been down at the square in the centre of Guelph and had come upon a group of girls who were having a huge fight because one girl had tried to steal another's boyfriend. They had made a ring of girls so that the boyfriend-stealer couldn't get away, and the other girl was beating her up. Sarah went in to save her. She was planning to rip the fight apart. When she was telling the story, "she was almost shooting off sparks," Aunt Jean says.

This is the first story of Sarah trying to help the underdog, rushing into a dangerous situation and trying to see that right was done. It was not what a fourteen-year-old girl who was visiting her aunt and her grandmother should have been doing in the wee hours of the morning, but it is true to her character.

A few nights later, she was gone again. Grandma didn't call the police right away that time. She tried to leave it up to Sarah to come home on her own, but at 4:30 she lost her nerve. "I cannot, I cannot stand it, Jean," she said. "She could be anywhere. She could be hurt." Once again, the police found Sarah and brought her home. There was no dramatic story this time. She had met up with some people, she said.

Sarah also stole from Aunt Jean and Grandma. She swore at Grandma and was generally rude when confronted with what she had done. I cannot imagine swearing at Grandma! She was a dignified, kind woman who had been a big part of Sarah's life and whom Sarah loved dearly. And Sarah *had* stolen from her. It seemed Sarah had taken all her pain and resentment with her to Ontario and was dumping it on Grandma and Aunt Jean.

It was tough on both women and they were totally unprepared— not for the fact that Sarah was troubled, but for the depth of her anger and the lengths to which she would go. Aunt Jean would phone Mum to unburden herself, but she got not a whit of sympathy. "She just was not going to listen," Aunt Jean says. Mum was having a month away from it. "She had worried herself sick and she was taking a month off."

I remember that: Mum's desperate need for a break. Mine too. Aunt Jean's calls broke into that small peaceful time, throwing us back into the worry and snatching away any hope that that summer in Guelph was going to be the cure for what ailed Sarah. We all had so little strength and energy left after trying to cope with Sarah; we had nothing to offer one another.

The last letter that Sarah ever wrote to me was sent from Ontario that summer. She was fourteen. I was about to turn twenty-two.

Dear Maggie,

I'm really sorry that I can't be there for your birthday, but I have something for you when I get back. I made it for you at camp. I had a really good time, but I can't wait to get home. Anyway, a present I can give you right now is that I really love you a lot, no matter how mean and nasty I am to you, and when I think how mean I was, I feel really bad, so I LOVE YOU. I wish I could tell Mom how unhappy I am, but I myself don't know. But I do know this. I love you and Mom so much that I start to cry when I think about you. Well, I met Lisa again and she's doing really well, but her brother is a real jerk. I went roller skating a couple of times. It was really fun. I became an expert at Pac-Man, Frogger, Centipede, Turbo. I learnt the words to some of my favourite songs, Straight from the Heart, Total Eclipse of the Heart, What a

Feeling, Our House, Candy, Every Breath You Take and much more (songs I mean).

I have had a really good holiday so far (actually that's a lie). Forget it, anyway. At least I have a really nice tan that I got at camp. It's fading now, but it's still there. Camp turned out okay, but I didn't really want to go that much. I didn't get any of the classes I wanted and the ones I got were not worth going to. The purple bathing suit Mom bought for me got stolen or lost, but it was too small in the top half anyway and my black bathing suit is falling apart. Do you think Mom would give me Mark's record player, because he has one at Dad's house and one at Mom's house. Would you talk to her for me, please?

Happy Birthday! Well, it's 11:32 p.m. here so, love you.

Ever loving, Sarah de Vries

IF ANYTHING CHANGED NOTICEABLY after Sarah came home to Vancouver that August, it was that the bad episodes became longer and more frequent. Sarah ran away more often. Gradually, she began to believe that she was not able to live at home at all. The transition did not happen overnight, and it was not a transition directly to living on the street—an odd expression because, in Sarah's case, I don't believe that she ever actually did live on the street.

During that year, from the summer of 1983 until the summer of 1984, when I was living with Mum, Sarah was home a lot. Then she would be gone. Then she would be home. She was trying. We were trying. I had lost weight in Montreal the previous year and was slim for a while (rare, for me) and I remember trying on Sarah's clothes. Sarah and I had such fun that day. The eight years between us disappeared and Sarah became the one with something to share. She was a much more sophisticated dresser at fourteen than I was at twenty-two, and she was always willing to put much more effort into her appearance than I was.

Only recently, after I had been working on this book for months, did I remember how I spent much of that year while Sarah was moving farther and farther away from us. I was escaping in my own way.

It was the last year of my degree. I kept up with my courses and did well enough, but I still gained fifty pounds. I would skip classes from lunch on, buy Häagen-Dazs ice cream, then come home and sit in Mum's bed watching soap operas. *All My Children, Another World* and *General Hospital*. I followed all three storylines that year, a regular three-hour escape! No wonder my memories of Sarah's repeated running away are vague. I was running away too.

MINDY WAS A CLOSE CHILDHOOD FRIEND of Sarah's. She remembers an event from the fall of 1983, the last time she spent time with Sarah. Mindy was in grade eight; Sarah was in grade nine and still going to school occasionally.

One night, Sarah suggested that she and Mindy go downtown. Mindy remembers Sarah loving it and being caught up in the energy. The two of them walked around on Granville near Robson and later sat at a bus stop and watched the nightlife, people coming and going from arcades and bars. Mindy doesn't remember Sarah talking to anyone that night. "I was amazed at how comfortable she felt and how interested she was," Mindy says. "It was almost as if she had found a place that was hers." Mindy, on the other hand, hated it. She could tell that Sarah had been there before and was struck by the chasm between Sarah's comfort and her own discomfort.

It wasn't that Sarah was truly happy downtown. Always there was a pull in both directions. Sarah would continue to spend periods of time at Mum's house until 1989, and she continued to visit for birthdays and Christmas until Mum moved to Ontario in 1993. But from the fall of 1983 on, she was drawn ever increasingly to the downtown life.

Mindy saw her once more after that, from a distance, in the Pacific Centre Mall. "I was on the escalator," Mindy says, "and I saw her in

Radio Shack. She was very skinny. She had tight clothes on, jeans and a jean jacket. Her hair was very big. It took me a minute to recognize her. When I got there, she was gone."

Mindy then brought up her own confusion about how Sarah was making money downtown. For us, her family, the realization that Sarah was making money by selling sex came in fits and starts that fall and winter. Her school friends, though, were oblivious.

At University Hill Secondary School, they talked about Sarah's absence, about trying to help her. They knew that she was hanging around downtown and had a pretty good idea that she was using drugs. "We were doing drugs at school," Mindy says, "marijuana and speed. But I don't think that we clued in that she was working as a prostitute." Mindy and her friends were concerned, but they didn't know what to do. "No one wanted to do what she was doing. We had the feeling that it was weird and not healthy. But we didn't go to our parents. We didn't go to our school counsellor. We didn't have a support network to turn to and ask for help.

"I think that's really unfortunate. It's like she sort of slipped away. What stopped us as her friends from reaching out to her? I didn't know how to not let her do this."

I now understand why Sarah was drawn into selling sex. She had to make money to survive. Although Mindy mentions drugs, I don't think that they were a driving force for Sarah at that point. She was not truly addicted for at least three years. Until she was seventeen she was able to come home for periods of time without going into withdrawal. And it was not necessary to go downtown to do drugs. As Mindy mentions, they were common among kids everywhere.

I know that Sarah used drugs recreationally, possibly more than her peers who remained in school. It seems to me that people have the idea that it is the drugs that lure kids to the street. I honestly believe that in Sarah's case, what lured her was the excitement and the sense that here were other people like her, and what pushed her was her unhappiness at home.

Mum's journal provides a record of Sarah's running away over and over again through the second half of 1983, sometimes brought home by police or social workers, other times arriving under her own steam. Mum's building frustration and helplessness comes through in her writing. Sex work comes up twice.

JUNE 2   Sitting in Mother's attic. Tomorrow I go back. I've spent so much on phone calls it is horrifying. Sarah keeps running away. She was picked up in a house where there are people who are into armed robbery and heavy drugs. I don't know if we can protect her from herself or not.

Sarah ran away again after I came back on Tuesday night. She was picked up Friday morning. She is so full of anger. It is strange that hearing how she mutilated Peter's school annual crystallized for me some conception of the turmoil she has going on in her . . . Tomorrow morning she has an exam to write. I must make sure she's up in time. I've booked off sick this week just to see her through.

Wednesday a.m. Sarah is still asleep. The night before last we went to see *The Return of the Jedi,* Sarah and Mark and Maggie and I. Sarah told me, "You'll love the animals, Mum, the teddy bear ones." And I did.

SEPT 3   Visiting in Victoria with Maggie and Sarah. Four rounds of Mille Bournes [a card game]. It was really fun. Last night Sarah went out her window and was gone most of the night. It is good to be here.

SEPT 7   Patched Sarah's pants. Spent two nights on her essay. Talking, talking, talking. Trying to get her to relate it to a book. She says she hasn't read any of the books in her room. They bore her. I get sick of trying.

OCT 3   Sarah has been gone all night. Still not back this evening.

OCT 7   Sarah's case number is 83-64281. She phoned last night and talked to Mark. Peggy Beck [her school advisor] phoned too. Sarah has not been attending school. She sure is making it hard for herself. Sarah and Tina came for supper. Sarah "just wanted to visit."

OCT 12   Sarah came back yesterday at about 5 p.m., having left on Saturday. Crazy. Thank goodness I have the next four days off. I tried to talk to her and ended up shouting and arguing.

OCT 16   Talk with Sarah. Tears from me. So very tired.

OCT 17   Sarah cooked spaghetti.

OCT 18   Mark cooked. Three games of Othello with Sarah and she creamed me every time. We moved the old record player up to her room and she is blasting away on it right now. I cut her hair at her request. Friendly. Relaxed.

OCT 19   Trying to ignore Sarah's conversation on the phone advising someone to punch some girl in the face. The police finally brought back the car keys that were stolen [by Anne] last spring.

NOV 5   Sarah didn't come home last night. She fell asleep at a party. Shit.

Nov 20   Last night I went to bed early and at 11:30 I got phoned
         by a social worker from Emergency Services who returned
         Sarah home and sat and talked for a few minutes. Same
         old story. I'm sick of it.
         Evening: She left. She is gone.

Nov 24   Sarah was picked up by the police for possibly soliciting
         on a street corner Tuesday at 6:30, just after I left for
         Victoria. They took her home. She is gone again now.
         This time, Maggie says, she is getting more practical. She
         took the toothpaste and the conditioner.

Dec 6   Sarah phoned. I wasn't very enthusiastic.

Dec 17   Sarah has come home with tonsillitis and has gone again.
         I had flu.

Dec 18   Sarah phoned and we talked about prostitution.

Mum's feelings are clear, but Sarah's I can only guess at. The one person who might be able to tell us what Sarah went through, felt and thought is Sarah herself, and she is not around to do so, so we must piece her story together, gathering material from everywhere. But no matter how much material I gather, I do not end up with tidy answers. Still, I continue to hope, even in the face of hopelessness. I read Sarah's childhood letters and write about them and I find myself hoping that things will work out differently this time. As if I can put to use what I have learned. As if I might reach out to Sarah. As if we'll talk. Really talk. And finally, she'll be all right.

It is like when I reread a sad book that I love or watch a favourite movie for the fifth time. Maybe Rhett won't walk out on Scarlett this time. Maybe Boromir won't try to steal the ring; maybe he won't have to die. But every time, the outcome is the same. Sarah is not a book or a movie—she is a living, breathing person whom I love, a person who is not living and breathing any more. It is hard to accept that the outcome will always be the same, to accept once and for all that she is gone.

Sarah called several days before Christmas that year and asked to bring a friend for Christmas Day. Mum said no. Then Sarah said that she didn't want to go to Vancouver Island as planned. Mum insisted. Sarah didn't come home the next day, but in the end, she was at the house on Christmas Eve and she and Mum had a lovely time together, wrapping and delivering gifts to the residents at the Extended Care Unit where Mum worked. Mum wrote in her journal, "Then she made popcorn and we climbed into my bed and watched Alistair Sims be Scrooge. Perfect. And we liked all the same parts best and laughed and cried and were warm together. A good evening. Really good for me. I hope for her too. Then Jan came up with a lovely sweater for Sarah at 11 p.m. Green with a hood and pockets and rainbow stripes around the middle. She really likes it."

I have fond memories of Christmas Day that year. Mum, Peter, Mark, Sarah and I travelled to Victoria with Sybilla, our tricolour collie, to spend Christmas with a family friend, Liz. I liked our having all four kids together for once. And Christmas dinner at Liz's, though different from our traditional Christmas dinner, was delicious and festive. I gave Sarah a pink beret and Peter gave her punk gloves. She is wearing them in many of the pictures from that day.

On Boxing Day Mum tried to talk to Sarah about what was going on in her life. "She seemed so ghostlike about the house," Mum wrote later. "Doing nothing but watching TV and snacking. She cried. I cried. We hugged. No, she was not angry at me and did not feel I was snooping or being critical. That was not why she was silent. Was it fear, then? I asked. That she never answered." Mum told Sarah that the coming and going had to stop, that she couldn't just leave and return at her whim. Mum told her that she would have to live a legal existence, which included school, and that she believed Sarah could do it.

Then Mum made a lemon meringue pie, Sarah's favourite dessert. But when Mum called Sarah to set the table, Sarah was not there. She had left by the cellar door. She had packed all her Christmas gifts and some of her other things into Mum's largest suitcase, and she was gone. All the time Mum had been talking to her, she had already been packed to go. That leaving—planned, packed for, secret—seems to have been a more conscious act than the earlier running away.

I don't remember that Boxing Day supper, pork chops and lemon meringue pie. It must have been a sad meal. That night Mum phoned Emergency Services. Then she phoned Missing Persons and finally persuaded them to take down Sarah's name. Then she went to bed.

A few days after Christmas 1983, Mum wrote in her diary, "Last night crying over my inability to be loving enough and wise enough, crying about Sarah. Terrible, painful crying, my face hurt so badly, a ripping feeling, but I've got to get through it, not bury it all. How does one reach self-acceptance? Crying is not enough."

From there, things moved quickly to the next stage. Mum had told Sarah that she couldn't stay at home if she was going to be running away all the time and if she was not going to attend school. Sarah had made it clear from her actions that she was not considering returning to school, at least not then. On January 24, 1984, Mum and Dad signed papers that stated that Sarah was apprehended on January 23. Sarah was taken into care, put into a group home. The papers from that January state that Sarah had been involved in prostitution for several months and that whenever she was taken home she always returned to the street scene.

Sarah described the process herself in her interview, almost three years later, with photojournalist Daniel Gautreau: "I ran away first. I ran away for about a year and they kept taking me home and I kept leaving, so they got me a social worker, Holly Prince. She put me in a group home and I was happier in the group home than I was at home. It was great. I liked everyone there. They treated me the way I wanted to be treated." She went on to explain that she already knew everyone at the group home. She had met them on her trips downtown with Anne, when much of Vancouver's street prostitution was happening on Davie Street in Vancouver's West End.

Sarah talked about how slow she was to trust Holly. "When I first meet people, I'm not too sure about them and I stay away from them. Sometimes I'm really rude. I had a social worker. I watched her for a while. I didn't trust her too much. And about the day I got to trust her, they transferred her to working with handicapped children. Every time I start talking to someone and I let them know how I'm feeling, they either leave or they die or something. I don't like talking to people that much."

Mum says, "Nobody understood her. Nobody understood her. And I would say, 'Well, help me. Talk to me.' And she would say, 'No, no.'" Sarah may have thought that she would find people who understood her better in a group home and that she would be living with kids like herself. I don't think that she had ever felt deeply understood by someone her own age. Maybe in some ways she had never felt deeply understood by anyone. That is such a common feeling among teens, I think, because they don't even understand themselves.

After moving into her first group home, Sarah was involved in a purse-snatching that January and spent some time in the Vancouver youth detention centre, Willingdon. She then moved into a new group home, Rainbow House. In February, she said to Dad, "I like it here. They don't fucking preach at me." Sarah was reportedly doing well, although she was uncommunicative. She was healthy, but she wouldn't come to the phone when Dad called. She was talking about going back to school in September and was getting involved in the running of the group home.

But a few days after that, she was back in Willingdon, this time for stealing the Rainbow House car. She was out again by April, apparently, because she was picked up on April 24 by a police officer and then again in May when she had been injured by a knife across her palm. She was barely fifteen years old.

The group homes varied in terms of what they were able to offer Sarah and she was ambivalent about them as well. In her interview, she emphasized her independence: "I like being by myself a lot of the time, and you don't get that in a group home. People are always pushing you into talking about stuff when it really hurts to talk about it. They are always telling you to do this or that. I'll do it on my own time, you know. If someone pushed me into something, like school, I quit. If someone's telling me I have to do it, I won't do it, but if someone doesn't tell me I have to do it, I'll do it and I'll do it till it's right."

By December 1984, Sarah was spending time at another group home, Cypress House, which seems to have been a supportive, happy place in many ways. Barbara, the mother of a childhood friend of mine, worked at Cypress House. "I was working with a lot of kids that were third- or fourth-generation kids on the street," she told me. "Sarah wasn't part of that. She had that spunky kind of centre. There was a light to her. She wasn't a whiner. She didn't stage big scenes to get her way. She had incredible dignity. She could be quite bratty, but she could be dependable. She could be responsible. She helped someone when they were hurt. She wasn't a group-home junkie. She would leave. Or get dignified and saucy and toss her head and look at you like you were the riff-raff. She knew what was happening to her, so that made it harder. She had a conscience."

Barbara's words offer the first picture of Sarah in that new world—the honourable, dignified Sarah who made such an impact on so many people. Sarah would continue to commit crimes, and she would continue to struggle to change her life. But from this point on, a picture of her begins to emerge—a picture of a young woman of great beauty and with enormous potential for love and caring for others.

The tragedy is that she never seemed to be able to turn that love and caring toward herself or to accept it from others in a way that would allow her to change her life as she always wished she could. Often in her journals, Sarah writes about her place in the world. In the following entry, she talks about her struggle to fit in, a struggle that she believed was partly precipitated by being adopted into a white family.

Man, I don't understand how the adoption agency could let a
couple that are both of the opposite colour as the child become
this child's legal guardians. I understand that they were not as
strict as they are today on things of race, gender and traditions.
But, come on, did they honestly think that it would have
absolutely no effect on my way of thinking or in the way I
present my persona? I'm not accepted into the Caucasian social
circle nor am I accepted in the black social circle, for I am
neither white nor black. The blacks say I act too much like a tie
and tails, and whites say I act like a homeboy. I'm stuck in the
middle and outside to both. I have no people. I have no nation
and I am alone.

That sense of isolation followed Sarah wherever she went, I think.
I don't want to believe that she really felt that way. Did she wish that
she had not joined our family? That breaks my heart. The child who
loved to play on the beach, who swam like a fish, who loved to laugh
and who seemed to know her own mind so well—that child was not
alone. She had people. We were her people. But reading her journals
reveals that she felt differently, at least at times. In her interview with
Daniel, she said, "I felt like I was always on the outside looking in,"
although she went on to say about Mum and Dad that "they were
really nice, they gave me everything I wanted," and that she was
happy in our family until she was ten or eleven.

In another journal entry, she writes,

I'd like to go home if I had a real home. I've never really had
one, yet I've always wondered what a real home and family life
and brothers and sisters and mother and father would be like.
But there is no such thing as the perfect family. Dysfunctional
families are everywhere. The old saying, the grass is always
greener on the other side of fence. Well, it's not once you get

over to the greener side and turn to say goodbye, you find that everything is much greener on the side you left, but it's too late. You're already on your way and don't want to hear the words "I told you so" again.

When she turns to say goodbye, she sees that the grass is greener on the side that she has left, the side where we are, the typical dysfunctional family. I cannot bear it that she says she never had a real home. She did so, she did so, she did so!

I have to accept that, although we were hers and she was ours, there was a place at her core where she knew she was different, a place that we hardly knew existed, let alone understood. Even downtown, where at least at first she felt a part of things, she was still lost between two worlds.

1984   October   *Linda Louise Grant last seen*

1985   August 1   *Laura Mah last seen*

1985   August   *Sheryl Donahue last seen*

four

EARLY FRIENDSHIPS

In 1984, Sarah was beginning to forge bonds with other girls, bonds that would last. In September, she met a girl who would be her friend for years. Alex had run away from home with a friend in late August and come to Vancouver. When the two girls went to Social Services for help, they were told that they could have bus tickets home, but that was all. They walked out the door, met a male prostitute, and started working.

Not long after that, Alex noticed a young woman walking up the street at a furious pace, a young woman in stilettos and a black spandex miniskirt. Alex described her as beautiful and compact and looking much older than fifteen.

The girl was Sarah and her pace matched her mood. Alex watched fascinated while Sarah hauled off and hit the guy she was after. Her purse flew. "She was dynamite," Alex said. "This little compact woman with one hell of a blow." Moments later, Sarah and Alex were introduced. Sarah was still angry at the man she had attacked, but she shrugged that off and gave Alex her full attention.

Within weeks, Alex was apprehended and put into a group home, Cypress House. Sarah wasn't living there at the time, but she would come over and hang out. Alex remembers one evening when Sarah was on the couch wrapped up in a blanket, miserable. It was a comforting place, a place that drew kids whether they were living there or not. "Kids would come along on outings," Alex says. "I loved that place."

Alex continued to hang out with Sarah when she was living downtown again. Granville Street was the hangout at the time. They spent time at McDonald's and at local hotels. They partied together. Sarah smoked marijuana and she and Alex did some cocaine, but it was recreational drug use.

They squatted with other young people in a condemned hotel that would later become Granville Cinemas. One night an unattended Hibachi started a fire. Sarah and Alex had to climb down a broken-down fire escape. Alex was afraid of heights and almost didn't make it, but instead of running off into the night, Sarah stayed and coaxed her down.

Alex remembers a telling line of Sarah's, perhaps spoken that night: "You can't show people that you're scared." Sarah kept true to that policy most of her life, but in her own writing, she acknowledged those fears that she would never let anyone see.

At school we had a gerbil in a cage. In that cage he had a running wheel. I used to daydream as I became hypnotized by the spinning of the wheel, around, around and around. Does this little guy realize that he is going absolutely nowhere? Huffing and puffing, he runs his little heart out.

I think I'm that gerbil in another universe outside of his on my own running wheel, going absolutely nowhere fast.

I'm getting scared inside.

Sarah got into a serious relationship in 1984, perhaps her first and perhaps her best. Nick* spotted for her, writing down the licence plate numbers of the cars of her johns so that if something happened to her, he would have some information for the police. Spotting works as a deterrent too, letting the john know that someone can identify his car. To Alex's knowledge, Nick never took money from Sarah. "They were really into each other," Alex says.

Mum remembers Nick too. He came with Sarah to visit on Christmas Day, 1984. I wasn't in Vancouver that Christmas; I had moved to Montreal in the summer. Mum told me later that Sarah and Nick arrived during dessert, Sarah wearing slinky black clothes and high heels. Sarah seemed to enjoy opening her presents in front of him. Mum gave her a sewing box stocked with supplies. When Sarah saw what it was, she turned to Nick and said, "Now I can fix your jacket." Mum had made lemon meringue pie, and this time Sarah was there to eat it. They played a game of Kensington together, her favourite game, and everyone had a good time. Then Mum drove them home, to Vancouver's densely populated West End.

Sarah had a front tooth knocked out that year. She said that it was knocked out while she and Nick were swimming together, and we always doubted that, suspecting violence, but Alex referred casually to Sarah's tooth being knocked out in a pool. Sometimes our suspicions were unjustified.

The relationship lasted a year. In November 1985, Nick was arrested and sent to jail for bank robbery and Sarah was evicted from her apartment. It was horrifying to hear that Sarah's boyfriend was guilty of robbing a bank, but one of the things that made him better for Sarah than some of the men she got involved with later on was the fact that he was, as Alex put it, independent. He did not live off Sarah. She didn't have to work more to support him. He was with her because he liked her. And vice versa. Most of Sarah's later relationships would be much more complex and exploitative.

From late 1985 until the middle of 1986, Sarah spent much of her time with another friend, Angela*—a girl who had run away from home the way Sarah had. They lived together in four different locations, two apartments and two hotel rooms in the West End. Angela was a year younger than Sarah, just fifteen when they met.

By that time, Sarah had been selling sex for about two years. I know very little about how she got involved in prostitution herself, except what I can glean from women like Angela who share their stories. Whatever it had been like for Sarah, she wanted to share what wisdom she had gained and offer what protection she could to a young girl who she believed needed her help.

Sarah met Angela in an arcade near Granville and Nelson, the arcade where Sarah and Angela would later play endless games of pinball. Angela had been downtown before. She had worked for an older woman who had taken care of everything. Angela just had to show up at the house and have sex with men there. In the morning the woman would give her money and Angela would leave. "It didn't really count so much," Angela says, meaning that it didn't count as prostitution.

Apparently an older girl or woman had "helped" Sarah in the same way that the older woman had helped Angela, but that woman was gone by the time Angela arrived. Sarah described the woman in positive terms, Angela says; Sarah felt helped by her. The woman taught Sarah the rules and Sarah passed them on to Angela. I wish that I knew more about the nature of that relationship and about Sarah's experiences in those early months.

I try to imagine a fourteen-year-old girl taking the bus downtown, making her way to a particular house and having sex with men there for money. I try to imagine the pain and desperation that would drive her there and the reinforcement of that pain when men would use her body—she was still a child. When Angela said that it didn't count so much, she meant that she wasn't working the streets on her own; everything was arranged for her. She had not yet started to think of herself as a sex worker. Girls don't start defining themselves as prostitutes overnight. When Angela turned her first trick the night after she met Sarah downtown, she was consciously taking on the identity of a prostitute. From that point on, it counted very much indeed.

When Angela met Sarah, she was not headed to the house to make some money. She was set on self-destruction. "I just wanted to die," she says. "I wanted to turn a trick, get a hotel room and slash my wrists." She didn't know what else to do. All other options seemed closed to her. "I was a lost cause," she adds.

Sarah saw her in the arcade, a young girl wearing flat grey runners, jeans, a grey-and-yellow striped rugby shirt with the polo collar flipped up and a jean jacket. Somehow, Sarah knew that the girl was in trouble. She approached Angela and asked if she was all right. Something possessed Angela, perhaps a last flash of hope, and she said, "No." She was not all right.

Sarah was the same height and build as Angela, close to the same age, obviously experienced, but, says Angela, she came across as genuine. For some reason that Angela did not understand, Sarah cared. She offered concern and protection on Angela's terms.

Later, Angela went with Sarah to turn a trick. Sarah checked that that was what Angela really wanted to do, but did not try to talk her into or out of it. She also made sure that Angela knew how to go about it. She told her what you charged for what you did. How you did it. Where you went. "You don't grow up learning these things," Angela points out. "Parents don't tell you. You're told, cross at the sidewalk. You're not told, sixty bucks for a blow job or a hand job or whatever. You're not told these things."

The first man who pulled up "was this great big fat guy. He was huge." He just wanted Angela, but Sarah wouldn't let Angela go unless she came too, to make sure that it was all right. Angela was launched into a difficult life that night, but she did not take the money she earned, rent a hotel room and kill herself.

Sarah and Angela were almost instant friends; they played pinball for hours back at the same arcade where they had met, one of the nicer arcades in the area. They always played Comet. If they got separated, they always met back at Comet. They had all the high scores. It was their game.

Sarah and Angela had entered street prostitution at a critical time in its history in Vancouver. A vigilante group was in the process of pushing prostitution out of the West End, the start of a move that would eventually drive sex workers to the Downtown Eastside, the area where Sarah lived for the last decade of her life, the area from which sixty-three women have gone missing in the past twenty-five years. In 1983 and 1984, Sarah worked in the West End, but by the time she met Angela, the trade had moved a few blocks east to the less residential neighbourhood around Granville.

For a couple of months Sarah and Angela lived in a hotel on Robson Street, now one of the most expensive shopping streets in Vancouver. The hotel is still there, but it's a tourist-oriented hotel now. Back then it was one of the few hotels willing to take kids. After that, they lived in an apartment so small that the beds were built to slide into the walls. It was in terrible shape. The mattress stains were so bad that Sarah and Angela got a piece of foam to put over it. "It was cheap and it was disgusting and dirty," Angela says, "but you could get a place without a whole lot of questions."

I have mixed feelings when I hear about these hotels and apartment buildings, filthy places willing to rent to children at low rates and to turn a blind eye to what was going on in their rooms. Those were the years when Sarah was a child, a child who was sexually exploited every day by men who either didn't care how old she was or who actively sought out underage prostitutes. If those hotels had turned her and Angela away, what would the girls have done? Would they have been forced to work for a pimp who could put them up somewhere? Would they have ended up working on the street with nowhere to sleep at night? Or would they have been more likely to seek help?

Considering how things are today, when so many kids are forced to live on the street, in Vancouver and other cities, I'm glad that Sarah had a roof over her head, a safe place that she controlled, at least for a while.

Not only did Sarah find a safe place for herself and Angela but she constantly invited others to share that space. "Our new family was each other," Angela says, "and the odd person that Sarah pulled into our hotel room. She pulled in lost souls, but I couldn't say too much because she had pulled me in."

At one time Sarah invited five people to share their hotel room, a room with only one double bed. Altogether, there were five women and two men, or five girls and two boys, to be more accurate. One of the boys sold marijuana by the gram, calling out, "Gram of pot, gram of pot" on street corners. The other was a squatter, as was one of the girls, Squirrel. Angela was not sure about the rest of the girls, but figured that they were soon to be working the streets or that they already were. "I don't know," she says. "They were just . . . people in my room!" Three would sleep normally in the bed, with a fourth across the foot. Squirrel slept beside Angela at first, but when she got her period unexpectedly and bled all over the bed, she was relegated to the bathtub. Whoever was left slept on the floor.

First thing in the morning, everyone would slip out to the McDonald's nearby where Sarah and Angela would meet them later and buy them breakfast. One morning Angela asked Sarah why they were paying the rent for the room for all those people. The two friends always split their bills fifty-fifty. Why were they supporting these people? Angela wanted to know.

"Better us than somebody else," Sarah said. "They have nowhere else to go."

Angela understood, but she craved privacy. She wanted to be able to roll over in bed. She wanted to have the bathroom to herself. In the life they were leading, they did not have many personal possessions. "What you do have becomes really important," Angela says.

Subterfuge was required as well, because they were only allowed two people in a room. Sarah and Angela would walk in the front door and then one of them would go let everyone else in by the fire door. They always made sure that they didn't have a room near the front desk; the building was old and footsteps carried, so they had to be near the back of the building. That made it easier, when Sarah and Angela had the room to themselves, to get tricks in and out. They had removed one of the screws from the room number and whoever had a trick in the room would turn the number upside down to alert the other to stay away.

I love hearing about Sarah's generosity when she invited other homeless kids to share her room. She took care of people. While downtown, she had something to give others—something I don't think that she felt she had at home. I wonder how big a role that played in keeping her there. On balance, could it be that she felt better about herself sneaking tricks into a hotel room and sharing that room with half a dozen kids than she did in her comfortable West Point Grey home? I think she must have; otherwise she wouldn't have stayed. At the same time, I know from her journals that that life wore away at her, that she despised herself for what she was doing, that she judged herself harshly, and that the longer she spent there, the harder it got to come home.

Angela remembers Sarah with great fondness. She keeps Sarah's photo on her desk and credits Sarah with her life. Still, the line between help and recruitment must be a fine one at times. I don't believe that Sarah recruited Angela. Sarah did not have a pimp at that time and she never made money from Angela. The two of them shared expenses as roommates do. But girls do, and I'm sure at that time, did, recruit other girls.

A woman who did sex work from 1993 until 2000 described to me how she used to recruit girls who were just a year or two younger than herself. She would look for girls who were sitting alone, not tough-looking girls, but those who looked vulnerable, lonely, naive. She said that the girls that are the easiest to recruit are not the most beautiful or the most confident, but those who have been bullied or ostracized and who crave friendship. She would ask if she could sit down, strike up a conversation, suggest a movie, take the girl shopping, share confidences, find the girl's weak spot. She would take the girl to a bar, somewhere the child couldn't go on her own, introduce her to new experiences, shower her with attention. Finally, after a week or two, she would introduce her to the pimp. "Here's a friend of mine," she would say. He would be attractive and friendly. The two would start dating. "At that age, people become instant friends," she pointed out. "And if

I'm spending my time recruiting, then I don't have to turn tricks." The style of recruitment that she described sounded to me like what I believed went on, except that it never occurred to me that girls would be doing most of the recruiting. Angela referred to recruiting as well, to picking out the vulnerable girls, but she was adamant that pimps and drugs are not the key forces at work when girls turn to sex work.

She points out that parents prefer to believe that their child is a prostitute because she's hooked on drugs rather than looking to what is troubling the girl at home. "It's easier to believe drugs did it," she said. "Drugs and an evil person got them. But they're not fish."

The language, "trolling" and "luring," is indeed that of fishing. But she is right; girls and boys are not fish. Angela does acknowledge that pimps, and women and girls working for pimps, troll school grounds and malls looking for vulnerable girls. She herself can still pick out girls who would be easy to lure away. "Puberty sucks," she reminds me. "If some child is having that much fun and looks that happy, it's usually a mask. I was a perfect student and a perfect jock. It was a perfect mask." She says that teenagers get good at pretending, but that if they are miserable deep down, they can usually pick out another miserable person—recognizing the misery and vulnerability beneath the mask.

Kids are not only responding to tempting bait on the outside, they are driven by some deep discontent on the inside. To me, Angela's statement that they are not fish is a powerful deconstruction of a metaphor. We create a language set around a particular activity that reinforces the beliefs we are comfortable with. Bad people are trolling for and luring away our children. Catch the bad people, solve the problem. Such a strategy will never work for two reasons: more "bad people" will appear in their place; and, as long as we do not solve our problems at home, our children will continue to leave.

Char Lafontaine, who worked in the sex trade in Vancouver from 1969 until the early 1990s, told me a different story. She said that while that kind of deliberate recruitment does take place, often it is much less formal than that and less malicious in intent. She described a common scenario in which a girl will run away downtown, meet some people, spend some time there, and then either decide to go home or get taken home by the authorities. Soon, she wants to go downtown again, but not by herself. She describes what it's like to her friends, glamorizing it a bit, wanting them to be impressed. And eventually, she is able to persuade another girl to go with her—just as, I believe, Anne did Sarah.

In personal writing about her own life, Char has described the first days she spent downtown at the age of thirteen: "I learned what all poor people have to learn. When you're poor and have no formal skills, if you're too young to work, you go underground into that economy that is as foreign to most straights as money is to us. I started out panhandling. I could get enough for pizza, a piece of chicken, sometimes even a room for the night. Men started to offer me money to relieve my problem. But I wasn't ready to go there. I knew it probably wouldn't be long. Too many wet and destitute nights on Hastings Street were driving me right there."

I don't think that Sarah was formally recruited: as far as I can tell she didn't have a pimp in the early years. Sarah said in her interview with Daniel, "I first started working because I needed the money and I didn't want to ask anybody else to help me out. I thought, I'm independent now and I can do it myself. Once I started working, it was like every time I'd pull a trick, I'd end up in the shower for about ten minutes, washing myself and making sure I was clean and everything. It's rude. It's gross. You don't really think about it while you're doing it, but after you do it, every time you do it, it scars you mentally, it leaves you with a kind of empty feeling. It hurts."

Sarah taught Angela all that she had learned. She taught her how to wear makeup to work the streets. She taught her how to choose shoes and outfits. And she taught her how to stay safe— where to get condoms, for example. Which drugstores would sell them without questions. Which condoms were best. Which ones tasted bad.

For a long time, Angela never did a trick without Sarah. Sarah came along to make sure that Angela was safe. She would sit in the living room or somewhere nearby, keeping an eye on things. Eventually, Sarah decided that Angela didn't need that degree of care. After that, they spotted for each other, each keeping track of the other's licence plates, of where the other had gone, arranging to meet up afterwards at a particular time and place.

One of the things I learned from Angela that surprised me was how long it took Sarah to get into heavy heroin use. Some time after she and Sarah met, Angela did heroin for the first time, threw up all over Sarah, went to bed and never did heroin again. She says that at that time, Sarah had done heroin only a couple of times.

I did not get the sense from Angela that anyone had ever tried to get her or Sarah addicted to heroin or to other drugs. In her interview with Daniel, Sarah said that the first time she tried heroin she got sick too. But the next time, "it made me feel more relaxed. I was in control of everything. I didn't have to think of stuff I didn't want to think about, and I could act more like myself and people wouldn't think I was weird or anything."

The night Angela tried heroin, she and Sarah were staying on the North Shore with a man whom Angela called her Sugar Daddy. A party was going on, but Angela went to sleep. In the morning they all had steak and eggs for breakfast, after which the man gave Angela money and dropped her and Sarah off downtown.

They bought matching pink and blue boots. They couldn't decide on one or the other, so Angela bought both, one for her and one for Sarah so that they could trade. "We wore each other's clothes, shoes, everything," Angela says.

Sarah and Angela shared a lot during their time together. I'm glad to know that they had each other. Eventually they were able to get an apartment with two bedrooms. Rather than have one room each, they would share a room and use the other room for work, so that their sleeping room would be free of the taint of the men they brought home.

They worked the renegade corners, the corners where girls and women worked who didn't have a pimp. It sounds to me as if those corners were tougher in a way, because the pimps would be trying to get those girls to work for them, but at least the girls on those corners had a degree of independence.

Sarah told Daniel that sometimes she had to fight for the right to work on those corners. "They tell me to move and I'd say, 'I'm not going to move,' and they start pushing me around. You got to fight back. If you let someone come up every time you're working and take your corner away, pretty soon you're not going to have anywhere to work to make your money. You got to defend your corner."

Daniel asked her what she thought about pimps. "Pimps?" Sarah said. "There's no use for them. When it comes down to it, you're standing on the corner. You're risking your life every half hour to give somebody a free ride. It's not worth it when you can put the money in your own back pocket and do whatever you want with it. Give yourself a good time instead of paying for somebody else. You deserve it. You worked for it. It's yours. You can do whatever you want with it." Here she confirms what many people told me: Sarah never had a pimp. She had boyfriends who took her money, but she never got into a formal arrangement where she had to give her money to a pimp.

Independent or not, the risks were always great. The worst risk was violence and exploitation at the hands of johns. At least twice, Sarah rescued Angela from such situations.

The first time, Angela let herself be talked into going to a man's apartment with another girl. The girl got extra money and didn't have to participate herself if she brought other girls. Men took pornographic pictures of Angela against her will. "You had to tell this guy that you were twelve," Angela said. "That was the first time I ever had pictures taken of me. I didn't want them, but at that point I was scared."

Angela knew that it was dangerous to have photos of herself in circulation, but she didn't know what to do. She went back to the arcade and found Sarah at the Comet game. Sarah told her to wait right there. Off she went and came back within an hour with the pictures. Angela never knew what she had to say or do to get her hands on them, but get them she did.

The other time was much more serious. Sarah and Angela were in a hotel with two different men in two different rooms on the same hallway. The man that Angela was with tried to hurt her, and Sarah heard her screaming. Sarah ran into the room, jumped on his back and started beating him. With Sarah on his back, he dragged Angela into the boiler room and adjusted the valve. Scalding steam poured out of the boiler. He had to let go of Angela to fight off Sarah. Sarah screamed at Angela to run, but Angela wouldn't. He flipped Sarah off his back and tried to stick her face in the steam, but Sarah managed to kick him in the groin, and when he bent over he burned his face, and they escaped.

"Sarah was willing to stay there and get hurt to save me," Angela says. "I couldn't leave her. At that point she was all I had."

Their lives were very dangerous. Yet, when someone tried to hurt them, as the man in the boiler room did, they did not turn to the authorities or to any adults. They believed that they could depend only on one another.

When teens feel that way, it is a great challenge for any adults, relatives, social workers or police officers, to reach them. One group that had regular contact with teens like Angela and Sarah was police officers known as the "kiddie cops."

Angela remembers one kiddie cop, Jack, fondly. She believes that he cared about her and about other youths. And he knew there were limits on what he could do if he wanted to retain Angela's trust. He would stop the car, she told me, and open the door. She would get in, knowing exactly what to expect: a drive to Emergency Services, a mug of hot chocolate and a doughnut. She could trust him not to apprehend her. It was like a check-in.

"Are you okay?" he would ask.

"Yeah."

"You need a doctor?"

"No."

"Where you living?"

"I don't know."

She would sit in the office for twenty minutes to half an hour and then she would leave. The police were supposed to take her into care, she told me, but once a kid had been taken in a certain number of times and ended up back on the street each time, they would just pick her up to check on her and then let her go. "It was warm in the car," Angela says, indicating that she welcomed the respite as long as no threat was attached to it, "and I knew I was going to be out in twenty minutes." Also, regular cops would leave youth alone if they were taken care of by the kiddie squad.

Once, the kiddie squad treated Angela differently, though. Jack had told her that if he picked her up again, she would be leaving the city and going back into care. She could not bear the thought of another foster home. So when Jack did pick her up the next time, she knew that she was going to fight for her freedom; she just didn't know how. He drove her to Emergency Services, where her shoes were taken away and she was put in a back office.

Angela did the only thing she could think of, drastic though it was. She picked up a black vinyl chair with metal legs, threw it through the window, jumped out and got straight into a cab where Sarah was waiting for her.

Sarah had seen her get into Jack's car and knew that this was the "one more time," the time when they would take Angela away. She got a cab and followed, circled the block until the chair flew through the window, and then the two girls were together again. Angela had to stay out of her usual part of town for about a month after that.

It's a story straight out of a movie. The capture. The bare feet. The swinging chair, breaking glass, loyal friend, waiting cab. Yet it has so much heartache built in: the kids, both so desperate, so unhappy, yet so unwilling to accept help from adults; the adults, all well meaning, I suspect, in this instance if not in others, but with no idea what might actually help these girls. Maybe if Sarah hadn't been there in that cab, Angela would have failed in her getaway and she would have been placed with foster parents who could have helped her. But that seems unlikely. I think that it is rare that teenagers (or any of us) can be forced to change, to make new choices.

What triumph Sarah and Angela must have felt as they made their getaway! I felt triumph hearing about it. But it wasn't really a triumph for anyone—just another failed intersection between the authorities and the kids on the street, a further erosion of trust.

Less than a year before she disappeared, Sarah wrote a cryptic journal entry about her transition from childhood to the streets.

When you're a child, you spend your time playing with dolls and toys. All this is apparently getting you ready for adulthood. Childhood dreams for some can and will last forever. Some happily come true, for others they get blurred and turn into different dreams.

For the rest of the dreamers, their dreams get shot down, shattered into tons of little pieces never to be dreamt again. More sadly, these children never pick up those pieces. There are too many and they're not all found. Somewhere along the line they are plucked from the security of family life and sent rapidly into adulthood even though they are still babies.

You have to grow up to protect yourself from elements that are not under your control. Things that most adults redden to speak of.

Sarah saw the tragedy of her own transition from childhood innocence to a set of childhood experiences that most adults cannot even bear to discuss. When she came home periodically during her teens, she was reaching out for that innocence again, but it was beyond her grasp. She couldn't find all the bits any more.

She often used weather metaphorically in her writing. In a piece she wrote much later, she refers to a lost child, and a child's grief:

I watch in wonder and awe
As the raindrops fall;
Like a child's pain-filled tears
They roll down my window.
I hear an empty loveless whimper.
How sadly this little one sings!
So hurt and empty, it howls through the night.
No rest, no comfort,
No mother to hold onto or put out the light.
In the morn the world is calm.
Maybe the little one found a mom.

Some of Sarah's experiences were so horrific that they must have changed her permanently, deep down. In an attempt to protect Angela, she tried to teach her to avoid danger. One of the first rules that Sarah taught Angela was never to get into a van, especially a van without windows. If a van had windows, it was all right to consider it, but first you had to open the door and look in the back. Sarah learned that rule in the hardest way possible. "She had a bad experience before I met her," Angela says. "There were more than one man, so she couldn't get out of the van. They took turns. They made her perform oral sex on them and they ejaculated on her face. To this day I hate vans."

Ever since Sarah disappeared, long before Angela told me that story from Sarah's childhood, I have looked at vans with a certain horror, wondering if Sarah had been held captive in one, if she might have died in one. But I had not thought about the other things that might have happened to my sister in the back of a van. Sarah was only sixteen when she gave Angela that warning, and Sarah was describing a scene from her past.

Over time, Angela tells me, it grew harder and harder to work, more and more demoralizing. So, she turned to alcohol: "The only way I could work was to be drunk. I couldn't stand the men any more. So I'd have to go get drunk before I could do it." It was a natural progression. She was bothered by what she was doing, and everyone around her was getting high, so she got high. "And you realize, hey, you're actually smiling or laughing, and yes, it's all fake, but it doesn't hurt any more." Gradually drugs or alcohol become essential. They take away the pain, so the worse the pain gets, the more important the drugs become.

Sarah was starting to use drugs more regularly then too, in 1986, as Vancouver was preparing for a world's fair, Expo 86. Suddenly the parts of the city where Sarah and Angela lived and worked were getting cleaned up. Cheap hotels were renovating in preparation for an influx of tourists. And the city itself began to enforce municipal laws to "clean up" the streets. Vancouver already had "no go zones." The courts could prohibit individual sex workers from being in certain areas; they still can. As Expo approached, the law was applied more frequently and the restrictions were enforced. The "no go zones" were difficult because they often included the street where a woman or girl actually lived and spent her non-working time. Angela needed to go into her "no go zone" one morning to pick up keys from someone. She was wearing flat shoes, sweatpants and no makeup, yet she was arrested for communicating for the purposes of prostitution. Her lawyer told her to plead guilty so that they would let her out of jail. Otherwise she would have had to stay and go through a trial— and all for walking down a street in her own neighbourhood in broad daylight.

Angela didn't tell me what it was that got her to leave downtown, except that Sarah always encouraged her to do so. She had some tough times, lived in other cities in Canada, worked for pimps, found herself in dangerous and scary circumstances, but always if she went downtown in Vancouver, there was Sarah. And always, Sarah was willing to help her.

Once she finally made the break, got off drugs and left sex work behind, she found it hard to stay away. It wasn't the drugs that lured her back, it was the money—the knowledge that in one night she could make enough to get herself out of a tight spot.

Several times, she got on a bus and rode downtown, intending to make some quick money and head home. Every time she sought out Sarah first. She told me that it was safer to do that, that things changed quickly downtown so that simply choosing a random corner and trying to make money was dangerous. Sarah could help her. I think that she sought out Sarah for other reasons as well. She knew that Sarah would protect her from herself.

Every time Angela went downtown, Sarah sent her home before she turned a trick.

"We'd spend the night drinking or talking or sitting in the park," Angela tells me, and then Sarah would see her off on the bus back home.

The last time that Angela saw Sarah was the night of the cats.

It was a beautiful, clear early-summer night. Sarah and Angela went to a big park among towering apartment buildings, sat on the swings and talked. All of a sudden they realized that they were surrounded by cats.

"I have never seen so many cats in my life," Angela says. "I hate cats and there were probably thirty cats coming at us and we were swinging. It was bizarre."

Sarah took on the voice of one brave cat. She had Angela howling with laughter.

"Watch these stupid humans," Sarah the cat said. "They'll bend over and go meow, meow, and expect me to come. Watch, I'll take a step and sure enough . . ."

Eventually the cats dispersed and Sarah and Angela went back to more serious talk. They were on the swings for hours that night.

"Why are you here this time?" Sarah asked Angela. "What happened?" And Angela tried to answer her.

Sarah was forgoing a night's income, but she was willing to give Angela the time she needed. "Keeping me from working was keeping her from working," Angela points out.

When morning came, Sarah gave Angela money for the bus.

"She went back to her life and sent me back to mine," Angela says.

That night in that park, that last talk, the prowling felines, all happened some fifteen years ago. Angela has now completed a college degree and is busy raising her children. Sarah would be glad to know that Angela is doing well. I am glad to know it too.

five

SEX WORK IN VANCOUVER

J OHN LOWMAN, professor of criminology at Simon Fraser University, has been studying prostitution in Canada since the late seventies.

As part of criminal law, he explained to me, laws around sex work are federal in this country. And they are hopelessly hypocritical and confused. Pierre Trudeau argued that the state should keep out of the bedrooms of the nation, but in the case of sex work the state has held on to the right to bar the bedroom door. Prostitution itself, "the act or practice of engaging in sexual intercourse for money" *(Random House Dictionary),* is legal in Canada, but all the acts connected with it are not. Before 1972, the Vagrancy C Law had been in effect for decades. It prohibited a "common prostitute from being in a public place where she could not give a good account of herself." That law was unenforceable and contrary to basic human dignity because it was a status offence. It was the status of the person, not the act, that was criminalized.

In the late sixties, sweeping cultural changes took place in society that made sex work more prevalent or caused it to take place more openly. The Vietnam War, the civil rights movement and the women's movement all played a role. People were leaving home earlier. Society was growing more permissive. Perhaps in a reaction against that permissiveness, the Vagrancy C Law was replaced in 1972 with a new law prohibiting soliciting in a public place. That law was widely interpreted to mean that prostitutes could not communicate with customers in public.

While street prostitution did exist in Vancouver prior to 1975, many sex workers, "about fifty on any given night," according to Lowman, were working out of a club called the Penthouse Cabaret. When the owners were charged in 1975 and the club was closed, many of those women started working on the street, mostly in the West End. Before that, between 1960 and 1974, only one homicide of a sex worker was recorded in British Columbia. Between 1975 and 1979, three homicides of sex workers were recorded.

Then, in the historic *Regina v. Hutt* case, the judge looked up the word "solicit" in the dictionary and threw out a charge before him on the grounds that to solicit, one would have to be "importuning or pressing or persistent." The acquittal was upheld by the Supreme Court of Canada in 1978. Thus the 1972 law was no longer enforceable. Sex workers rarely importune, press or persist. While it was argued by local residents and politicians that the Hutt decision caused the problem of street prostitution in Vancouver, in reality women had been on the street in greater numbers since the closing of the Penthouse in 1975.

Lowman explains the "problem" in different terms: "The dilemmas posed by the street sex trade reflect the ambivalence of prostitution law and the inability of Canadian legislators to decide whether prostitution itself ought to be legal or illegal." If legislators had been willing to take a clear position, it might have been possible to address the concerns of neighbourhoods and sex workers at the same time. Instead, the issue has been left to communities themselves, creating adversarial relationships. To this day, prostitutes are pushed from one neighbourhood to the next, with little changing in the grand scheme of things, except for the most important thing of all: street prostitution in Vancouver has grown more and more dangerous. An increasing number of prostitutes have ended up dead.

In 1981 a group of people unhappy about prostitution taking place in their community formed a group called Concerned Residents of the West End (CROWE). At that time there were five strolls in Vancouver—five areas where prostitutes worked on the street, all of them in the downtown area. CROWE took steps to discourage prostitution around Davie Street. A kindred group called Shame the Johns wrote down licence plate numbers and posted them, and stood near sex workers to discourage men from stopping to talk to them. They threw things at the women such as pennies, eggs and even rocks. In addition, the city put traffic barriers in the West End to create "traffic calming" zones, primarily to make it more difficult for prostitutes to work in their neighbourhood by making it difficult for clients to negotiate the area in their cars. Such dead ends and one-way streets have since been used in other areas of the city for exactly the same reasons.

In response to CROWE, the provincial government issued a nuisance injunction that said that prostitutes could not meet customers on West End streets west of Burrard. Later, the injunction boundary was moved farther east to Granville Street. By 1984, prostitutes had been pushed out of the West End entirely. Prostitutes could no longer work in the residential area, but had been pushed into a largely commercial area of the city.

That same year, a film called *Hookers on Davie* was released. It was a documentary about women, transvestites and transsexuals in sex work around Davie Street in Vancouver's West End, a non-pimped street where prostitutes worked with each other to keep safe and demonstrated against efforts to drive them out of the area and against the criminalization of prostitution. They started a group called Alliance for the Safety of Prostitutes. "We're trying to live a normal life instead of being in the gutter," one woman said in the film. "We don't allow pimps down here. We protect ourselves and each other." They talked about pimps trying to take over, the use of violence, and conflicts with a pimp from the U.S. They talked about drugs, but drug use was not for everyone. A number of them had started selling sex as children, but others had not. Sadly, the statistics tell us the effect of their efforts. In the face of the forces against them, they were out of the West End within the next year, probably by the time *Hookers on Davie* hit the screen.

But what they were trying to do was exactly what was needed then and is still needed today. "We need a process that includes the people we need to regulate," John Lowman pointed out. In other words, we must not try to figure out the answers without talking to the people who are most affected, the people who know what will work for them and what will not. In most industries, regulations are made, processes put in place, through consultation with those concerned. Because our society has deemed sex work unacceptable, it does not occur to us to consult with sex workers when making decisions that affect them.

At the federal level, a Special Committee on Pornography and Prostitution was formed in 1983. The committee reported in 1985, finding that Canadian prostitution law was "at odds with itself," and that street prostitution was created largely by local authorities clamping down on indoor prostitution. They recommended an overhaul of our laws that would make it legal for prostitutes to work out of small licensed brothels or for one or two prostitutes to work out of a single location without a licence. Their recommendations were ignored by the Progressive Conservative government of the time, according to an article by Lowman. Instead, in December 1985, a new federal law made it an offence to "in any manner communicate or attempt to communicate with any person for the purpose of engaging in prostitution or of obtaining the services of a prostitute." This is referred to as the "communicating law." The new law was more egalitarian than prior laws in that it made the activities of both the client and the prostitute illegal, although until recently it was rarely used against clients. At first, the enforcement of the new law did reduce street prostitution, but within six months the level of prostitution on the street was back to what it had been. In the long run, the law gave police the power to move prostitutes around the city.

When neighbourhood community groups call on the police for assistance in driving away prostitutes or when they turn to vigilante action themselves, they need to think about the consequences for the people they are pushing away, people who are also part of the community.

Their actions and attitude take an emotional toll. Sarah's friend Angela tells me how passersby often treated her and how it felt. "After a while of pennies being thrown at you out of car windows, people judging what you do and the life you live, you get worn down. It's degrading. You don't know how to let people in any more. You don't know how to get out. You want what you see, but you can't get there." She is referring not to the effect of sex work itself, but to society's judgement of her for engaging in sex work.

And society's actions take a more frightening toll as well because they drive vulnerable people into dark, industrial areas. If men are afraid of being exposed, they will not stop under bright lights to talk to a prostitute. Prostitutes must then go to where men are willing to stop—increasingly dark, isolated parts of the city, places where it is easier for predatory men to hurt women without being seen.

Today, more and more women are working along Kingsway in Vancouver. The strategy in that part of the city is to call 911 to drive away the prostitutes. Many of the women who are being arrested have been driven back to sex work because they can't pay their bills. Then they find themselves with criminal records, a further hindrance to success in the straight world.

I spoke with a young woman named Rusty. She is addicted and works to support her habit. She wants very much to get off drugs. Rusty has an area restriction against working on Kingsway, similar to the "no go zones" of the mid-eighties. The area restriction was put in place because Rusty was caught "communicating" by an undercover police officer who posed as a date. She was placed under arrest, taken to jail and then to court where she was given the restriction.

As a result, Rusty had to find a new place to work and ended up moving to an industrial area. When she was working there one night, several men drove by, saw her and circled the block. They entertained themselves by shooting at her with fireworks. Rusty was badly burned. Had she been standing on Kingsway, a major thoroughfare, such an event would have been unlikely.

Recently, I accompanied an outreach worker on her shift on a Friday night. Char Lafontaine, the woman who told me about how girls slip into prostitution, now works for Prostitution Alternatives Counselling and Education (PACE), an organization that counsels women who engage in sex work, particularly those whose work is better characterized as survival sex. Survival sex refers to prostitution with limited choice, to situations where people sell sex because if they don't they will not be able to eat, keep a roof over their head or get the drugs they need to feed their addiction. With limited choice comes increased desperation and greater danger.

I drove the car on the outreach shift, so that Char could speak to the women out the passenger window and offer them a few friendly words, along with condoms, needles and candy. We drove through the back streets east of the Downtown Eastside and along portions of main streets such as Broadway and Kingsway all the way into the suburbs. We also drove through parts of the Downtown Eastside itself. Almost everywhere, the women were working away from residential areas. And in many cases, they were working alone.

I was nervous as we headed out, sure that I was going to say the wrong thing, that I would put women off. I was glad to drive, to follow Char's instructions. And glad that we had an eight-hour shift to talk to one another, to get to know each other. She had known Sarah. She was experienced. I wanted to tell her what I was doing, get her reaction. And I wanted to listen, to hear about her work and her memories.

It turned out that I didn't need to be nervous. Women let us know if they wanted to talk with us or preferred for us simply to hand out what they wanted and drive away. I was struck by their dignity, their manners. It often felt as if what I had expected was reversed. Most of the women made a point of being welcoming and kind to us. The barriers that I had always felt between myself and women working on the street started, just started, to come down.

Organizations such as PACE are essential in Vancouver, more and more so in the past quarter century, as more sex workers have been pushed onto the streets and from there into industrial areas. PACE offers outreach, support and referrals without pressuring women to leave the trade. Many of the women who work for PACE are ex–sex workers themselves. They can look sex workers in the eye and understand their experience, and they can see the great strength and many skills that people in sex work tend to have.

Angela and I have talked about PACE. "I wish there was a PACE when I was downtown," she says. "A place that isn't just academics trying to make the world better. Academics know book answers but forget all the variables of life, feelings, emotion, pain."

The changes that have taken place in the past two decades have led to a dramatic increase in the rates of violence against sex workers. As mentioned above, between 1960 and 1974, one prostitute was a victim of homicide in British Columbia, and in the five years that followed, that number increased to three. Between 1980 and 1984, eight homicides were committed against sex workers. Between 1985 and 1989, that number rose to twenty-two, and between 1990 and 1994 it rose still further to twenty-four. Those numbers do not include the sixty-three sex workers who have disappeared from Vancouver since 1978, almost twenty of whose DNA has now been found on the farm in Port Coquitlam where Sarah's DNA was identified. Our attitudes, our laws and our approach to law enforcement have made life increasingly dangerous for those who work on the street.

We must provide places where all women who work as prostitutes can do so safely. Community groups, police and government need to consult with sex workers to find long-term solutions that work for everyone, rather than taking part in shortsighted, geographically specific efforts to relocate sex workers to anywhere else but here.

The egg throwing and traffic calming, the no go zones, the new 1985 law—all had a devastating effect. In the late eighties, a large part of the sex trade shifted down to the east side of Vancouver, an area where prostitutes had worked for decades, but an area that was to change dramatically as prostitution and drugs became increasingly concentrated there. By 1987, Sarah was spending much of her time on the Downtown Eastside, breaking one of her most important rules: never work on Hastings Street.

Today a debate rages about what to do about the Downtown Eastside—what to do about the poverty, homelessness, drug addiction, overdoses, violence, disappearances and death. In 2002, homeless people occupied the old Woodwards building for weeks, pressuring for subsidized housing, for the building itself to be used in some way that will serve the local community, revitalize the neighbourhood. Our new mayor, Larry Campbell, suggested giving incentives to contractors to hire people in the community when building happens in that area. Ideas are being put forward that are meant to help the residents, not to drive them elsewhere. Larry Campbell has pointed out that the popular four-pillar strategy championed by the previous mayor, Philip Owen, to help drug addicts—enforcement, harm reduction, treatment and education—is strong, but leaves out a critical fifth pillar, economic incentive. That makes sense to me. And housing is critical too, as the demonstrators outside Woodwards stressed over and over again.

As I follow the debate, I am always asking myself what changes that are being proposed or made now might have meant for Sarah, had they been made earlier. Sarah needed a safe place to live. She needed choices. She needed respect. And she needed to be able to continue what she was doing as safely as possible until she was willing and able to make other choices. Any revitalizing that would have brought the neighbours out with their pennies and their eggs to push Sarah down to the other side of the tracks, to push her out from under the streetlights, would have put her in greater danger. Any changes that would have forced her out of her house so that it could be renovated for more monied, respectable tenants would have placed her in greater danger still.

When community groups on the Downtown Eastside gather to discuss and bring about change, they need to involve groups that represent sex workers, such as PACE, and they need to involve sex workers themselves. When politicians and others work to bring about change in federal prostitution law and to decide what changes would help and which groups to fund at the provincial and municipal levels, they need to invite sex workers into their process. And give them an active role. The sex workers are out there. They are talking. They are as articulate and intelligent as the rest of us and they know what they need.

SARAH WRITES ABOUT SEX WORK several times in her journals, always in negative terms. I don't know if what she writes reflects how she felt all the time. I suspect that she didn't find it quite as painful with the men that she saw regularly, but she does describe how badly she felt and implies that the men she was with didn't care.

MAY 1997

Sometimes I start to take my clothes off and I feel a lump start to form in my throat. It starts to burn as I try to swallow it back down. I swear whomever I'm with can see it clear as day. It hurts my throat. They must hear me trying to swallow. My mouth and throat are so dry. I try to avoid eye contact at all times. It makes it easier for me.

As I lie on my back, I find that men's nipples look like two eyes and that their belly hangs down like a nose. The belly

button is a mouth. Sometimes these faces are hairy, bald,
wrinkly, smooth, fat, lean, dark, white, hot, cold, dry, sweaty.

When I hear women talk, as Sarah does in the above journal entry,
about the pain and humiliation they felt when they sold sex, I tend
to jump to the conclusion that sex work is bad and should be abol-
ished. However, that is not a useful conclusion. Sex work exists now,
has always existed and always will exist. And many sex workers,
including those who work on the street, do not do drugs. Some find
sex work provides them with a better income to support their families than any other work available to them. Even those involved in
survival sex do have some freedom to choose and cannot be forced to
change their lives. While they may be having sex for money because
it is their only means of survival, of keeping a roof over their head,
of getting food and feeding their drug habit, they are not slaves.

It is important to draw a distinction between survival sex and
sexual slavery. None of the women I've interviewed were being held
against their will. They were doing the best they could with a tough
situation; life circumstances had limited their choices. But they did
not need to be rescued in the way that one would rescue people who
were being held captive. They needed more choices, more connections with the larger world, more services, more education, greater
safety. When we equate one thing with another, such as saying that
all prostitution is sexual slavery, we limit our capacity to draw distinc-
tions, to understand the actual permutations of people's lives. And we
deny their agency.

My sister was engaged in survival sex. Her choices were limited as
long as she could not see a way out of that life. She was locked tight
inside her addiction. But she had dignity. Within the scope of her
life, she made choices every day. She had the right, I believe, to sell
sex whether she hated it or loved it. She had the right to do drugs,
to be a drug addict. She could only leave that life if she did so freely.
I don't think there is any way we could have helped her except by
increasing her freedom.

Criminologist John Lowman reminded me that the argument that all prostitution is sexual slavery is a radical feminist argument. He suggested that that belief permeates our judicial system in Canada and our own opinions about prostitution. The more I think about it, the more I agree with him. I remember studying radical feminism in university and exploring radical feminist ideals when I was involved with the Women's Union at McGill University in the mid-eighties. I had been well grounded in feminist principles before that, and remain so, I hope, but radical feminism is a whole different realm. It goes beyond notions of equality. One of the ideas of radical feminism that I remember struggling with was that all penetration is rape. There again is the equation of one act with another. The notion that all pornography degrades women also stems from radical feminism.

The idea that all penetration is rape eliminates the possibility of women being equal with men in heterosexual relationships. The idea that all pornography degrades women eliminates the possibility of women creating pornography for other women, or of women enjoying pornography in any context, or of women participating in the creation of male-dominated pornography because they want to. These ideas seem to me to suggest that women cannot participate in any way in the world with men without being enslaved, dominated and used. Such a notion is patronizing in the extreme.

Men (or women) who force women (or men) to sell sex are moving prostitution close to the realm of slavery, but still the differences are important. The relationships between men who live on the avails of prostitution and the women who support them are infinitely complex. Even the relationships between pimps and the prostitutes who work for them are complicated, and varied as well. And many, many prostitutes do not work for pimps.

Indoor sex work as it stands in Canada involves a whole other set of relationships. Women work for business owners who buy expensive permits and who pay taxes to government. We all, whether we like it or not, live on the avails of prostitution in the sense that our governments profit from it.

I saw a couple on *Oprah* recently who were unhappy in their relationship because the husband wouldn't give his wife money unless she had sex with him. She had to earn her spending money at twenty dollars per sex act. She felt degraded. He thought the system worked well because they both got what they wanted. He got sex and she got money. It made me sick to listen to him, and I was glad to see him set straight. At the same time, no one suggested that she should be arrested.

By making communicating for the purposes of prostitution illegal, we criminalize the way in which women working in the survival sex trade live. They are at odds with the system in which they live and thus are vulnerable. Men can hurt them and get away with it. And men do, every day. I heard recently that where the ratio of "bad dates"—dates where the john refuses the sex worker's guidelines, tries to coerce or hurt her or doesn't pay her—used to be one in ten, in Vancouver it has crept up closer to one in five. We are unwilling to acknowledge sex workers as a legitimate part of our workforce. Thus they are not protected by the structures that protect others. As a society, we almost believe that violence is just part of their job. I don't think most people feel the same horror when they hear that a sex worker has been badly beaten that they feel if exactly the same thing happens to a nurse or a lawyer or a cashier.

On the Vancouver Police Department's website, I found two lists on opposite sides of the screen of the missing persons page. Missing persons were listed on the right, missing sex workers on the left. Sex workers were excluded from the "persons" category. Historically, women fought long and hard to be defined as persons, yet certain women are excluded from that category all the time. As things stand, we have left those women working on the street, with few resources beyond one another.

MUST I ENDURE
THIS EACH TIME.

One of Sarah's sketches.

1986   *March 13*   *Elaine Allenbach last seen*
1988   *July 1*   *Taressa Anne Williams last seen*

six

FROM THE HIGH TRACK TO
THE LOW TRACK

In 1986, Peter was living in Mum's garage, which Mum had renovated into a room with a loft. On Sarah's birthday that year, her seventeenth, Peter remembers her bringing two friends, a girl and a man dressed as a woman, to Mum's house for dinner. Peter was struck by how weird the situation was, how impossible it was for him to relate to these people who were suddenly there at the dinner table.

Another time, Peter remembers going into the basement to use the washroom that was next to the TV room. A man was there, obviously high on cocaine. Sarah was sitting on the love seat, hugging her legs. Peter asked the man what he was doing there and made him leave. Other men came around in those years, I remember, during the times when Sarah was home.

I lived at home that summer of 1986, working for UBC Catering while Expo was on. I had been living in Montreal since August 1984, studying political theory and getting involved with the McGill Women's Union and the *McGill Daily Newspaper*.

Mum's friend Liz had moved into the top storey of Mum's house, so I lived in the basement that summer and whenever Sarah was home, she and I shared a room. I remember being vaguely aware of her arriving in the night sometimes, and seeing her there in the heap of bedclothes in the morning when I went off to work. I don't think that she was there a lot.

Her downtown world would follow her to our house, whether she wanted it to or not. She was afraid at times, I think, that we, her family, might be in danger. I find it hard to believe that we actually were, but that may simply show how hopelessly naive I am.

On October 2, Sarah talked to Daniel Gautreau, the journalist who had been trying to get her to speak to him for six months. He said that out of all the street kids that he interviewed, she was the only one he was nervous with. She was cautious with him and put up a protective barrier. Yet now, when I listen to her voice on the tape, I hear such vulnerability. Each word is crystal clear. She speaks with a lilt, but completely without bravado, as if she were the most innocent person in the world. In a matter-of-fact tone she describes horrors.

Sarah told Daniel that she had been clean for about five months, but that she had been using heroin heavily for months before that. He asked her what she thought of life on the streets. "Sometimes I like it and sometimes I hate it. I like it most of all for the people I meet that I like. The part I hate is where you'd be working the streets and you pull a trick and the guy could beat you up or rape you or try and kill you. When I got into heroin, I thought, 'Hey I'm cool, I can do it now,' and I did it for about three months and my best friend walked up to me and said, 'You look really ugly. You're not the same person you used to be. You've turned into a bitch and I don't want to talk to you any more.'

"After that I looked at myself in the mirror. My face was sinking in. I had lots and lots of zits. I was skinny. I looked at myself and I said, 'Hey, I am getting ugly, and it's because of the drugs.' I'd start ripping my friends off for money to get a fix, and if I wasn't on drugs I wouldn't do that, I wouldn't look terrible, I'd be a nicer person.

When you're addicted to heroin, you start doing stuff to get a fix. You don't care who you hurt, just as long as you make yourself feel better."

Daniel asked her what the bad things were about life on the street including being a sex worker. "The bad thing is that when you're working, the people who say that you're their friend only use you for your money, because sometimes you do make a lot of money. You could end up supporting somebody's habit. You could end up having a junkie mug you.

"I never really had anything bad happen to me till I was about fifteen when a trick tried to beat me up. And I got raped just last March. A couple of weeks later I didn't feel right. I was throwing up when I woke up in the morning, and I went to 575 Drake Street and got a blood test done. I found out I was pregnant, and I had to go in for an abortion. That's about the worst that ever happened to me, that I got raped by a bad trick and I was carrying his kid, and it doesn't feel really great, it made me feel really shitty. I was depressed for quite a while. I cried a lot for no reason. I would be walking down the street and I would start crying for no reason at all."

Daniel asked her why she thought that men would treat her that way. "They think that because they pay for you they can treat you like a sex tool. They think because they paid for it, you aren't going to tell anybody. They think it doesn't hurt you inside, but it does. They think because you're a hooker you don't feel any emotions, you don't feel any pain. You are just doing it for the money, and you don't feel anything, but you do. I'm not just speaking for myself; I'm speaking for everybody else. You know, they do. They are human, they feel, and just because you are paying them money doesn't mean you can treat them like total shit, because they have feelings too."

Sarah had been sent to Willingdon, the youth detention centre, in January of that year for entering her "no go zone," and she ended up there again in October. She told Daniel that there were two warrants

out for her for assault, one for mischief and one for breached proba-
tion. He asked her how she felt about the legal system. "I will have
to say it's fair, because I've done crimes," she said. "Don't do the
crime if you can't pay the time, you know. I did the crime, so I am
going to have to do the time sooner or later." Then she added with a
small laugh, "But I don't think I want to do it right now."

Daniel asked her what she thought about street people.
"They're not like they say in the newspapers, where they're all
violence and drugs. A lot of them have hidden talents and people
won't give them the chance to show them. And they're a lot nicer
than other people I've met. They understand a lot more. They
know what people are going through. They give you your own
headspace to think. They're there when you need them. They're
always there to party with. And most of all, they're really special
people. If you make friends with them, they're the best friends
that you can ever have."

In January Sarah had returned to Mum's house when she got out
of Willingdon and before going into a group home, but by the time
she was picked up in October, Mum's patience had worn thin. "I told
the lawyer she could not come home. They should keep her in
Willingdon until she had to appear in court. . . . God, I feel so badly
about Sarah." Sometime later in October, Mum visited Sarah in
Willingdon's large, low-ceilinged visiting room full of round plastic
orange and yellow furniture. She had to push a bell on the outside of
the fencing and wait for someone to come with a huge bunch of keys
to let her through first a gate, then a door.

Mum and Sarah had the best time together they had had in years.
Sarah was talkative. She was funny. She was open about her feelings.
She told Mum that she had started reading, and Mum promised to
bring her a copy of *The Hobbit*. Mum went back the next Saturday
with Peter, and Sarah gave them her poems to read. Some of the
poems were addressed to God, some to Mum and some to Jamie,
Sarah's boyfriend at the time—a decent guy, but a drug dealer. One
poem described how dreadful she felt about selling sex. Another was

about shooting drugs. They were explicit. "I can't talk about it, but I can write about it," Sarah told Mum.

One of the poems she wrote that year shows that she had read the book Mum brought her. She had been in Tolkien's Misty Mountains with Gandalf:

> Come, take my hand and travel to
> The heart of my mystic land
> Where waterfalls flow through the misty mountain
> To the edge of the sea and the sand.
>
> Where magical wizards roam the lands
> And cast their spells on every disloyal man
> Where demons and soldiers fight to the death
> To protect the laws that they know best.
>
> Where the lords love their ladies
> And the ladies love their lords
> While minstrels sit and play
> The most beautiful chords.

Another poem talked about life on the street:

> The street is a place where you're never safe
> It's not all just fun and games.
> The people here are quite unique.
> You may find the junkies smooth and sleek,
> But be careful they might try to stab you in your sleep.
> For when they're hurting inside,
> The heroin takes over the mind
> They don't care what they do to cut the pain loose.
> Don't ever trust a junkie
> He'll just turn around and use you for a monkey.

You may find the prostitute sleazy and easy
But I know for a fact they don't find it pleasing.
They're alive and breathing
With a functioning mind
And a heart that ticks in perfect time.
There is the odd one who wants it all
And will use everything, even her claws.
But if you're friends, you're friends for life
And fight side by side to prove your right.
In this business, you lose lots of friends
And that's where the terror begins.

Willingdon was like a cross between a high school and a jail, Peter told me. He noted that Sarah did well there, that she started to look healthier. Dad visited her there too in November. He tried to bring the Labrador retriever, Licorice, that Sarah loved so much. Sadly, though not surprisingly, they wouldn't let the dog in. Still, "We had a sort of a nice time, Sarah and I," Dad wrote to me. "I had never visited a person in a prison before. Sort of sobering . . ." All those visits must have meant a lot to Sarah, reconnecting her to us, her family.

By early January 1987, Sarah had moved into a group home called Balaclava House where she lived until June, a month after turning eighteen years old. In early March that year Sarah went to Mum's for dinner and told her that she was going to school, but I don't think that she attended for long. In June, Sarah left Balaclava House and moved back downtown.

Then came three months of silence.

In October, Mum went to a conference in Calgary. She was walking downtown, when all of a sudden, there was Sarah, "all dressed in pink, looking great and all excited to see me. I was excited and pleased to see her too and I invited her to lunch. We went shopping afterwards and I got her a warm jacket and some PJs. . . . I phoned Mother and Jean and they are all excited about Sarah being okay. Guess we expected her to be dead long ago."

Sarah came back to Vancouver sometime in the fall, because she was home for Christmas. By then, Peter had become involved with Troy, the woman who is now his wife. We were all together at Mum's house for Christmas dinner on Christmas Eve. "It was a fun meal," Mum wrote, "with lots of talking and remembering and sharing of ourselves with Troy, who was there." Sarah folded origami figures for the tree while we sat together reading Dickens's *Christmas Carol* aloud. We kids all had Christmas dinner at Dad's the next day. I still have a picture of us there, looking as if we are having a good time. We were.

That New Year's Eve, Peter, Troy, Mark, Sarah and I all went together to see the Red Hot Chili Peppers at a downtown bar. Troy remembers all of us in a circle, arms around each other's shoulders, swaying to "We Are Family" when the band was on a break.

Sarah seemed to be doing well. "She's so much more relaxed with herself and us," Mum wrote. Sarah had made it through puberty and into a time when she was a little more settled. We all, Sarah included, had hope. She stayed home for six months after that, the first half of 1988, the same months that I spent on a cattle ranch in Mexico teaching English to an eleven-year-old girl.

Sarah worked toward getting her driver's licence. She had an assessment done at a local college. They recommended that she take grade eight math and grade eleven English in the academic program. But in March, things started to fall apart. She was starting to party in the house. Noise and smoke infiltrated the upstairs from the basement. On March 20, Sarah came home drunk and high at 4:00 in the morning without the key to her room. Mum wound up outside in her nightshirt helping Sarah break into her own house. The night was cold. "It had a hilarious side," Mum wrote, "but also a sad one." Sarah didn't drink to excess often, but by that spring I think that she was starting to use hard drugs more regularly again. Still, on Mother's Day she gave Mum a stained-glass hummingbird to hang in the front window. It was to match the seagull, she told Mum. "I really like it," Mum wrote. "She's a very observant person, is Sarah Jean."

Also that May, the house would likely have burned to the ground had it not been for Sarah. Liz had left a wood-handled pot of chicken stock simmering on the back of the stove. It boiled dry and melted lids on coffee tins two shelves up. Sarah smelled the smoke, came up from the basement and put the pot outside. "It is so lucky that she was here and that she smelled it in time," Mum wrote. "Practical child!"

Within weeks, though, Sarah was gone, and Mum was running out of patience once again. Then, out of the blue, Sarah came home in the middle of the night crying wildly, high on cocaine and accompanied by a man. "I sit here and sit here and write nothing," Mum wrote. "I am trying to figure out whether I have to kick her out." The hardest thing, for all of us, was the cycle of hope rising, dropping through the floor and then rising again. Along with that came the utter helplessness and the anger at Sarah for the chaos and pain she caused in our lives.

Late in July, after I returned from Mexico, Peter, Troy, Sarah and I planned to go camping, but Sarah came home too late and missed the trip. By August 9, Mum was beside herself. She wrote:

I am in such a state I cannot function. So hurt, angry, sad, so vindictive, so coldly angry, so hotly angry, so sad, I want to cry and cry. I am sick to death of Sarah and her accusations shrieked at me. "Don't you know how hard it is to talk to you? You don't understand. You never talk to me. You don't listen." She lies to me and wonders why I don't talk to her. Last week her pimp, or someone who styles himself as her pimp, broke her hand. She didn't mention it until Leesa brought it up on Thursday when they were both here for a barbecue supper. Last night the same fellow threatened to break her other hand and then threatened to come and get me. She was terrified and got a friend of Dave's, who is a bouncer at Luv a Fair [a downtown club], to bring her home to see if I was all right. This fellow's name is Simon. And he is 31, and "not a pimp or an asshole," he says. He acted like a gentleman, but then, so did Nick, Sarah's former boyfriend, before he went to jail for armed robbery. I phoned the police. There was nothing they could do, which I knew ahead, but I needed to do it anyway. I'm so exhausted.

The next week, as I prepared to move to Ontario to live with Aunt Jean and Grandma and find a job in publishing, Sarah's friend Dave, whom she must have met when she was hanging out at the club where he worked, phoned Mum: he wanted to bring Sarah back to stay at Mum's for a while. Dave followed up the phone call with a visit. "I liked him," Mum wrote. "I liked his sense of humour, the twinkle in his eye when he told me his mother was Scottish Irish." They looked through Sarah's baby book together and he was impressed. Mum felt that he really cared about Sarah. He wanted to get Sarah into detox even if he had to "lay down the law" to do it. Mum told him that that wouldn't work, that detox would be no use to Sarah if she were forced into it. Joking, he said, "What am I supposed to do? Say please?" Mum suggested that that might be a good start. He flexed his muscles and said that he wasn't sure that he could do that, but he went away and did, and Sarah agreed to give detox a try. Once again, hope ran high.

This effort on Dave's part is the first mention of detox for Sarah, although she had told Daniel earlier that fall that she had already been addicted and cleaned up. Now, for the first time, she was considering getting help for her addiction. She had been using drugs for five years by that time; it is no wonder that dependency was becoming a problem.

After that, Sarah did not phone when she was supposed to, but Dave brought her to Mum's house on August 23 and Mum drove her downtown to pick up her stuff. She slept at Mum's house that night, before going into detox the next day. "I hope to God she can really make a go of it," Mum wrote, "lay off the drugs and gradually find a life for herself that she can enjoy." Dave picked her up the next afternoon and took her to Maple Cottage.

In Sarah's bag was a new diary from Mum. Later Mum found the diary with only one page filled in:

DAY 1. 7:55 A.M.: Everybody is up and awake for breakfast at 7:30 a.m. I found out you have to join in all the activities or you get kicked out. I can't believe it. I actually feel nauseous. I get these incredible headaches, eye strain, and I get very short-tempered at the smallest things. I didn't think I could get addicted, but I guess freebasing for nine months and fixing on and off for one will do the trick. I hope David comes to see me. I miss him already.

I don't think that she stayed at Maple Cottage for long.

By freebasing, she meant smoking cocaine, and by fixing, she meant injecting heroin. She was addicted and going through withdrawal, but nothing like what she would experience later, when she had been using heroin almost hourly and for years.

Sarah was starting to build more of a relationship with Peter and Troy through this time. The three of them spent a day up at Lynn Canyon, a beautiful, rugged park along a river that runs along the bottom of a narrow canyon between Grouse and Seymour mountains just north of Vancouver. And Troy visited Sarah in a group home that year. She said that it was a terrible place. "If I had to stay there," Troy told me, "I would have snuck out the window a long, long time ago. The women there were very tough. They claimed their territory."

That was the group home that got Sarah involved in a work-training program. She was supposed to sell vacuum cleaners, and did a practice demonstration at Mum's house in September. It seemed like a hopeful time, I remember. But selling vacuum cleaners door to door was not the solution to Sarah's problems. Troy put it more strongly: "They had her selling those fucking vacuums door to door. I remember thinking, here's your chance, Sarah," she said sarcastically. "That wasn't a chance!" It was a demeaning and difficult job, not one that took into account Sarah's strengths or interests and not one with much earning potential either.

That September, one of Sarah's best friends, Carrie, killed herself by overdosing. Carrie was only seventeen. Through endless tears, Sarah told Mum that Carrie felt so bad that she couldn't stand it, but that she hadn't really been trying to kill herself. Sarah was also upset because the night before, a man had driven Sarah across the Granville Street Bridge against her will, out of territory where she felt safe. When she tried to get out of the car, he stabbed her in the leg. She did manage to jump out of the car then, her leg bleeding, and escape.

Troy had bonded with Sarah early on and wanted very much to help her, as did Peter. In late October 1988, Troy and Peter arranged for Sarah to move in with several of Troy's old friends from college. They liked Sarah and were willing to let her into their circle. Sarah lived with them for just over a month, paying her rent through welfare. It worked well for everyone at first, but when December came, Sarah didn't have the money for the rent and the arrangement fell apart. It turned out that Sarah had been sneaking dates in as well, something her roommates were not prepared to tolerate.

It was a good time, though, for Sarah, horsing around with Peter and Troy regularly, and socializing with students—people who knew nothing of her downtown world. Peter and Troy went to a Christmas party with Sarah and Dave. "My feeling was that he was a pimp," Troy said, "but Sarah said, no, he was just a friend." He was drawn to Sarah and he wanted to help her. What the full range of his motives may have been, who can say?

When Sarah was evicted that December, Mum had a terrible dream about her. "She had beetles coming out of flesh-coloured eggs along the sides of her gums in her mouth. She was covered with rashes and sores. She was back downtown." And, of course, back downtown Sarah went. By early the next year, Dave was no longer part of her life. His efforts to help her had failed and he had moved on.

In early February 1989, Sarah phoned Peter and Troy and asked if she could move in with them while she arranged to get herself into some sort of rehab. She was using heroin more and more regularly; her addiction was growing more severe. Peter and Troy picked her up from a hotel close to Pender, where she was sharing a room with a dancer. As usual, her clothes were strewn everywhere, but it was a good room. Sarah crammed all her stuff into duffle bags and headed off to Peter and Troy's tiny apartment.

When they got there, Sarah said that she would like to take a bath. She soaked for a long time in their enormous old-fashioned tub. Afterward, the tub was brown with dirt. Troy told me that she didn't think that a bathtub would normally get that dirty in a year. She scrubbed it right away so that Sarah wouldn't see it. That dirty tub shows how tough life was for Sarah then, because cleanliness had always been very important to her. In later years, she would bathe daily. I even heard of her bathing in cold water when her electricity had been cut off.

That year, 1989, she was sliding downhill fast. She made several desperate attempts to stop the slide, but to no avail. The stay with Peter and Troy lasted only two days. As the drugs wore off, Sarah became more difficult to live with. Each night Troy asked her if she had phoned rehab, and each time Sarah said that she would do it tomorrow. Peter and Troy realized that without evidence that Sarah was actually making attempts to get into detox, they could not cope.

"She became intolerable," Peter told me. "I felt really bad about it, but I told her that we would find some other situation for her. She got really upset and left. I tried to hold on to her physically and she went crazy. She took off."

I know what Peter means by intolerable. Peter and Troy lived in a bachelor apartment in which they had constructed a loft bed above the dining area for themselves. Sarah would have had no separate space of her own, but wherever she lived, she spread her things around her. She could create chaos in a space in half an hour. And she was going through withdrawal as well. She needed more support than they could possibly give her, yet she was not prepared to seek out that support.

Soon after leaving Peter and Troy's apartment, Sarah was back in Mum's basement. She made a brief attempt at detox, but quickly ended up back downtown. And by now downtown meant the Downtown Eastside. Three years before, when Sarah was teaching Angela how to survive, one of the most important rules in her list was "Never go to Hastings. Never, never go to Hastings." Hastings is the main street that cuts through the Downtown Eastside from west to east. The area is poor and removed from the relative safety of the densely populated West End or the busy city core. Hastings Street is the Downtown Eastside, sometimes referred to as the poorest postal code in Canada—an area where people struggle to survive, and where the death rate from drug overdoses and violence is high.

In 1998, Sarah would be last seen on Hastings Street. "Never go to Hastings" was a good rule.

SARAH HAD KNOWN OF CHARLIE* for years. Everyone had. Everyone had known Miranda*, Charlie's girlfriend up on Granville Street before the exodus to Hastings. Everyone had seen how Charlie beat Miranda and how terrified she was of him. Sarah despised Charlie then. Yet, by the summer of 1989, Sarah was living on the Downtown Eastside with Charlie, and from then on, her life would remain entangled with his.

Charlie is first mentioned in Mum's diary in the spring of 1989. Sarah phoned in a miserable state, saying that she was pregnant (if she was truly pregnant then, she did not carry the baby to term), that she had been kicked in the head and had a lump over her eye, that she was having blackouts and forgetting things. Charlie wouldn't let her go out, she told Mum, and her friends wouldn't speak to her because they were afraid of him. She phoned Mum twice in the middle of the night, and Mum drove downtown first thing in the morning to pick her up while Charlie was still asleep. Mum took Sarah to Emergency, where Sarah pulled out a bag of candy and offered it around in the waiting area, apparently unfazed by those who shrank away from her. Mum and Sarah were told to return in the afternoon for tests. For hours Mum waited with Sarah in the car, in the rain, reading to herself while Sarah slept. When the time came, Mum left her at the hospital for the tests. When Mum phoned the hospital later, Sarah was gone, straight back downtown to Charlie.

Charlie hurt Sarah repeatedly. One woman told me, though, that she remembered Charlie himself getting beaten up a couple of times for mistreating Sarah. She thinks that he treated Sarah better after that. Another woman told me that she had paid a man to break her partner's arm when he hurt her, so I knew that this was a possible way of coping with spousal violence. Sarah was so well liked, I was told, that people would have been willing to help her.

However violent he may have been, Charlie's story was a tragic one. He was one of several children who were taken away from their family and placed in foster homes as so many Aboriginal children were at that time. He and one of his older brothers lived on a farm, where they were forced to work and were beaten regularly, even hit with a two-by-four. One day he went out to the barn to find that his brother, who had been his protector, had hanged himself from a beam. Charlie left the farm soon after and married as a young man, but his life was always troubled. I believe that he was functionally illiterate, another obstacle to add to all the pain.

His stories of childhood suffering were very important to Sarah. Perhaps the two of them bonded around those stories. Sarah may have felt that the rest of the world simply didn't know him. That would have allowed her to put aside other people's judgement and remain loyal—through everything.

When I teach Canadian children's literature courses at UBC, I often ask my class to read *My Name Is Seepeetza* by Shirley Sterling. It tells the story of Shirley's experience in a residential school, one of the boarding schools where Aboriginal children were sent ostensibly to integrate them with society as a whole. The effect, of course, was to tear apart families, and to stamp out knowledge of their language, history and culture in several generations of First Nations children in Canada. Charlie was not sent to residential school as far as I know, but his family was torn apart, he was separated from his culture and he was subjected to abuse. Many of the men and women on the Downtown Eastside are Aboriginal, a far greater proportion than in society as a whole.

When I can, I tell my classes about Charlie. My students are teachers. I want them to remember that while we no longer have residential schools and we no longer deliberately separate children from their culture, we live with the legacy of those acts. Charlie had at least ten children, but raised none. All of those children have to come to terms with the fact that they have been abandoned by their father and that they are separated from half of their heritage.

PETER AND TROY were still trying to maintain contact with Sarah, so they got to know Charlie a little bit that summer. Once, they met Sarah and Charlie at the Columbia Hotel—which was an awful place, Peter told me—and played pool with Charlie. People spoke to Charlie in hushed tones and parted to let him through. They seemed to be afraid of him. Charlie was middling then, I suspect—buying drugs from a supplier, cutting them and selling them again, keeping some for himself. Despite his reputation, he was friendly with Peter and Troy that night, solicitous even. He paid for everything, and Sarah seemed proud of his generosity, proud of him.

They went to another bar that night and then to a hotel room so that Charlie and Sarah could do some heroin. "It was a horrendous dive," Peter told me, "piled knee high in filthy clothes and sleeping bags." A man who was asleep in the corner woke up and asked the time. When told, he followed up with "Day or night?" and went back to sleep.

Peter and Troy invited Sarah and Charlie to dinner at around the same time, in July 1989. Sarah and Charlie came in a taxi, their standard mode of transport, and the visit was pleasant enough at first. Sarah was drawing in a sketchbook, but as time went on the drawing turned to scribbling, and the scribbling got more and more frantic. The cat kept trying to approach her. She would shove him away, turning page after page, scribbling with all her strength. Finally she stopped, pulled out a large pharmaceutical jar of morphine and asked if she and Charlie could use the bathroom. Soon after that they left.

On July 9, Mum wrote in her journal that Sarah's troubles were eating away at her. "I feel broken, used, abused, dropped. I can't cope with what she is doing to herself. What do I do with the anger? Every time she phones, part of me bleeds and part of me burns."

Peter and Troy got married the next month, and to our happy surprise, Sarah made it to the wedding. The couple got married in a church downtown. Mum and I were sitting by the centre aisle, the wedding already under way, when Sarah flew into the church and into the pew beside us. She was pulling on a little black sweater as she ran in. Sweat was beaded on her lip. She had run all the way across town and she had made it there on her own at the right time, more or less. She had even taken the trouble to dress for the event. She was wearing a white skirt that reached to mid-calf, flat shoes and a stretchy black top with a black jacket. She was also wearing less makeup than she usually did. She had made such an effort to be there and to fit in, to dress appropriately. But in the photographs she stands a little apart.

Mum and Liz and Sarah and I drove to the reception at Troy's parents' house. On the way, we stopped off downtown so that Sarah could leave a note for Charlie. She came to the reception for a little while. Peter remembers her gobbling the Vietnamese beef sticks. When I think back, I can see how she tried—her effort, her need to reach out to us, to connect.

Yet, after that night, no one in our family heard much from Sarah for the next few months.

Another sketch of Sarah's.

1989   August 28   Ingrid Soet last seen

1989   Elaine Phyllis Dumba last seen

1991   August 22   Nancy Clark last seen

1992   June 18   Kathleen Dale Wattley last seen

1992   October 16   Elsie Sebastian last seen

1993   April   Teresa Louise Triff last seen

1993   December 14   Leigh Miner last seen

1994   August 19   Angela Mary Arsenault last seen

seven

THE DOWNTOWN EASTSIDE

CRAZY JACKIE, as she was called on the street, had known of Sarah for years before they became friends in 1989. In the mid-eighties, Jackie was working the amateur circuit as a stripper and had an attitude. "I was really, really vain," she tells me. She felt superior to prostitutes. She thought that she would never sink to turning tricks. "I didn't know a lot," she says.

Vanity can spring paradoxically from self-loathing, a feeling that Jackie struggled with throughout her years downtown. Like Charlie, Jackie had a hard beginning. Her birth father sexually abused her until she was three and a half. Her parents abused alcohol and drugs. Her mother abandoned her and her twin sister three times. The last time, her baby brother was left with them, and she watched him die of hypothermia. After that, they were put up for adoption, but Jackie remembers telling her sister, "Don't love our adoptive mom and dad because they're only going to hurt us."

Jackie speaks lovingly of her adoptive parents now. Her story is different from Charlie's in that, although she was an Aboriginal child thrust into a white home, that home embraced her. And she had been taken from an untenable situation. I don't know if she shares Sarah's feelings of alienation and loss of her own heritage. Jackie's is another in the many and varied stories of interracial adoption.

Like Sarah, Jackie ended up on the Downtown Eastside. She was four years older than Sarah, though, already eighteen when she started working as a stripper in the Granville Street area at the end of 1983 and twenty-four by the time she and Sarah got to know each other well in 1989.

Jackie remembers when Sarah got involved with Charlie. Charlie supplied her with the clothes that she needed to work but kept her tightly controlled. "She had the boots," Jackie says. "The clothes. It was almost like Charlie had her in hiding for a while. She was out on the corner and then she was gone. You didn't see her down on the street scoring or anything. She was going straight back to Charlie." Charlie was making sure that Sarah brought the money that she made home to him. He would go out and buy drugs himself, controlling her money and her access to heroin.

Sometime during this period, Jackie and Sarah started talking on the corner one day. Jackie was drawn to Sarah. "There was something about her," she says. "She was friendly. She was bubbly. She wasn't standoffish or rude. She wasn't territorial. She'd share her corner." Jackie would buy a pop and chips and share them with Sarah as they chatted while they waited to be picked up.

Jackie was amazed at Sarah's confidence. Sarah knew that she was going to get picked up whether another woman was standing beside her or not. Jackie realized through Sarah that she didn't have to defend her corner. "I'm dark, Native, short, with long hair," she points out. "If I'm standing beside a white or a black person or somebody else, if they want me, they're going to pick me. I learned that through Sarah. Yet, you see girls scrap over corners." Jackie's description reveals a certain dignity in Sarah and a willingness to welcome other women in.

Sarah's openness remained even in the more competitive world of East Hastings, where the prices women could charge for various services were at least 20 percent lower than they had been up on Granville. It was unacceptable to undercut the going rate, though. Women would get beaten up for that. "The only way to stay on top was to stick to the rules," Jackie says. "Sarah stuck to the rules." At that time, most people did, it seems. Good drugs were readily available as long as you could come up with the money.

Changes in the availability, quality and price of heroin and cocaine as well as the advent of crack cocaine and speedballs are responsible for a lot of the deterioration that took place on the Downtown Eastside through the nineties, in Jackie's opinion. Talwin and Ritalin, Ts and Rs, had become widely available, for example. Talwin mimics heroin and Ritalin mimics cocaine. Put them together and you have the "poor man's speedball." Dealers had people working full-time, going from doctor's office to doctor's office getting prescriptions for the drugs. Pharmacies charged a dollar a pill, but one pill sold on the street for ten times that price. I remember Sarah telling us about the use of Ritalin as a street drug. Both Jackie's partner and Charlie sold Ts and Rs.

Throughout 1989, Sarah was living in various hotels along Hastings, but she was no longer finding it possible to use the hotels for turning tricks. Earlier in the eighties lots of hotels still charged ten dollars an hour, presenting a feasible and relatively safe alternative to getting into cars. "We tried really hard not to be in cars," Jackie tells me. "We actually didn't get pushed into cars until 1989 when the price dropped on drugs."

As the eighties ended and the nineties began, an influx of drugs from Mexico and Guatemala created havoc in Vancouver. Spitballs, the heroin was called, because small-time dealers carried it in tiny plastic packages in their mouths. Dealers wrapped it in a square of garbage bag, inside another square of garbage bag, closed tightly with dental floss. Jackie remembers that as a turning point. They sold heroin more cheaply, so the competition to sell became stiffer. The first spitballs sold for twenty dollars.

Dealers could no longer remain out of sight, secure in the knowledge that their clients would come to them. They had to get out there, or get people out there for them, and compete. And as the price of the drugs went down, forces of supply and demand pushed down the prices that some women charged for sex as well, and that in turn increased competition on the street, making life more difficult for everyone. Desperation grew. And the quality of the drugs became less consistent, less reliable.

Suddenly, the market for drugs crashed because dealers started to sell spitballs of cocaine or heroin for ten dollars, half price. A spitball contained an eighth of a gram of cocaine or less than half a point of heroin, "which for most addicts would straighten them out," Jackie says. That language, "straighten them out," is important. For an addict, heroin is not used to get high, it is used to function at a basic level, to feel normal, to feel straight. Realizing that heroin addicts are not people who want to be high all the time and have endless fun, that without their drugs they can't feel like the rest of us do, takes away some of my tendency to want to tell them to snap out of it.

Not only did the price drop on drugs at that time but hotels stopped renting by the hour. The police clamped down on hotels functioning as brothels. Thus women weren't able to command as much money as before, nor were they able to ask for the extra ten dollars for a hotel room. And the hotel rooms were no longer available anyway.

Papers and capsules of heroin all but disappeared. Everything was sold in spitballs. Women became more desperate, less willing to stand and wait for clients. Jackie calls it a "frenzy." Part of the frenzy came about because the quality of the drugs was no longer reliable. There was more speed in heroin. The cocaine wasn't pure any more. So, even though the prices were low, you couldn't count on getting high. "I remember spending hundreds of dollars one time and I only got high twice because I was getting really low-grade coke," Jackie says. "You would get just a little bit of a feeling and then it would go away. You'd have to go and score again." So, to the struggle to find a place to sleep and enough to eat was added the struggle to get good drugs. You had to work hard to hang on to your contacts, while it was often hard to find a particular dealer because everything had shifted out on the street. Dealers weren't sitting in bars any more. They were outdoors actively pushing drugs on the street and moving regularly from place to place.

Many people over the years have blamed the economic downturn on the Downtown Eastside on the shifting of the drug trade outdoors. However, I recently read an alternative point of view. The Carnegie Community Action Project produced a report that hypothesized that the opening of malls and big box stores in Vancouver led to the closing of key businesses along Hastings Street, including several banks. In addition, large stores such as Woodwards and Woolworths closed their doors. The higher the vacancy rate grew, the harder it became to attract business back into the area. And the higher the vacancy rate grew, the more abandoned buildings, the fewer people coming to the neighbourhood to shop or bank, the greater the vacuum, the more room for open drug use. Now, of course, the drug scene does deter business, but when I was a child we shopped regularly at Woodwards, one of Vancouver's major department stores and slightly cheaper than the uptown Hudson's Bay. The store closed, I believe, because of competition, not because of problems in the neighbourhood.

Within that frightening and rapidly changing world, Sarah and Charlie had a system that worked pretty well in its own way. By working the street, Sarah could accumulate a quantity of money that would allow Charlie to buy a bulk of drugs, which he could then divide into smaller portions and sell at a profit to make more money. Eventually both money and drugs would be gone and the cycle would start again. Sarah's work and Charlie's complemented one another, even if Charlie dominated Sarah throughout.

At Christmastime 1989, at the end of Sarah's first year with Charlie, she came home to Mum's house in rough shape. She was missing her false front tooth; she was high; she was frantic for sugar and food, fidgeting and coming apart, falling against things or falling sound asleep in a chair. Yet, she brought beautiful carved argillite pendants for everyone. She was wearing a jacket made by the man who had made the pendants; he had meant the jacket for his son, but his son had overdosed a few days earlier. I was living in Ontario at the time and spent that Christmas at the other end of the country with my aunt and uncle, deep in the Cape Breton snow.

By 1990, fear was beginning to mount on the Downtown Eastside as women noticed increasing violence against sex workers. "All the girls on the Downtown Eastside knew that there was somebody, probably more than one person, out there hurting girls," Jackie says. "It was so unbelievable. It was so unfathomable and so heinous. It was so hard to believe that someone was targeting us. We were so desperate and we were so lost, struggling beyond imagination. To actually try to fathom that somebody picked us to hurt . . . We just couldn't believe it."

In February 1990, Sarah called home to tell Mum that Charlie had been diagnosed with several serious illnesses, in particular a degeneration of the spine caused by poor diet and excessive use of drugs, including codeine. At one point he was hospitalized and had his spine fused in about five places. Sarah got Mum to look at his back once, because the wounds from surgery wouldn't heal. I believe that he has been in pain ever since. When Sarah called that day, she wished Mum a happy Valentine's Day and invited her to have dinner with the two of them. Mum did have dinner with Sarah and Charlie, but then didn't hear from Sarah again until Sarah phoned to wish her a happy birthday in mid-April.

On May 11, the night before Sarah's twenty-first birthday, she phoned Mum in tears and asked to come for the night. She arrived in the wee hours. Charlie had hit her on the ear and it was swollen and bruised. Mum had already invited her for a birthday supper that night, so Sarah stayed for the day, had dinner and later headed back downtown. After that, there was only phone contact until seven months later, on the morning of December 22, 1990, when St. Paul's Hospital called to tell Mum that Sarah was in labour.

I had moved back to Vancouver at the end of August and was living in Mum's basement while I did my master's degree in English at UBC. When Mum called me upstairs to tell me that Sarah was having a baby, I cried and cried. I spent the day in a fog, driving friends who were visiting from Montreal around the city. My friends were baffled by the depth of my grief. I was baffled by it too, baffled by the whole event, the fact that Sarah had been through a whole pregnancy without our knowledge, that she was going to have a child, and so aware that that was going to bring change. It was overwhelming, as was so much interaction with Sarah.

Mum spent the day in the hospital with Sarah. The baby, Jeanie, was full term, so when Sarah had come home on her birthday she was already six weeks pregnant. "No wonder she threw up her birthday dinner in May," Mum wrote in her journal while Sarah slept. "The baby's heart rate is normal at 130 to 150. Strange to hear it beating at me through this monitor. I wonder what she'll name this child. My first grandchild. I called Mum. Her first great-grandchild." Sarah Jean the second was born at 5:24 p.m., December 22, weighing six pounds, thirteen ounces. We called her Jeanie, after Aunt Jean. "Her hair is wavy when wet," Mum wrote, "but now it is totally straight."

Mum phoned home to tell us that Jeanie had been born and I cried again, but this time with wonder that a brand-new little person, my niece, whom I had known nothing of twelve hours earlier, was now there at the hospital beginning her life. Once Jeanie became real, our feelings focused on her with hope and joy.

I met both Jeanie and her father, Charlie, the next day. I had to look at Jeanie through glass because she was in the babies' Intensive Care. She was born addicted to heroin and cocaine. Mum was allowed in there and so were Sarah and Charlie. I stood on the other side of the glass and watched.

As soon as I met Charlie, I understood Sarah's attraction to him. He had gleaming long black hair and a radiant smile. And he was sweating profusely, a result of having abstained from drugs and allowing himself to slip into withdrawal in order to come to the hospital to meet his new baby and her mother's family without being high. I believe that he also brought Sarah drugs to see her through the day. I sensed that he cared for Sarah. And I sensed wonder and tenderness in him as well, when I watched him hold Jeanie in his hands. Sarah was not as familiar with babies as he was. I had heard about Charlie's dark side, but that day I saw the best in him.

Dad visited Sarah and Jeanie the next day. He and Sarah walked together to see Jeanie in the glass-enclosed Intensive Care ward for babies. A nurse held Jeanie up on the other side of the glass so Dad and Sarah could see her. Dad walked Sarah back to her room, said goodbye and made his way downstairs toward the exit.

Sarah chose the exact same time to try to leave the hospital without being checked out. The next thing Dad knew, a nurse ran into the lobby in a panic. Sarah was gone. Then an elevator door opened and there she was. While Dad watched in shock, two security guards grabbed Sarah and wrestled her into the elevator.

"Dad! Dad!" she cried. "Help me!" But Dad could do nothing. He stood in horror, unable to assist his youngest child.

"I left," Dad says. "I couldn't do anything. I could not interfere in that situation."

He never saw her again after that day.

"I NEVER ATTEMPTED TO SEE HER in the nineties while she was on the street," says Dad. "It was my perception that she didn't want to see me."

Sarah needed help in so many ways. Dad pointed out to me when we talked about it later that her cry to him in the hospital was much, much bigger than the moment that contained it. But at a more basic level, she wanted help so that she could leave the hospital and get a fix. She made her way down the back stairs minutes after she was wrestled back up to her room. I don't know why she wasn't allowed to sign herself out, what the hospital thought could be gained by keeping her there against her will.

After that, Jeanie had to go into a special ward for drug-addicted babies at Sunny Hill Health Centre. She was there for twelve weeks. Mum visited her almost every day. If ever Mum could not go, I would go in her stead. I learned how to give Jeanie the special care that she needed, how to wrap her tight in a blanket and sit with her, feeding her and just being there with her, providing human contact. Murmuring to her. And then settling her back down in her crib. Often the room was noisy with other babies crying. Drug-addicted babies cry a lot. But the room was dim and the nurses and the doctor who looked after the babies knew exactly what they needed—tight swaddling and lots of calm, loving human contact, for example.

During that time, Mum made arrangements with Sarah for custody of Jeanie. Mum seemed to know right away that she wanted Jeanie to live with her. There was no question of Sarah's taking Jeanie then, although I think that Sarah thought about it a lot after that. Sarah was not leading a stable enough life. She didn't have a support system. Charlie ended up in jail in January and asked both Dad and Mum to bail him out. Both refused. "It's hard to say no to the father of your new grandchild," Mum wrote. Sarah was staying at the Brandiz Hotel for a while at that time, so Mum was able to reach her, and the discussion back and forth about the paperwork for custody went on a bit. Sarah and Charlie visited Jeanie at Sunny Hill when Jeanie was almost a month old, but they did not show up in court for the custody hearing. Sarah phoned Mum that night to say that she had mixed up the dates. "Possibly," Mum wrote. "Perhaps it was just too painful a thing for her to go through."

Jackie wasn't around much when Sarah was pregnant with Jeanie, but she remembers Sarah talking about Jeanie later and she remembers pictures. "She was proud of her baby," Jackie says, "proud of the fact that Jeanie was in a safe place with Sarah's mum."

While we waited for Jeanie to come home in March, we worked on changing the house around to receive her. The dining room became the nursery. Mum hired a young woman to look after Jeanie while she was at work, and I babysat once a week so Mum could have an evening off.

The day after Sarah's twenty-second birthday, on May 13, 1991, Charlie phoned to ask if they could come to see Jeanie. The visit was a success. Sarah and Charlie arrived just in time for tortellini, with a mocha roll standing in for a birthday cake. They looked at Sarah's and Jeanie's baby books together, and were pleased to see Jeanie so healthy and happy. "I gave Sarah two of the nicest pictures of Jeanie laughing," Mum wrote in her journal. "She liked the same ones I liked."

After that, the evening deteriorated. Sarah went out to "look at" the garage and came back in with her eyes rolling, obviously having had a fix. She passed out in the car when Mum drove them downtown. From that day until Thanksgiving, we didn't hear from Sarah.

I looked after Jeanie during the day that whole summer while Mum was at work. That fall, Mum hired a woman who looked after Jeanie for almost two years, until Mum and Jeanie moved to Ontario in June 1993.

In November 1991, Sarah was sentenced to six months in the Burnaby Correctional Centre for Women, BCCW. Strangely, none of us can remember what she was sentenced for—taking part in a robbery, perhaps. Her first several weeks there were terrible because she had to go through withdrawal with no support. The way she described it, she was put into a room by herself and left there until the drugs were out of her system. She wrote about withdrawal at great length in her journals:

Withdrawal is my biggest downfall. I'm terrified to death of that word; as far as I'm concerned it is a swear word. It's not like I haven't tried it before. Sometimes I was behind bars and that was the only reason why I did. Man, oh man, was I sick! A sick little puppy I was. There are no words on earth that can describe the feeling of being junk sick.

I have honestly fallen to my knees on the cement floor begging the Lord to strike me dead. He failed me again (thank you, Father).

I start off feeling okay. The few hours that I have before I awake I treasure, they are so precious. Then you should get done what needs to be done. Make your bed perfectly. Put a plastic bag in the garbage can. Put cigarettes, ashtray and water to rinse mouth after vomiting nearby. Have a bath or shower. Tie hair in ponytail. Wear pants and a shirt or shorts and a shirt. Lots of tossing and turning: ponytails save the hair from tangles and knots. Pants or shorts save from embarrassing poses.

A bath or shower make the worst of days seem a tiny bit better. If you're lucky you can go through withdrawal hot-bathing it. With Epsom salts. Epsom salts, my hero! Thank you, Lord! You like me, I think. Well, maybe a little. If you can get me in the water I could stay there forever, but if it's a quick dip, good luck to you and your army. I hate water when I'm going cold turkey. It feels weird, gross; it's hard to explain. But if I have the time to soak for an hour or so, it's one of the only things that makes me feel better. The Epsom salts send up little bubbles that scratch my joints and temporarily end the never-ending itching, tickling and aching in my joints, every joint, every joint means every god damn fucking joint. Fingers, toes. Insanity. Sometimes they must think I'm crazy, but by the end of the first twenty-four hours, I'm banging my head against the brick wall of my cell. It makes me forget one pain and concentrate on the one in my head. And I've only gone one day. It gets worse before it gets better.

Try to imagine hot and cold flashes like from sauna to igloo, sauna to igloo and then add sweating bullets non-stop, then go to a little tickle in the back of your throat, along with an itchy feeling in all your joints along with a little tickling with a feather that can't be scratched or stopped for seven days. Now the little tickle has become a cough which is making you heave which is making you convulse. Itchy, tickling in every joint heaving up nothing but yellow mucus that burns your throat. Then, oh joy, come the seizures.

All this with no sleep. If it takes seven, or fourteen, or twenty days to get off the physical sickness that is how many days I'm awake. No sleep, not one wink. It wouldn't be so bad if I could just relax and sleep a peaceful, restful, undisturbed sleep if only for thirty minutes, even thirty seconds, I wouldn't care.

It is so painful and cold, so cold, no matter how hot you feel on the outside, I'm cold inside just like an ice cube. I am so tired, cold, clammy, sweaty and I ache from head to toe. I just want to go to sleep and sleep and sleep. So tired. So thirsty. Water. I gulp that glass back in one gulp and then thud it hits the bottom of my stomach so heavy that I start to puke. As fast as it goes down it comes back up. Stupid. Fuck, was I dumb, I know better than that. I can never drink or eat anything. I throw it back up by the bucketful. I dry-heave yellow slime that burns all the way up and out. By the time it's finished my abdomen is so sore that it hurts to breathe.

By the end of day two, seizures have taken over. Now every time I try to stand I get the jerks. No control. I get scared to fart because if I do I start the waterfall of shit that burns like I'm spitting razors from my ass.

So tired. Bang, bang, bang. My head must be covered in bumps from knocking it against the wall, for a few seconds of relief from one agonizing extreme to another. Please somebody shoot me. By the time I'm at day four it's all going at the same time, never-ending itching, tickling, coughing, aching, hot-cold sweats, shits, sneezing, puking, seizures, no sleep. Weak. Weak. Weak. Still not able to eat, no appetite yet.

Once the drugs were out of her system, Sarah seemed to thrive in prison. I remember my visits fondly—that is, after I had made it through the long check-in process, all the security. We had to sign in and they would check that we were on the list of visitors that Sarah was willing to see. We would put our things in a locker before going through a metal detector and several locked doors. We would then wait in the visitors' room for guards to open the door to let the women in. I remember seeing Sarah through a little window in the door before they let her through.

She would come through the door full of energy, her face growing rounder, her hair full and healthy. But, of what she was going through, both inside herself and on the other side of the big door with the guards and her fellow prisoners, we knew very little.

Sarah wrote several poems while she was in jail. She gave copies of several to Mum, neatly typed. One was called "Death":

> *When I think of death*
> *I see the faces*
> *And remember certain*
> *Times and places.*
>
> *I hear the laughter*
> *And feel the tears*
> *And become more aware*
> *Of my inner fears.*
>
> *For every new day*
> *Another one's gone*
> *But life down here*
> *Just goes on and on.*
>
> *You can numb your mind*
> *And cover the scars*
> *By pumping the drugs*
> *And reaching the stars.*

You think you're cool
You think you're fine
But what you're doing
Is committing suicide.

While we were there, we would share photos of Jeanie. Sarah would tell us about the high school equivalency courses that she was taking. She talked about drawing and writing. She wrote a piece about drawing too, about its power in her life:

I've liked to draw ever since I was a little girl. It was my own secret doorway to escape, someplace only I knew and only I could get to. It was my own sanctuary from the storm. No matter what I drew on a piece of paper, it was me, it understood me, it was real to me. To others it was just a drawing, but to me it was my laugh, smile, thoughts, feelings, ideas, pain (lots of pain). My drawing was every emotion that I could ever dream to know.

When I draw I feel relieved like a great weight has been lifted from my shoulders. I have spilled my guts out on paper. My anger is bottled up inside mixing like oil and water because of the things that have happened to me. My lonely life is something I'm far from being proud of, any of it, but it just happened. I have to cope with life and my drawing is the most understanding, reassuring friend. My drawing will never turn around and stab me in the back. My drawing will always, always be there waiting patiently. Sometimes when I draw, I use a charcoal pencil. It might seem strange, but when I draw, it's like the charcoal pencil is screaming, really screaming. I like to think it is doing that for me. Like it knows the pain I've gone through and it is trying to release it for me through our work.

Yes, I love to draw and it is my very own sanctuary from the storm.

She also fattened up a bit while she was in there. And she seemed to be considering changing the direction of her life once she got out.

In early 1992, Sarah was still doing well in BCCW. She got her CPR certificate. As her release day neared, she phoned Mum and told her that she had to stay in a bit longer and would be able to write her grade twelve equivalence exam. But in February, being incarcerated got harder for her; the approaching release date brought up thoughts of drugs again. Apparently this is a common experience in prison: as the release date nears, the obsession with drugs becomes overpowering. And the women reinforce each other's cravings with endless talk about getting high.

The day before Valentine's Day, Mark and a friend of mine and I went to see Sarah. Mum sent along a Valentine's present, a card with a picture of Jeanie, telling Sarah that we knew she could make it; two rap music tapes and a book called *White Rabbit* about a young female psychiatrist who started on drugs at twelve and finally accepted help and treatment seventeen years later and made it. Sarah had seemed depressed the last few times Mum had visited her. As the day loomed, she told Mum that she had five days added to her confinement for mouthing off to a guard. Anxiety about what she would do when she got out must have been building.

Sarah gave me a Valentine's card to take home to Mum. "To Mom," she wrote in it. "I don't ever say anything to let you know I love you so very much." Then, at the bottom, she wrote, "I love you, Mom!!! Love, Sarah Jean de Vries." On the back is a photo of Sarah staring directly into the camera, utterly serious. She is wearing black leggings and a purple shirt.

Now that I've spoken with a woman who was in jail with Sarah at that time, I'm not sure I believe that five days were added to her confinement. According to her friend, she deliberately gave Mum the wrong release date so that she could go back downtown. Perhaps she saw it as a way of minimizing our hurt. For by the time Sarah got out, nothing was more important than getting downtown for that first fix.

On March 23, 1992, Mum went to visit Sarah one last time before her supposed release, but she wasn't there.

AGAIN, ONCE SARAH HAD LEFT BCCW, we did not hear from her for months. The disappointment, the heartbreak, was profound. It was so difficult to remain open to hope over and over again and have it dashed every time.

We were angry at Sarah, but I remember focusing my anger on the prison system. Why didn't they tell us? Why would they simply give her cab fare? Didn't they make any attempt to provide her with options when she was released? But Sarah's friend said that Sarah deliberately gave Mum the wrong date. "I remember her giggling about that," the friend said to me. And I wanted to yell at her or hang up the phone.

If we were honest with ourselves, we always knew that Sarah chose to go downtown rather than come home. It wasn't as if she was told on the spur of the moment, "You're free. Here's cab fare. Off you go, now!" If she had wanted to come home to us, she could have. All it would have taken was one phone call. She didn't want to. I imagine that she was torn up about it. The fact that she had no contact with Mum for eight months following her release supports that.

Those were particularly hard years for Mum. Grandma died the year before, and Uncle Hugh, one of Mum's brothers, died in October 1992. Mum was dealing with her grief and was also worried about Aunt Jean all alone in the house in Guelph.

I was a bit at sea that year as well. I had completed my master's degree in April and was unsure what to do next. I taught a couple of children's literature courses that summer, one at UBC and one at the University of Guelph, but decided to stay in Vancouver and write for the next year instead of beginning a PhD at the University of Alberta as planned. That decision was fortunate because in November I met my husband-to-be, Roland.

Sarah came to see her daughter on Jeanie's birthday, December 22. Jeanie was turning two. Sarah brought two duffle bags full of gifts.

"She dropped on her knees in front of Jeanie," Mum wrote in her journal, "hauled out a toy clown and pushed a button on his back and he started to play a tune and bend about. He has a sweet smile, but his legs are broken already." The clown's legs were made of Styrofoam. Sarah also brought clothes for Jeanie, none of which fit, and a plastic Indian doll all done up in "genuine leather and deerskin." Sarah's attempts to involve herself in Jeanie's life were heartbreaking because her desire to connect was so strong, but her efforts so often misjudged.

She came for Christmas too, my first with Roland. A crowd was at Mum's for Christmas dinner and Sarah showed up late with heaps of gifts—many of them stolen, I suspect. They were an odd selection, but she had things for Mum, Peter, Mark, me and Jeanie. It was so important for Sarah to give us those gifts, to shower us with them, to be in a position to give. She gave Peter an expensive London Fog jacket with a zip lining. She was worried it wouldn't fit him, but it was just the right size. He loved it. I think that was the Christmas when Sarah gave me a pair of earrings that I still wear: hollow, gold-plated hearts about a centimetre across, with a single pearl above each heart. I wear them when I particularly want to keep Sarah close to me. I lose earrings all the time, but these I still have.

That evening, "Sarah's eyes started closing and she almost tipped off the sofa," Mum wrote. Mum wrapped up a tray of turkey and ham and other food, and some pictures of Jeanie for Sarah to take to Charlie. I drove Sarah back downtown that night. The drive was quiet. Sarah was slipping away, her head nodding against the window. I was tense. I had never driven her downtown or visited her there. I did not go with her into her room. She was still living in a hotel at that time.

The next year, 1993, was a dangerous year downtown. Many, many people died of drug overdoses because of an influx of pure heroin, much stronger than most people were used to. CBC Television ran a story on May 28, two weeks after Sarah's twenty-fourth birthday, in which they reported that the sixty-eighth death of the year from an overdose had happened the night before. Their reporter, Margo Harper, visited a Chinatown rooming house because a fifteen-year-old girl had overdosed. There, she met and interviewed Sarah.

Sarah began the interview by shooting up on camera and explaining that the amount of heroin she was injecting would most likely kill a non-addict. She said that the quality of the heroin was getting higher and higher, "but I probably don't realize it as much, because I'm pretty much numb to it. I don't get high off it any more. It just makes me normal. It just makes me able to function."

The interviewer asked her if she wanted to stop. "I want to, but I'm not ready to yet," Sarah said, then acknowledged that the drugs could kill her but that that wasn't enough to stop her from doing them.

On the tape, Sarah speaks clearly, softly, directly, although she often pauses to consider a question and sways slightly from the drugs. She doesn't evade questions or put on any show of bravado. She ponders her experience and communicates it as best she can. The camera zooms in on her scars now and then. While I understand why it does, I wish that it would not.

When she says that fear of dying is no deterrent, she goes on to explain that the fear of getting sick overpowers all other considerations. "It drives you insane," she says. "It's like having the flu, a cold, arthritis, times a hundred, all at once.

"I went to jail for six months a while ago and they made me quit cold turkey and I would rather have been dead. It hurts. When you don't have the drug, it physically hurts."

The reporter asks her if the drugs make her feel good. Sarah thinks about that one for a long time. "I feel good," she says at last, "but I'm not particularly happy. It's like carrying a big ball and chain around with you for part of your life. I'm scared to go to sleep, because I know I'm going to wake up sick."

Finally, Sarah tells viewers what her thoughts are about people trying heroin for the first time. "I'm not the one to tell you not to do it," she says, "because I'm sitting here doing it myself. I'm definitely not proud of it. It may sound strange or stupid coming from me, but just stay away from it.

"It is dangerous. It is addicting. You got three ways that you can go. You can go to jail. You can end up dead. Or you can wind up being a lifer down here. It's not a nice life. It looks fun when you come down here, but it's not. There's a lot of stuff that you don't want to see."

"Are you a lifer?" Margo Harper asks her, a cruel question.

Sarah's eyes slide over to one side as she considers that question. The pause is long. "I can't really say that, but I've been down here since I was ten years old, just about. And that seems like a long time to me already, because I'm twenty-four."

Sarah had not been downtown since she was ten, but she had been down there for ten years, on and off. That interview was an early example of Sarah's sharing her experience with the world in the hopes that others might learn something from her. The same impulse was at work in much of her journal writing over the years.

I read a column in the paper about safe injection sites that used the expression "the moral cost." The writer argued that if we help drug addicts at all, in any way, we make it easier for people to become drug addicts and we make it more appealing, and thus it becomes a worse problem. It made me very angry when I read that. I suspect that leaving addicts to hit bottom leads to at least as many deaths as it does successful detoxes. The misery that addicts experience is caused not only by their poor choices made way back when they decided to use hard drugs but by society's criminalizing of their behaviour, by their poverty, by the things that they have to do to get the money to obtain the drugs. Many movie stars, rock stars and other wealthy people use the same drugs and become addicts, but because they have money and society's approval, they rarely have to deal with the justice system. They can shell out the money required to go into treatment when they want, where they want.

Too often, the bottom for a Downtown Eastside drug addict is death, a high moral cost indeed.

THE MONTH AFTER SARAH DID THE INTERVIEW with the CBC, Mum packed up, sold her house and moved to Ontario to live with Aunt Jean. Aunt Jean was finding it difficult to live alone and Mum was finding it a strain to work full-time and raise a child. After all, she was fifty-five years old. I had been helping a fair bit, but my relationship with Roland was serious and it was clear that I was not going to be living at Mum's house forever. Mum and Aunt Jean bought a huge stone house on ten acres outside of Guelph, and moved there with Aunt Jean's three dogs and Mum's one.

When Mum left, Sarah stopped calling the family. She didn't start to call me or Peter. She just stopped contacting anyone. So, from then on, I visited her regularly, at least twice a year, once around her birthday and once a few days before Christmas. Peter came with me the first few times, at least through 1994, but then I started going by myself.

By that time, it was easier to visit her because she wasn't living in hotels any more. Sarah and Charlie had rented a little grey house on Princess Avenue about half a dozen blocks east of Main and Hastings and two doors north of Hastings, in the heart of the Downtown Eastside. From then on, Princess and Hastings was Sarah's corner. She spent many hours a day standing on the street that she had so firmly warned Angela against. Sarah tended to stay east of Main. She earned money, gave it to Charlie, and he went after the drugs. So people who knew her downtown didn't see her that much unless they dropped by her house or passed her on the corner. She established a regular routine and a regular clientele.

Jackie is impressed by that. "The one thing that I had to have was my reputation," she tells me. "And that was what Sarah always had: her reputation with her clients. Sarah had lots and lots and lots of regulars. Sarah had that reputation of following through and being good to customers."

Jackie, on the other hand, was struggling. She was on her own and doing as much cocaine as she could. She would spend her last hundred dollars with no thought to where she would sleep that night

Sarah at Lighthouse Park, not long after she was adopted.

All photos courtesy of Maggie de Vries unless otherwise noted.

The whole family, including Katy the dog, in the early seventies.

Sarah with Mindy and Julian, late summer 1974.

Sarah and me reading a birthday
book on May 12, 1973.

Peter, Mark, Mum, Sarah and me.

Sarah's grade seven photo, 1981.

Mum with Sarah on Christmas morning, 1983. Sarah is sporting her new beret.

Grandma, Mum, me and Sarah in 1974.

Sarah with Licorice in
dress-up clothes, circa 1981.

Sarah holding Lucy on
a visit home in 1985.

Sarah with Peter and Troy at Mum's, Christmas 1987.

Sarah with Alex at
a downtown bar, 1985.

Sarah in prison. She put this
picture in a Valentine's card
to Mum in early 1992.

Sarah in slippers on her last
Christmas visit when she
was very high, 1992.

Sarah with Jeanie in my home, 1994.

Sarah with Ben in his foster home, 1996.

Sarah with me, 1997.

The Princess Avenue house all boarded up, 2002.

Jeanie leading the march to the second part of the missing women memorial in May of 1999. Wayne is to her right.

The bench dedication for Sarah in March of 2000.
I am at left in the foreground.

Craig Hodge/The Vancouver Sun

or what she would eat. "Everything got so fast and scary out there," she says. "I didn't know what Sarah had learned about maintaining. I was a suicide runner. I used to think that Sarah had the right thing going, because if anybody messed with her, Charlie was out there, stomping down the street and beating the crap out of them. If you owed her a smidge of dope, he was out there getting it out of you. A lot of the time, I didn't see how high she paid for that. My thinking is that it was a really high price." The more I learn, the higher I realize that the price was. Still, as Jackie suggests, having an "old man" worked for Sarah in many ways.

At the same time, the fact that Sarah was able to stay relatively stable within her world may have kept her from trying to get out. Jackie entered recovery houses and treatment centres repeatedly, until finally, a long way down the road, she was able to leave the Downtown Eastside permanently. For some years, except for when she was in jail, I don't think that Sarah had ever seriously tried to get off drugs, although I believe that she thought about doing so daily.

As the years went by, Charlie became ill; the illnesses that Sarah had mentioned to Mum in 1990 grew worse. He had some sort of growth on his back and his spine continued to deteriorate. By the mid-nineties, as far as I could tell, he rarely left the immediate vicinity of the house. He wasn't stomping anywhere to do anything.

Sarah had a number of men in her life to whom she could turn when she needed to get away—some of the regular clientele that Jackie mentioned so enviously. If she got sick, she could go stay with someone. She could usually get away for a few days, particularly after she met Wayne. As Charlie grew more debilitated, it seemed to become easier for her to let other men into her life in a bigger way. So when she met Wayne in the early summer of 1994, the relationship had room to grow.

Sarah was sitting outside in the sun with Charlie one day in June. They were on a tiny patch of grass, leaning against the stucco wall of the corner coffee shop, soaking up the heat. Wayne, an automotive technician in his mid-forties, was out for his usual Sunday afternoon drive, headed east along Hastings on his way out of town. "I saw her sitting on the grass," he says. "And I thought, this is an incredibly beautiful woman." He pulled over, ostensibly to get a Pepsi at the corner store opposite where she was sitting, and he started talking to her. He asked her if she was working and she said that she was. She agreed to come along with him, he picked up some coolers instead of a Pepsi and they drove back to his place.

For a number of years after Wayne started talking publicly about Sarah and about his relationship with her, he skirted the fact that he first approached Sarah as a john. More recently, he has begun to talk about that fact more openly so that people can begin to understand that men who visit prostitutes can be ordinary, caring people, just like anybody else. At the same time, he says that he would never pay for sex again. He has gotten to know many women in the sex trade in recent years as friends and he has seen the dark side of sex work as well as the disgust that many sex workers feel toward many of their clients.

On that day, though, in 1994, he was simply drawn to Sarah. He told me that he was not in the habit of paying for sex, although he admitted that he had stopped at the Mustang Ranch in Nevada once on a road trip with a friend. "We had always read about the brothels in Nevada and heard about them, and we stopped one time. So it's not that I had never done it before," he says, "but I . . . It was a tourist attraction. All the girls would line up and that sort of thing; you would see tourists coming in from Japan. It was crazy."

Prostitution as a tourist attraction is particularly repugnant to me. Men go, as Wayne did, because it is a novelty. The women who work in such places are subject to all kinds of rules and controls, and only keep about half of the money they bring in, which is then subject to taxation. The establishment itself gets the rest.

Wayne's first meeting with Sarah sounds to me like a more authentic interaction than any he would be likely to have with a woman he picked out of a line at a brothel on a road trip, or any that a woman chosen from a lineup would be likely to have with him. In many ways, Sarah had more control throughout the evening than women would have in a brothel or massage parlour. At the same time, of course, she was not as safe as she would have been in a controlled establishment.

The two of them spent a lot of time talking that night. Sarah told Wayne about Charlie, about her life. "She overwhelmed me with what she shared," Wayne says. "I didn't know what to expect, but I didn't expect somebody to start pouring out how they were really feeling, and she did." Sarah seems to have had a real need to talk that night and she saw in Wayne someone she could safely confide in, someone unconnected with her world and someone who was deeply interested in what she had to say.

That night Wayne also paid Sarah for sex.

After that, Wayne dropped by to see Sarah regularly. She started to show him her poetry. Once, Charlie asked Wayne to look for some bolts for him. He wanted to use them for weightlifting to strengthen his back. Wayne took a look around at work. "We sort of got to know each other, Charlie and I," Wayne says. "I got to know Charlie and various characters that would come in the place."

At first Sarah and Wayne saw each other every couple of weeks, but as time went on, they saw more of each other. Wayne began to hope for a relationship, and later that year they did try living together, a change that Charlie—despite his somewhat open situation with Sarah—did not appreciate. Sarah only stayed at Wayne's for a couple of weeks, however. His apartment was too far away from the Downtown Eastside, too far away from where Sarah needed to be, both to earn money and to buy drugs. But although Sarah moved out again, she kept most of her belongings there from then on.

Wayne lived in a 475-square-foot bachelor apartment with a Murphy bed. After she moved out, Sarah stayed there regularly, sometimes dropping in for a few hours, other times staying for several days. Whenever she was there, her stuff would be scattered everywhere. "That was her comfort zone," Wayne said, "in the middle of her stuff." She would do crossword puzzles and fill out bingo cards. They went to movies together, including *Trainspotting*, a film about drug addiction in Great Britain. The last movie they saw together was *Titanic*, which Sarah loved.

Sometimes Sarah would cook, both at Wayne's apartment and at her house—once it was pork chops in gravy with string beans, and lemon meringue pie. They went grocery shopping together, usually heading first for the candy aisle. Sarah loved Maynards wine gums and Panda licorice. She played CDs and did lots of writing and drawing. Sometimes she mended clothes. Once she found some acrylic paints in a Dumpster and she and Wayne spent a whole evening trying to unplug the holes so she could use the paints. "We never did get them open," Wayne said, "but we made an awful mess."

It strikes me that the things Sarah liked to do to relax as an adult are related, in many cases, to interests she developed as a child. Her life may have gone off course but she remained devoted to the things that she loved to do. It also strikes me that judging by their leisure pursuits, Sarah and Wayne could have been any happy couple. Neither what Sarah did for a living nor her addiction was all she was, just as neither my career nor my various addictions—food, coffee, too much TV, a martini or glass of wine too many on occasion— define me.

The time that Sarah could spend relaxing over a crossword puzzle or baking a lemon meringue pie was limited by the threat of with-drawal, always lingering in the background. It had become terribly hard for Sarah to make enough money to support her habit. As Jackie explained, women were making less and less money on the street, yet right up until the end, Sarah could easily spend several hundred dollars a day on her drugs. Even though she had more of a regular clientele than many women did, she still must have found it a terrible grind. She must have found it increasingly difficult to make enough money to avoid getting sick.

And through it all, she was supplying Charlie's habit too. Charlie wasn't a pimp, exactly, but, as Wayne pointed out to me, every girl-friend Charlie's ever had has been forced to support his habit.

He lived off Sarah and off other women. He protected Sarah and other women. And he beat Sarah and other women. Somewhere around 1994, before Sarah met Wayne, the relationship between Sarah and Charlie changed. She was no longer his partner, although she still lived with him. After that, he always had at least one other woman living in the house, but still he kept Sarah fairly close to home. She spent much of her time in that house when she wasn't working. Yet, she was free to stay with Wayne or with others when she wished. She was free to come to my place for a visit and I was free to visit her there. I still do not understand the exact nature of the hold that Charlie had on her, but the fact that he was Jeanie's father must have been part of it.

The combination of that steady, though troubled, relationship, Sarah's careful maintenance of her appearance and her health, and her network of relationships with others who genuinely cared about her helped to keep Sarah safe, I believe, although it also kept her locked in the world of the Downtown Eastside.

I DREADED MY VISITS to Sarah's house.

On each occasion, I stored my emotions away as carefully as I could, but still, as I drove closer, my body would tense, my gut would twist. I would anticipate. I brought gifts and photos, a store of anecdotes: a plan to fill the time.

I made a point of going early in the afternoon, when less desperation and hopelessness was evident on the streets. I looked away from the people who stumbled, who yelled obscenities, from the women with bare, scarred legs and shaking bodies standing on corners trying to make a few dollars for their next fix. I drove down Main Street one block north of Hastings and turned left, passing Oppenheimer Park. When I came to the Union Gospel Mission, I had reached Princess Avenue, where I turned left again. There was Sarah's house, a little grey bungalow, one of two, a matched set. Sarah lived in the one on the right.

I parked the car, walked around the back of the house, climbed the six steps or so to the back door and hesitated, listening, trying to get a sense of what might be going on inside. When I was ready, I knocked loudly.

"Who's there?" a voice would shout, usually Charlie's.

"It's Maggie, Sarah's sister," I would shout back through the door.

A minute or so later, the door would open and I would be ushered in. The kitchen was always a shambles. Dishes and pots would be piled high, evidence of cooking without the cleaning up. Pudding was a regular dish in that house—instant pudding that you mix with hot milk but don't have to cook. Sarah knew that she needed nourishment, but often didn't have the stomach for much in the way of "real food." She loved instant chocolate pudding mixed with Dream Whip—long-standing heroin addicts eat sugar endlessly. And Sarah liked to crunch on ice, again feeding a craving.

While Sarah contributed plenty to the disorder in the house, she always wanted to make it a home as well. I was told that she sometimes put up signs in the kitchen. "Wash your dishes," one said. "This is not a flophouse," said another. A long-time friend of Sarah's who was also a john, Ken, says that once someone brought a big roast of beef to the house and traded it for drugs. Sarah cooked that roast, the word spread, and people flocked to the back door for a taste. "She was a good cook," Ken says. "But she cooked like she kept house. She would be in her glory while she was doing it, oblivious to the grease flying around." She showed Ken how to rid the drippings of some of the fat when getting ready to make gravy. She would put ice cubes in the drippings and the fat would congeal around the ice. I don't know where she learned that.

The TV was always on in the living room when I was there. The floor in the house had been stripped several years earlier and then re-covered with nailed-down pieces of linoleum. Sarah would show me the latest improvements every time I came: walls painted, a new couch . . . Once she had cleaned and organized her room. All her clothes were hanging up. She had put pictures on the walls, put her makeup and jewellery in order. Such order was rare for her.

Sometimes there were kittens.

Also needles. Sarah would warn me to watch where I sat and stepped. She was protective. She told me to hang on to my purse if others were present. People came and went in the same way I did, shouting through the back door before being granted or denied entry. I might share the couch with a person on the nod from a recent fix. Other times, people would be gathered in friendly chatter; I would be drawn in, included. Once, Sarah searched a woman before she left, sure that the woman was stealing from her. When I visited at Christmastime, decorations would be up, a tree in the corner, and several times I took away wrapped gifts.

Sometimes, Sarah and I would be the only ones there. I liked that the best.

We would sit and try to talk to one another. I would bring photos if I could, stories at least. If Charlie was there, Sarah would call out to his room at the back of the house to pass on the stories about Jeanie. He loved the stories too. From what I could tell, neither of them knew how to relate to real live in-the-flesh children, although I have a photo of Charlie holding a day-old Jeanie so tenderly that I can hardly bear to look.

Dreaded though those visits were, I treasured the time together. I missed seeing Sarah at family gatherings and hearing from Mum that she had called to wish Mum a happy birthday or Mother's Day. I needed the contact.

1995   March   Catherine Louise Gonzales last seen

1995   April   Catherine Maureen Knight last seen

1995   July 30   Dorothy Anne Spence last seen

1995   December 27   Diana Melnick last seen

1996   April 6   Frances Ann Young last seen

1996   October 29   Tanya Marlo Holyk last seen

1996   December 6   Olivia Gayle Williams last seen

1997   January 1   Maria Laura Laliberte last seen

1997   January 10   Stephanie Marie Lane last seen

1997   April 23   Kellie (Richard) Little last seen

1997   April   Sherry Leigh Irving last seen

1997   June 15   Helen Mae Hallmark last seen

1997   June 25   Janet Gail Henry last seen

1997   August 14   Jacqueline Marie Murdock last seen

1997   August   Marnie Lee Frey last seen

1997   September   Cindy Louise Beck last seen

1997   November 26   Cindy Feliks last seen

1997   Andrea Fay Borhaven last seen

1998   January 7   Kerry Lynn Koski last seen

1998   February 26   Inga Monique Hall last seen

1998   April 14   Sarah Jean de Vries last seen

eight

THE FINAL YEARS

SARAH HAD BEEN A HEROIN ADDICT since the late eighties, but in the mid-nineties her addiction took on added complexity when she started doing a great deal of cocaine. She wrote in her journal about what drugs did for her and how hard it was to let them go:

Drug addiction is a very serious disease. It's not easy letting go of something that makes you feel so, so powerful, so good, so at ease with every little part of your flesh and bones.

Drugs make people the opposite of what they are in their reality. Do you know what it means to be able to be the centre of attention in every social circle, party, whatever, when in reality you are a hermit, a turtle sort of guy who hides every time someone looks at him sideways? Being funny instead of boring, being able to speak your mind with no fears; it's another addiction. When you're high you don't have to experience horrible things like not being able to carry on an intelligent conversation or not having the brass to stand up for yourself when some dork intimidates you to death, fear, fear that makes your throat dry, makes it hard to swallow, your heart seems to be beating double time in your throat and in your ass. Thud, thud, thud. Oh God, it's a gross feeling. You can't let them see you sweat. Then it's bye-bye for you. As soon as they see the fear they play on it. You've got no choice. Your defences are gone.

But on cocaine. Damn. I'll take the whole mother fucking world on and its army and win too. That's how I feel. Nothing, not nothing on God's green, well, sort of green acres, can stop me. I'm so god damn bad. So to maintain this, you must stay high. To stay high, you must work. Bear with me, people, but if I'm jumping from topic to topic I can't help it. I write what flows onto the page. I have no control. My thoughts are stains on paper. What is written is what I'm thinking.

Heroin is hard to give up because it is so addictive, but after a time, it doesn't make the addict feel good any more, just ordinary—as close to the way a non-addict feels as a heroin addict can get. Cocaine is almost worse because it makes the addict feel so wonderful. Greater physical deterioration takes place over time on cocaine than on heroin. And cocaine is much more damaging to a fetus. But it creates that incredibly powerful feeling that Sarah describes, a feeling hard to resist for people living the kind of tough life that she was.

Roland and I got married in July 1995, and Sarah did not make it to the wedding. So much had changed in the six years since Peter and Troy's wedding. One of the biggest changes was Sarah's deeper drug addiction. Another was the presence of her four-and-a-half-year-old daughter in our family, all set to be my flower girl.

When Mark went to pick Sarah up that day, she wasn't ready. She told him that the church was too far away. She was worried about having to shoot up in the bathroom. "She said that she was really sorry," Mark says. "She really wanted to go."

I had planned the day for a year. I wore a big white dress and a veil. Jeanie wore a scaled-down version of my dress. Eighty family members and friends attended and we had the reception at Dad's house, lots of flowers, white tablecloths, dancing, finished with a glorious display of fireworks, part of the yearly fireworks competition in Vancouver, visible from Dad's upstairs balcony.

Sarah had not been to Dad's house for six or seven years. Her daughter, whom she hardly knew but in whom many of her dreams—her guilt and her hope both—were invested, was taking part in a ritual that had had no place in Sarah's life. In the early nineties Sarah and Charlie had lived together as common-law husband and wife, but the family had never gathered to celebrate their union. I think that it would have hurt her terribly to be there, to feel connected but separate at the same time. And to feel like the family failure.

This journal entry that she wrote two years later expresses some of her ambivalence toward us, her family:

I find it strange how I instantly feel as if I am only six or seven years old whenever I talk to any one of my family members. I get nervous and start to fidget and can never keep my eye contact. I feel as if their eyes are burning holes in my body, as if cigarettes were being put out in an ashtray. I fumble in my mind for words. Swallowing almost seems like an impossible task, for instantly my mouth becomes so dry and pasty. My palms become cold, sweaty and clammy and my heart's thump thump thump in my throat feels like a piece of apple stuck in my windpipe.

The gap between us was too large. We wanted her in our lives, but it pained us to see her living the life that she was living. And so our eyes burned holes in her. However hard we tried to understand, whatever efforts we made not to judge, she still felt diminished in our presence. I wanted her to come to my wedding and was hurt when she did not, but I know that she would have felt like an alien being there.

An important part of what made Sarah feel so miserable in our presence, I think, is the shame that she felt about selling sex. She felt judged by society as a whole and by her family specifically. And she was right. Each of us responded differently to what she did, but we were all horrified by it. Sarah was horrified by it too, at least at times. She often despised herself for selling sex and she despised likewise many of the men who bought it from her:

> I close my eyes.
> I can see the sky, the stars, so bright and gay
> Dancing just for me, they say.
>
> Penetration snatches me back.
> I count every pumping drive as your pleasure begins to rise.
> I fight to hold the tears in.
> I clench the sheet, body, and teeth.
>
> "Don't fight it. I know you like it.
> Go with the flow. Come on, baby, just let go."
>
> These words, how they make me sick.
> How could you actually think
> I like having your hard prick inside me, using me?
> You make me dirty, you make me ashamed.
> I think you're to blame.
> I think you should be locked away
> Never to see another sunny day.
> You're the dirty sinner and warped sex fiend.
> You, you had to pay me money.

I've talked to men for whom not paying for sex is a point of pride. A real man doesn't have to pay for sex, they say. But some "real men" would rather pay for it and be done with it. For other men, perhaps, paying is, or seems to be, their only option. Sarah is trying to place her own feelings of self-loathing firmly on the backs of the johns. She hates what she is doing. She cannot bear it. Yet, she must do it again and again and again. She wrestles with that in her writing.

Sometimes, though, her tone is much more matter-of-fact:

> I sit here in this house, listening to the world outside go by. Raindrops tap dance upon the roof; it sounds like tiny feet. I'd rather have snow than rain when it's cold. Being wet and cold is worse than just cold; standing in one spot doesn't help much, neither does wearing heels or high-heeled boots. There's no protection between the snow and ice and your feet. My feet get cold and my whole body freezes. Yet if my torso is warm, the rest of me will stay warm as long as my feet are dry. Two pairs of nylons, thick socks, plastic bags tied around my feet help big time.
>
> Supporting a heroin and cocaine habit is not fun and games; you have to make the money. No money. No drugs. No drugs, you go sick. You go sick, forget trying to pull a trick. They seem to see the desperate look upon your face. I've stood there for hours before I've broke. No patience, no tolerance, feeling like death warmed over, wishing you would just drop dead instead of gagging giving some guy head.
>
> It wouldn't be the first time or the last I've been giving beak and woofed my cookies in his lap. It's embarrassing, but at the time I didn't give two fucks, didn't even apologize, he got what he deserved. Yet still the ears go a little red after I'm feeling a bit better. Needless to say, he never stopped for me again. Don't blame him in a way.

In this piece, Sarah is not complaining about turning tricks in general, she is complaining about having trouble getting a trick when she is sick. She gives this bit such a light touch. I love the way that she says simply, "still the ears go a little red." She is talking about extreme desperation, about having to work when she is drug sick, about vomiting on a man (more than once) while she is performing oral sex (something that he will not soon forget!). Then she slips in the slightly red ears, an acknowledgment of embarrassment, but not too much embarrassment. And finally writing, "don't blame him in a way," brushing aside the whole event while recognizing that the experience might stick in the man's mind.

Wayne was often disgusted with the men who bought sex from Sarah. "I've seen some guys come over there to pick her up that are absolutely horrible looking," he says. "They stink. I found that diffi-cult. This one fellow whom she considered a friend would always talk about her. He was lewd. He wouldn't say things in front of her, just when the guys were around." Those men offended Wayne. "Because I loved her," he says. "I really loved her, you know. I know that she wasn't in love with me, but she loved me as a friend and I saw some-thing in her that I have never seen in anybody else in my life."

Wayne's words are particularly important because men who visit prostitutes are unknown even though they're all around us. Prostitutes aren't all around us. They're over there and yet we can see them, at least the ones who are outside on the street. We know that they are prostitutes, yet we know nothing about them. We have very little insight, just stereotypes. Men who visit prostitutes are invisible, yet they could be your husband, your son, your co-worker, your friend. They're everybody.

Men who go to prostitutes must be as complex and varied a group as sex workers themselves; their motives must be as varied or even more so, because prostitutes are almost always working for economic reasons. Men can be trying to meet sexual needs, or to meet a need for a sense of power or for companionship or for touch.

Then there are the men who seek out prostitutes to hurt them.

Sarah was badly hurt by men many times, at least twice to the point where she feared for her life. She was very aware of the danger that she was in. In December 1995, she wrote about the women who were missing:

Warmer than it was a couple of days ago, thank you, God. It's hard standing out there in the cold. My toes get so cold they actually make me cry when they start warming up again. My hands aren't much better. The tips of my fingers, yikes: ouchie, ouchie, ouchie. Business has been okay. Can't really complain. I've done better. I've done worse.

I can't shake it. It's this feeling that creeps over me all the time. Loneliness, emptiness. Lost in a vast void of nothingness. Groping my way through life like a blind woman with no cane, crawling on my hands and knees afraid to stand, unsteady upon my feet. No sense of direction, balance or time. Drifting endlessly through these icy cold nights trying to hide my pathetic growing fear that maybe just maybe my time draws near.

Am I next? Is he watching me now? Stalking me like a predator and its prey. Waiting, waiting for some perfect spot, time or my stupid mistake. How does one choose a victim? Good question, isn't it? If I knew that, I would never get snuffed.

So many women, so many that I never even knew about, are missing in action. It's getting to be a daily part of life. That's sad. Somebody dies and it's like somebody just did something normal. I can't find the right words. It's strange. A woman who works the Hastings Street area gets murdered, and nothing.

Yet if she were some square john's little girl, shit would hit the goddamn fan. Front page news for weeks, people protesting in the streets. Everybody makes a stink. While the happy hooker just starts to decay, like she didn't matter, expendable, dishonourable. It's a shame that society is that unfeeling. She was some woman's baby girl, gone astray, lost from the right path.

She was a person.

Although she almost certainly didn't know it, Sarah was three months pregnant when she wrote the above passage. My knowledge today of her son's presence inside her adds another layer of meaning to her writing.

When Sarah defines the "happy hooker," she is defining herself and many women that she knew. When she talks about the john's little girl, she reminds us of one link between her world and ours, the link through the invisible johns.

I love Sarah's cry of "ouchie, ouchie, ouchie"; it is so human, so universal, and handled with such humour even in the face of pain. Yet, I am sad that she had to stand on the street with freezing fingers and toes, hour after hour. It makes me want to bundle her up, safe and warm and loved.

I wish we could all go back to being curled up together on Mum and Dad's bed while Mum reads us poems from *When We Were Very Young* or *Now We Are Six*. I wish that we could go back to being held in a cocoon of love, that we could travel together into the wonder of a poem or story, looking for rabbits at the marketplace or begging through the castle for a bit of butter for the royal slice of bread. Instead, Sarah spent her days and nights on a street corner, with frozen toes, waiting to get into a car with a stranger so that she could earn the money to buy her next fix.

And now she can't even do that.

SARAH'S SECOND PREGNANCY WAS HARD. A trick had forced her to have sex without a condom and, while it was not uncommon for women to have tricks' babies, Charlie was furious with Sarah for carrying someone else's baby to term. He turned other women against Sarah, women who lived right in the house with them. "She used to get beat up," Jackie says. "Girls would throw rocks at her. She used to fight for her right to be standing on the corner and to be having this baby. She was a lot more on the run during that time." Sarah started moving around more and working in other areas. But sometimes she would just stand on the corner of Princess and Hastings, her corner, holding her head high.

"She was such a beautiful person," Jackie says. "Regardless of who the father of this baby was, Sarah had a right to this child, and I couldn't understand how her own people, Charlie and the girls, could do this to her."

On May 1, 1996, Sarah gave birth, one month early. She ran into Ken, the man who told me the story about the roast of beef, and told him that she was having pains. But she didn't think that she was in labour; it was too early. Ken took her up to the emergency room at St. Paul's and dropped her off. When he got back from parking the car, she was standing at the desk and "her water broke right there," he says. "I was there all that night. She had a terrible time."

The same nurse who had been there when Sarah gave birth to Jeanie was there this time. "She was nice," Ken says, "but Sarah wasn't." She shouted things like "Hit me over the fucking head and do what you have to do." At one point she started to pull Ken's hand toward her face. "She had such a look in her eye," Ken says. He had to use all his strength to keep his hand back. "She was going to bite me. She wanted me to feel the pain too."

Sarah had gone to the hospital prepared this time. She had a needle, all ready to go, woven into her hair. She did the fix before she went into heavy labour. It seems obscene to write this: the deliberate pumping of drugs into the body of a tiny baby, about to be born. But Sarah had been doing drugs throughout the pregnancy. At this point she was doing what she had to do to survive.

Once Ben was born, she held him for a minute or two. "She had a beautiful look on her face," Ken says. I don't know what she would have been thinking. She had planned all along to leave the baby in the hospital, to turn him over to "the system." Maybe she was just relieved to have the pain over with, or maybe she was caught up in the new life in her arms, created by her, and able to push the future aside for the moment. After that, she fell deeply asleep.

A few hours later, Sarah started to experience a lot of pain and withdrawal along with it. Tylenol 3s were little help. Drug addicts' pain is more difficult to control because they tend to be immune to ordinary painkillers, but the doctors would not prescribe anything stronger for Sarah or give her anything to keep withdrawal in abeyance. She signed herself out against the recommendations of the hospital. Unlike the first time, they did not try to restrain her.

Wayne didn't find out that Sarah had given birth until Charlie called him and told him. Sarah was at the house then, recuperating on the couch, and she wanted to see Wayne. "She was ill," Wayne says. "She was drained. She was lying on the couch all curled up." He asked her why she hadn't called him when she went into labour. "It just happened," she said.

Later that day, she started hemorrhaging. Ken took her back to the hospital briefly, but she left again without making any arrangements for her son and she did not tell Mum or me or any family member that she had had a baby. Ben—Baby de Vries at the time—spent his first weeks at Sunny Hill Health Centre in their special detox room, just as Jeanie had done. Unlike Jeanie, though, he did not have a family member visiting daily, bonding with him from the beginning of his life.

And after Ben was born, Sarah stayed at Charlie's house even less than she had before. She spent more time at Wayne's apartment, at Ken's place and at the homes of other regulars, and more time in downtown hotels as well. "She had a whole underworld of places to stay," Jackie says. "People that cared about her enough to put her up. Those were her safety zones," she says. "And you didn't share safety zones or you were liable to lose them."

Safety zones or no, Sarah's world was becoming less stable and she was unhappy. Jackie noticed a new melancholy about her. No matter what, Jackie had always counted on Sarah for a smile, an upbeat conversation. Now Sarah was looking at the ground. She was sad. And she had a blank look in her eyes. She must have felt betrayed by Charlie and by the others who had not stood by her through her pregnancy. I wonder as well if she was struggling with her bond to a little baby boy who was out there somewhere. She had turned her back on him, but he was still there.

She stayed at Wayne's place for a while that summer. "It took a lot out of her," he says. "She just lay there and recuperated." By that time

Wayne and Sarah had known each other for two years. He was no longer paying her for sex. Sometime earlier, Wayne had told Sarah that he would still help her, but that he wouldn't expect sex for it.

"I helped her out from then on," he says, "without expecting anything in return." She would phone him in a desperate state, well into withdrawal. He would drive down and give her money if he had any, so that she could get a fix so that she could work. "I did that many, many, many times," he says. "I could never stand to see her sick. I couldn't."

At times, though, even after the relationship had settled into a largely platonic pattern, Wayne would still ask for sex. Given the dynamic between them, the fact that Sarah, while she cared for Wayne, never returned his feelings, sex between them could not be equal. It was an obligation on Sarah's part, I suspect. And that is what Wayne cannot take part in any longer.

"I could never ever be involved in buying sex off a woman again. I just couldn't do that. It's almost like a certain circuit in my brain was cut out. Sarah taught me a lot. Knowing Sarah and reading her journals and knowing how she felt. I said, 'God, Sarah. That's how we're relating when this happens between us.' And she said, 'No, I'm not talking about you.'"

In addition to the passages already quoted about johns, Sarah pondered in writing who they are, why they do what they do and what they might think about her:

> *I can't comprehend or start to understand*
> *what actually makes the man.*
> *How does one think?*
> *How does one feel?*
> *Do they actually realize that I'm real?*

Wayne did know that she was real, of course, which is why she said that she wasn't talking about him.

SUSAN HAD HEARD ABOUT SARAH. She had seen her around. Sarah's reputation was notorious, Susan says. People said not to mess with her.

But when she saw Sarah coming down the street toward her one day in late May 1996, less than a month after Ben was born, she had to approach her.

Sarah was wearing Susan's shoes. Susan's oxblood leather oxfords with pink ribbon laces complemented Sarah's outfit, her little white turtleneck, her kilt and her white knee socks pulled up neatly to her knees. Sarah was bopping down the street in a great mood on a spring day. She had money in her pocket and was on her way to get high.

"Where did you get those shoes?" Susan asked.

Someone had given them to her, Sarah said.

"Those are my shoes," Susan replied. "Somebody stole them out of my room at the Regency."

Without missing a beat, Sarah bent down, unlaced the pink ribbons, slipped the shoes off her feet and handed them over. Off the two of them went, up to Susan's room to shoot up together and to get Sarah some shoes to wear home. That was the beginning of their friendship.

"Sarah was my inspiration," Susan says. "We were close."

Susan was almost fifteen years older than Sarah and did not start doing drugs and working in the sex trade until she was thirty-eight years old, a fact that horrified Sarah because Sarah always wanted to get off drugs, to get *out* of that life. It scares me too, because it demonstrates that none of us can know where life circumstances are going to lead us.

The two women remained friends for the rest of Sarah's life.

WHEN I VISITED SARAH on her birthday in mid-May that year, she didn't mention that she had just had a baby, but in August she did mention him to Mum when Mum came to visit from Guelph.

"So, I had another one, eh," Sarah said to Mum, apparently casually, when they were together on August 23. She may have intended to tell her. She may have hoped that Mum would intervene and take the baby, whom Mum named Benjamin John. There is no way to know.

Mum waited until a family birthday celebration was over the next day before she told me. I could not bear it. I still don't know exactly why I was so utterly devastated. Shock, I suppose; we had a new person in our family whom we hadn't known was coming, a new person who had been in the world for almost four months without our knowledge. Confusion about what it would all mean for us, how our lives would change. Grief that Sarah was so separate from her family that she wouldn't let us know that she was pregnant. And jealousy? It doesn't seem like quite the right word, but I have not managed to fit children into my life. Roland and I have made the decision not to have children. For me there is a long-term grieving process associated with that decision. Sarah's casual production of two children and their subsequent journey into our lives has both provided me with the gift of two children to love and highlighted my own childlessness.

Mostly, though, when I cried in response to the two births—Jeanie's in December 1990 and Ben's five and a half years later—it was simply because these two babies tapped into all my grief, grief about many things that have nothing to do with Jeanie or Ben.

In the months that followed we all struggled with the knowledge of this new little person and with questions about how to incorporate him into our family. Roland and I met him first in a social worker's office in Vancouver. After that, Sarah, Wayne and I drove out to his foster home in the Fraser Valley. Seeing her son again meant a great deal to Sarah, as the photo of her holding a grinning Ben up in the air shows. By then, Sarah knew that Ben was going to live with Mum, that Jeanie was thrilled to have a little brother. It was wonderful for Sarah to see Ben thriving, to see how cute he was, to feed him and make him laugh. Other than immediately after his birth, that was Sarah's only visit with her son.

Dad and I drove out to visit Ben that fall as well. Then, when Mum came back to Vancouver to be with Sarah while Sarah had a tubal ligation, Mum met Ben and his foster parents too. I think she knew before she met him that he was coming home with her. He was Mum's grandson and Jeanie's brother; he belonged with them.

The rest of us weren't so sure at first. I wondered if an open adoption with a younger family would work, allowing him to know us and us to know him. Mum was already fifty-eight. I was worried that she wouldn't be physically able to parent for another twenty years. Jeanie was almost six, soon to be in school full-time; Mum was just getting to the point where she would have some time to herself again. Also, I had the idea that if Ben stayed in B.C., I would be able to see him all the time. I didn't want him to go off to Ontario the way Mum and Jeanie had.

Those feelings are a thing of the past. Ben has now been living with Mum, Aunt Jean and Jeanie for years. He is an active, demanding, charming, furious, curious young person, as cute as they come. Sarah passed her beauty on to her children along with her creativity, her intensity and passion.

She also set them up for more than their share of troubles. They were born drug addicted and went through withdrawal as small babies in the dark room at Sunny Hill Health Centre. And Sarah was only in their lives in the smallest way, even before she disappeared.

They are left with a set of questions not unlike those that Sarah herself grew up with, and to those they must add their awareness of the worst in human beings: the fact that a person would deliberately kill another, somebody's mother, and then chop up that person's body to dispose of it.

MOST WOMEN, MEN TOO, INVOLVED IN sex work and involved with drugs live by a code of behaviour, just as the rest of us do. We all live by some rules because we have to—we don't want to take the consequences of breaking them—and by others because we believe that we should, that we will not be the people we believe ourselves to be if we break them. Our society is made up of a set of institutions and thoroughly ingrained beliefs that keep enough of us in line that our society can function. Our institutions both reflect and reinforce who we are.

People who live outside of those institutions set up their own codes. Honesty, loyalty, treating well those who are weaker are common virtues; by living according to them, women such as Sarah and Jackie held on to some of their self-respect, and as long as they had that, they had hope. Over time, for many, the code will deteriorate. Each time one breaks one's own rules, it becomes a little easier to break them the next time. That is true for all of us.

Jackie survived in part by adhering to a set of rules about how she should treat others, especially youths. She had to help others, point them in the direction of services and avoid exploiting them. As time went on, though, she had younger women working for her. She would give them two hundred dollars for drugs. Once that money was spent, they had to work to earn the money to pay it back. She tried to tell herself that she was really helping those women who were suffering from cocaine psychosis. She tried to convince herself that taking care of them by getting them to eat and to sleep justified having them working for her or at least helped to compensate for it. She no longer feels that way.

Those women were part of one of the most terrible changes that happened on the Downtown Eastside in the nineties: the advent of crack cocaine. Crack cocaine is cheap, cut with substances that can be very damaging to the body; it doesn't have to be injected the way heroin does, so it is easier to ingest; and it is far, far more addictive than heroin. When crack cocaine entered the Downtown Eastside, the quality of life for everyone declined. Today, the people who are weaving around or picking at the ground or digging holes in their own flesh are crack addicts.

I thought that Sarah didn't do crack cocaine and thus avoided cocaine psychosis, or tweaking as it is also called, a state in which people deteriorate physically very fast. But Sarah's friend Susan says that she and Sarah smoked a rock together sometimes. Sarah "would go through her purse obsessively, looking for drugs," Susan says. "She would take her lipstick apart, for example." And Jackie referred to staying up with Sarah for days on end. I do not believe that Sarah was in cocaine psychosis when she disappeared, but she was doing a great deal of cocaine in her final years and she was dabbling in crack cocaine. She had less control of her life, and was more likely to place herself at risk.

Dr. Stanley de Vlaming writes about cocaine psychosis. Crack cocaine addicts binge for days without sleep. "The range is up to a dozen days," de Vlaming says. "An addict in cocaine psychosis is easy to spot . . . They are the ones listing to one side with bizarre limb movements and gestures, or frenetically picking at some imagined hole in the sidewalk or part of their body."

To my knowledge, Sarah never had other women working for her, as did Jackie and several other women I talked to. Although it was very hard at times, she was always able to meet her need for drugs. If she hadn't been, she might have resorted to more extreme measures as well.

"I always thought that as long as I wasn't hurting anybody else," Jackie says, "I could get out. That's why I had all these rules." Once she started breaking her own rules and seeing other people doing the same thing, she couldn't see the way out as easily. Ironically, that eventually frightened her into getting out once and for all. "I saw people changing, going down, crossing their own boundaries." She was seeing more violence, more death, more disease, more desperation.

It was very important to Sarah also to believe that she wasn't hurting anyone but herself. "I've done no one harm except myself," she writes. And I do think that she did her best to avoid doing harm, but it must have been harder for her to believe that she was an island after she walked away from Ben in the hospital.

Sarah did harm on a societal scale as well. She committed property crimes. She stole from clients. I believe that she took part in one or two muggings and at least one robbery when she was younger. She spent time in juvenile detention and in prison. Much as she would like to isolate herself and say that the way she lived her life harmed only her, she is wrong, just as each of us is wrong if we think that we live in a vacuum, that we can hurt ourselves without hurting others.

Sarah felt terrible that she was unable to raise her children. She felt that she had failed them. And I suppose that she had. I am glad, though, that she made no attempt to take either of her children into the Downtown Eastside. They did not have to contend with neglect during their early months or years, although they were subjected to drugs in utero. They did not suffer abuse at the hands of those who passed through Sarah's life. They did not have to deal with being wrested away from Sarah by the state when they were old enough to know what was happening. I like to remember how Sarah loved to hear about them. She carried their photographs everywhere she went; she talked about them to some of her friends downtown and she sent them presents when she could. But none of that changes the fact that she could not or did not raise them herself.

Sarah had to deal with shattering news that fall. She had already given birth and gone through four months with a baby out in the world. She had told Mum about her baby, and, in so doing, had turned him over to Mum's safekeeping. But changes had happened in her body that she was not aware of. When Sarah was in the hospital giving birth, the doctors learned that she had HIV and hepatitis C, but did not have a chance to pass the information on to Sarah before she left. In September, early on in Mum's process of becoming Ben's guardian, the hospital told her about the two diseases. They had sent a letter to Sarah's address, they said, but Sarah never received it. Later, Sarah suspected Charlie of having kept it from her.

Mum told me first. Then she called Wayne and asked him to get Sarah over to his place so that she could talk to her. Sarah had given her Wayne's phone number, providing us with an important link to her. Mum told Wayne about the HIV so that he would be ready to offer Sarah whatever support she asked for.

A day or two later, Sarah phoned Mum. She broke down as soon as Mum told her. Wayne held on to her while she finished her talk with Mum. "It was a quiet night," Wayne says. "She stayed the night and we just sat there." Then, she did her best to put it out of her mind.

Sarah knew that a lot of people in her community had HIV, but she didn't want anyone to know that she did. The two things that she needed to do to survive—sell sex to get the money for drugs and then inject drugs to feed her addiction—were the two most high-risk activities for getting and for passing on HIV. If people knew she had it, both her source of income and her source of drugs would be jeopardized.

She did talk about what she could do for the HIV. She read brochures. "It totally devastated her," Wayne says, "because she'd been so careful. And she didn't know a lot about it. Who did, really? Other than the fact that you can't get it by shaking hands or drinking out of the same glass."

From then on, Sarah needed to go to doctors' appointments and it fell to me to facilitate those visits with Wayne's help. Wayne was a link between our worlds. It was easier for Sarah in practical terms to manage visits when he went to pick her up and when he gave her money so that she had enough heroin to get through the day, but it was also emotionally easier for her, I think. She was more comfortable with him than she was with me. And he normalized things for her. I could visit her at his house away from the corner where she stood to make her money, away from other drug addicts shooting up in the back room, as was often happening at her house. She had made a home for herself at Wayne's and he welcomed her there.

Providing that Mum promised to come out to Vancouver to be with her for the surgery, Sarah had agreed to a tubal ligation. Mum phoned around and with some difficulty found a doctor who would perform the surgery despite Sarah's HIV. Then I needed to get her to his office for a preliminary appointment.

His schedule was tight. He had one opening, but she would have to be there or the surgery would be cancelled. I went to get her, only to be told by Charlie, with a self-satisfied smile, that he didn't think I would be able to get her up.

He was right. I couldn't. She was on the nod on the living room couch. She shifted when I shook her, opened her eyes a bit, mumbled, "Go away," and that was that. I begged to use the phone at the corner store across the street and finally got through to the doctor's office. Further begging and pleading and the appointment was changed.

The next day when I came to get her, she was ready to go. We stopped at the corner store and she picked up licorice and Pocky biscuit sticks and a stack of lottery tickets, a kind I wasn't familiar with that take hours to fill out.

Downtown, as we walked from the car to the doctor's office, I was conscious of men looking at my sister in a way that I do not see men look at other women. Sarah was wearing jeans that she had carefully torn and shredded, and high heels. She was heavily made up and her nails were done, just like always. I don't know how the men could tell that she was a prostitute; maybe they couldn't and I was paranoid. But to me, their looks expressed interest, disgust and possession. They were not looking at a human being. I felt a mixture of rage and protectiveness.

As we sat in the upscale doctor's office among the pregnant women and the small children, Sarah munched on her candy and worked endlessly at the lottery tickets. She was matter-of-fact, even friendly with anyone she needed to talk to, but in between she shut out her surroundings. I felt sad for her, watching her sit among the wealthy, happy women who edged away from her, who had no comprehension of her life. She was there to get ready for an operation that would stop her from having more children, while they were there to prepare for welcome births. Sarah's was a responsible act, but not a happy one.

I went with her into the doctor's office for the consultation. He was polite to her, but the distance between them was palpable. He wanted to take a Pap smear—standard procedure, it seems, in preparation for a tubal ligation. She refused, absolutely refused. This man was not going to lay his hands on her, not while she was conscious. I was surprised by her adamance and he probably more so, but it was telling.

He may have thought that she could have no objection to his examining her; after all, men who were strangers to her saw and touched her body all the time. It seemed to me, though, that it was *because* she knew that he knew she was a prostitute that she refused the procedure. She demonstrated dignity and a complete refusal to cross her own boundaries. The compromise we reached was that she would allow a Pap smear to be taken during the surgery, when she was under a general anaesthetic.

It was DNA from that Pap smear that the police eventually used to identify Sarah's DNA on the Port Coquitlam property.

Mum came out to Vancouver on September 16. The next day she took Sarah to the hospital, along with enough drugs and needles to get Sarah through her time there. The procedure went smoothly, but I don't know how Sarah felt about it. Three days later, Mum went with Sarah and Wayne to the HIV clinic. Mum had brought photo albums from Ontario, so Wayne and Sarah were able to look at them together. And Mum, who had been sick all week, read parts of Sarah's journals. "Pretty depressing," Mum wrote in her journal. "Talk about an emotionally draining week. I haven't seen Sarah three times in one week for years."

She had no way of knowing that she would never see Sarah again.

SARAH WAS SHAKEN by all that happened in 1996 and she never entirely regained her equilibrium, but she never gave up on herself.

Constable Dave Dickson remembers Sarah fondly. He keeps in close touch with many of the women on the Downtown Eastside and knew many of the missing women. His pager is always on and he is always willing to talk or offer support. Sarah's good nature stands out for him. "She was always polite," he says. "I don't remember her saying a bad word toward me or being hard to deal with." I think that good manners were part of her code.

Dave also thought it was remarkable that she kept her looks through all those years. "I take my vitamins," Sarah said to him when he asked her about it once. "I try to eat right." Taking care of herself was part of her survival strategy on every level. She even managed to incorporate exercise at times. In 1997, she was spotted regularly on Downtown Eastside sidewalks, whizzing along on her Rollerblades.

"It was an oddity down there," Dave says. "Along came this beautiful girl on Rollerblades!"

Sarah's good health and attractiveness helped her in several ways. They kept her safe and hooked into a network of people who were willing to help her, including regular clients. And they helped her to feel good about herself.

As I MENTIONED, Peter came with me the first few times I went to see Sarah. Then I realized that it was perfectly safe for me to go alone. Peter decided to visit Sarah on his own sometime in 1997.

"I got on my bicycle and rode down there," he says. "Sarah was on the porch."

She stared at him for several moments without recognizing him. She was high, Peter said, out of it. Finally she said in a flat voice, "Oh, hi." Peter said hi back. After another few moments it dawned on her that she had a role to play. She invited Peter inside and they chatted awkwardly. After a while, Peter made his excuses and went home.

He never saw her again.

AFTER BEN WAS WITH MUM, Sarah always had photos of Jeanie and Ben in her purse. "She was well known for her really tiny little clutch purses," Jackie says, "but she always had pictures on her." Jackie remembers one special afternoon in 1997. "It was almost like stepping back in time," she says. "My room was clean. The clothes were all hanging up. I had draped metallic scarves over the lamps. We were joking around, doing each other's nails, hair, makeup." Then Sarah pulled out her photos. It was hard for

Jackie to look at them because she had given her own son to her parents when he was a year and a half old. She would visit him only on his birthday and at Christmas, just as Sarah had done before Mum moved back east. "I remember thinking that at least she had pictures," Jackie says. "I was so tormented that I couldn't close my eyes and see my son's face. That just tore me apart. I felt like a bad person."

Some women downtown don't carry pictures of their children because they are afraid of placing their children in danger or because their pain about the loss of their children is too great to bear. Sarah always seemed to be glad to get the pictures I brought her, but she must have felt pain as well. How tangled up her feelings about Jeanie and Ben must have been!

Jackie saw more of Sarah in 1997 because they shared a regular client who happened to be in town a lot that year. "Sometimes he picked us both up," Jackie says. "Once, the three of us went to the bathhouse. He was a decent guy. There were some nice tricks out there."

But, although Sarah and Jackie still had some good times together, "all of a sudden a shell came up around her and she stopped sharing herself with us. Before she had seemed wide-open, bouncy, bubbly, alive. In 1997, there was a quietness about her."

THAT SUMMER, I PICKED SARAH UP ONE DAY to take her on several errands, to the welfare office and to replace her Social Insurance card. Her garden was gorgeous; tall sunflowers bloomed; bean plants grew up above my head between the two houses; large flowerpots stood on either side of the front step. The beans were enormous, but green and tender. Sarah picked one for me and one for herself and we munched happily as we headed for the car.

The last few years I visited her there, Sarah's house was beautiful, despite its peeling paint and sagging frame—adorned with hanging flower baskets, climbing sweet peas, tomato plants and geraniums that obscured the boarded-up windows. Despite his many shortcomings, Charlie could not keep his hands out of the soil. Whatever he planted grew sky high.

Sarah and I spent the whole afternoon together that day, the errands followed by a hamburger at McDonald's. We were comfortable together, happy in each other's company. I drove up in front of her house and turned to say goodbye.

Sarah looked at me, paused, looked away. Then she asked me if I had any money. That was the only time she ever asked me. I felt sick instantly. If I said no, it would feel like saying, "Go on out there and stand on the corner and get your own money. Go and have sex with a stranger." I couldn't do that.

I gave her thirty dollars and I told her that I could only do that once. I could never give her money like that again. Then I cried all the way home.

I felt terrible. It was one of those situations where, no matter what I did, I was going to feel terrible. She probably felt terrible too.

She never did ask me again.

Sarah's almost hourly need for heroin kept her tied to the Downtown Eastside where she could make money. If we wanted her to come away from that area for any length of time, the problem of how she would manage the drugs always came up. It was a real issue for her. Just like I wouldn't walk off into the desert without enough water to see me through, she couldn't go anywhere without enough heroin. Wayne solved the problem by giving her money.

I never felt comfortable about that, even though it was Wayne, not me, who was keeping her supplied. It felt to me as if I were facilitating her addiction. I was benefitting from Wayne's giving Sarah money for drugs. Yet through that period, Sarah's and my relationship was growing stronger. She and I were becoming closer. She felt cared for and a little better understood. "She was very thankful that she was getting closer to you, that you guys were getting closer," Wayne says. "You guys were talking more." I certainly felt that way, mixed in with all the pain, and I'm glad to know that Sarah did too.

Now, looking back, I don't feel so guilty any more. I think that what we did fit a "harm reduction" model just fine. Harm reduction involves helping addicts or dealing with one's own addiction more gently than in some other models. It accepts the limitations that we all have and the fact that we all make changes in our lives only when we are ready. It seeks to keep people alive by encouraging the use of clean needles. It seeks to ensure that people get the medical care that they need, that they are well fed and safe. It seeks to keep people in touch with professionals and aware of resources, so that if and when they are ready to change their lives further, they will be able to do so.

Later that summer, Jeanie came for her annual visit and I, as I always tried to do, planned a get-together with Sarah. We met Sarah at Wayne's place. She was on crutches with a hurt foot, but in good spirits. She had begun work on an alphabet book for Jeanie, a colour-ing book with a page for each letter. We photographed her and Jeanie kneeling on the floor, cheeks pressed together. Jeanie's discomfort shows in the photo.

Then we drove in Wayne's big old car to Dairy Queen and picked up food to take to the beach. At one point Jeanie took off and I found her at the top of a path down to the water, sitting and pulling bits of grass out of the ground. I sat with her for a minute and then we made our way back to Sarah and Wayne. Those visits with her mother were very important to Jeanie, but confusing and painful as well. Painful for Sarah too.

That summer evening at Kitsilano beach was their last time together.

JACKIE CALLED IT A SHELL, but Sarah called it a wall, a wall that she built up from the ground herself, brick by brick or stone by stone.

If you build a wall that is so god damn high that nobody can contact you, you might as well be in jail. Every time you've let loved ones down or loved ones let you down hard you insert another reminder, an etched memoranda of the event, so you never let yourself forget (not that you would).

A page from the alphabet book for Jeanie that Sarah was making when she disappeared.

Bb

AS IN
B——————

Sarah Jean de Vries

I find that I get so scared that I start to push people who care about me away. I try to get them upset with me or start false accusations to make them hate me. I can't let anybody in. Everything that is beautiful and happily free with the purity of innocence turns to shit around me. They leave me one way or another. Most likely they drop dead and are gone forever. And I try to be so tough and strong, but inside I just fall apart and cry like a little baby.

The image of the prison wall—high, hard, impenetrable and self-made—contrasts so painfully with the image of the frightened, crying child behind it. She says, *I've been in my own self-made jail cell constructed to keep the harshness of truth and reality away from the inner child still waiting to mature within me.* The brutal irony, of which Sarah was well aware, is that in her attempt to protect herself, she locked love away as well. And her inner child had little chance without love.

She writes that she pushes people away. She writes that everything good turns to bad around her. But I don't think that that was so, at least not from other people's points of view. So many give Sarah credit for their getting clean. Contact with Sarah gave many people joy. And I am sure that many touched her life as well, and more would have if she had let them in.

I've sentenced myself to life imprisonment, no chance of parole, no chance of release, no judge, no jury, no pre-sentence inquiry. My gavel's fallen and my sentence passed. From that fateful day on I am doomed slowly to fade away in my self-made prison. Self-erected, brick by brick. Day by day, I placed a stone to signify another event that is never to be forgiven or forgotten, always and forever cemented in time to tell me that another part of me has died. With every failure, letdown and misfortune, the wall gets higher and inside gets darker, emptier, colder.

A few days later she added,

> I made this big, empty, cold, senseless cell, escape proof. And, of course, I left no mistakes; in no part of my brilliant architectural plan is there a way for anybody to get in and realize who I really am, not that I know the answer to that question.

MY FAMILY IS NOT VERY PHYSICALLY DEMONSTRATIVE, especially, it seems to me, those of us who are related by blood. My brother Peter and I rarely hug each other, and when we do, it is with a certain level of discomfort. Mum and I hug when we see each other for the first time during a visit and sometimes at bedtime if I am staying in her home or she in mine, but when we were living in the same city or the same house, I don't remember us doing that often once I got past a certain age. Mark is different. I love his hugs because he grins and puts his whole self into them and he seems to like giving them. I like getting them too and I hug back hard.

I remember that when I was a teenager and our family was gradually self-destructing I felt that Sarah needed touch. I remember holding onto her when Mum and Dad were fighting, hoping that love and security could reach her through that hug. Later, when Sarah was living downtown and selling sex, I felt that she needed loving touch to counteract all the selfish touch—the touching to get, not to give. I tried to touch her as much as I could. And I loved the feel of her solid, strong body. She hugged back. I hope, I hope, I hope that she felt my love. I felt hers.

In the fall of her last year, she brought a john who was also a drug addict back to Charlie's place. She nodded off in bed with him and when she woke up, he was dead from an overdose. She cried for a long time about that, Wayne says, soaking his shirt with tears and rocking back and forth in his arms.

That September, she wrote about her fears:

Somebody's going to leave us tonight. I don't know who and I
don't know why. I feel it, I fear it, it's in the air. It's so just . . .
well, just there. It makes my flesh tingle from goosebumps and
sends my heart through a flash of panic.

What's the fucking use of trying to be so rock-hard cold,
emotionless, empty yet too tough to show that you're cracking
inside and are starting to cry? Deep, deeper, and deeper still, way
down in the abyss of my heart a spark shows through all the
empty cold and darkness.

It is no wonder that Sarah feared someone would die that night.
Jacqueline Murdock, Marnie Frey, Janet Henry and Helen Hallmark
had all disappeared that summer and Cindy Beck disappeared that
September, 1997.

Around that time, Sarah began to write about the erosion of feeling,
of response to touch. She is referring mainly to sexual touch, but I
suspect that the deadening extends to other kinds of touch as well.

You learn to put your feelings on and off at a drop of a rock. I've
become so good at it that telling what my heart mourns about is
a lost cause. Caring becomes a faint memory of a legend of days
of yore. I used to be able to really enjoy having somebody touch
me. Now it means nothing; I feel nothing. It's just a daily thing
now like brushing your teeth. It's the karma payback. I guess
that's the price I pay for my actions. I fear the response of my
body. Inside I feel dirty, slutty and cheap. I know I'm worth
more, but I'm a whore and that's not all, but a junkie as well.

Sarah did tell what her heart mourned about, at least some of it. She
told Wayne. I think that she told one or two women that she trusted.
And she wrote it down. Sarah had an escape mechanism. She had a
place to go inside her own head, and maybe the barriers she put up
helped her to protect that space. And she had a place to go on paper.
Always, always, she expressed herself in written words and in images:

I've held myself together and managed to stay sane in a little cubbyhole in the corner of my mind, my space to go and hide and let my love and emotions be free. I've learned to hide my every thought and feeling to protect myself from the world and all its ugly reality and hate. People are all in the same position, trying to survive, in a place where there is no trust, dedication, honesty, faith, compassion, affection, respect or friendship.

To let anybody that close is too crazy.

They only want something. Nobody cares about anybody down here. Nobody. Everybody just uses everybody else to get what they want.

All that they are concerned about is the next fix. Who cares who they hurt to get it? People's feelings or emotions don't matter. Not even their own. No respect for yourself. No respect for others.

When she writes "not even their own," I think that she gets to the heart of the matter. When you care nothing for yourself, you sometimes begin to care nothing for anyone else, and drug addiction on top of self-loathing drives people to a place where the drugs matter more than themselves or others. I suspect that Sarah found herself in that place more than once.

That cubbyhole in the corner of Sarah's mind was an important place. Her journal writing was a way of exploring that private space; so was her art. And while she may have learned to protect herself, she also wrote as if she were eager to reach out to those around her and beyond, to share.

Aunt Jean says, "I remember the pictures that she did with the tears. She used to draw faces, but she always drew tears. I had some for a long time. Women's faces. And animals. I remember one in particular, a blue face and then a tear going down the cheek. There would always be a tear going down. I don't think I ever saw her do a laughing one."

On Christmas morning 1997, Wayne brought Sarah to our apartment for breakfast. Sarah had a little trouble getting herself ready in time, but when Wayne suggested that perhaps they weren't going to make it, she said, "No, we've got to go. We're going."

That day she wrote in the new journal that Mum had given her:

DECEMBER 25, 1997

Christmas Day!!

So nothing's different, everything still feels the same. It's just another day, another day that I'm left here wishing for something that I guess was never meant to be. I'm not happy at all. In fact, I'm dying inside myself, slowly but surely wilting away into nothingness. I'm alone at soul, breaking at heart, and living a life of bullshit!! I know what has to be done and part wants to, yet the other half is so scared. I miss my baby and wish I was with him at this very moment. But I'm not and it hurts. I wanted to spend today with him and only him, but life goes the way that it is destined to go. Not that I'm complaining about the way I spent today. Not a problem there.

I had a very pleasant time at Maggie's with Roland and Wayne having blueberry pancakes and talking to my children on the phone. It was fantastic talking to Jeanie. It put an uplift to my day. And Wayne made it all possible. Without a worry for dope. Thank you, God, for everything you have blessed my messed-up existence with. Merry Christmas to all and to all a good year!

After that Christmas breakfast, Sarah and I would never see each other again.

JACKIE REMEMBERS SEEING SARAH in January and February 1998. "I saw her in her fur coat and her high-heeled boots, clean, long nails, makeup, hair done, nice clothes. She had a habit when it was cold, a way of moving her feet to keep warm, of bouncing from one foot to the other foot, making it look good."

Sarah sent me an e-mail on March 1, 1998:

Dear Maggie,

Hello there! How are you? Good, I hope. I'm in good health,
except for just getting over the flu that had me down and out
for four days, with headache. It was like my head was going to
explode every time I stood up. A fever that made my fingers
hurt to touch, I was so hot. So I stayed in bed at my friend
Bryan's for about a week. Now I just have the tail end of a
head cold and sinus cold. Please make a doctor's appointment
for me at Oak Tree Clinic and accompany me there as soon as
possible. Thank you. Hello there, Roland. Hope you are fine
too.

LOTS OF LOVE, YOUR SISTER SARAH!!!

Sarah was confused about her schedule and was not due for an
appointment. If she had been, I might have seen her once more.

On March 12, 1998, Jackie found herself seeing the people, the
suffering, on Hastings Street as if for the first time. She called out to
Sarah from half a block away and Sarah returned the greeting, their
last encounter. Suddenly Jackie wasn't entirely of that world.
Everything that had seemed normal, now scared her. And when she
went to stay with a friend the next day, on March 13, she was too
afraid to come back. Each day followed the last until she realized that
she was beginning a new life. She has not done drugs since and now
has a little girl and is involved in helping other women to get off
drugs and out of survival sex.

Susan saw Sarah in early April. A girl had stolen some money
orders that Susan had intended for her daughter's April birthday
present. Sarah and Susan lay in wait in a hotel room for several days,
waiting to ambush the thief. They didn't catch the culprit, but they
had fun together. At one point, Susan's high drew her out of the

room to wander the halls of the Brandiz Hotel. When she came back, the room was spotless and there was a note from Sarah, saying that since Susan had taken off, she was going to go too, but that it had been a good time. Sarah had cleaned the room and done the last of the drugs.

On April 11, Roland and I set off on a flight to Fort Lauderdale. On April 12, we boarded a cruise ship, the *Veendam*, and set off on a tour of the eastern Caribbean.

The next night, April 13, 1998, Sarah called Wayne at about 7:00 from the Beacon Hotel. She and a friend and two men had been staying there together for about two weeks. Jay had been her on-again, off-again boyfriend since the fall, abusive and unreliable, but still around. She asked Wayne to come pick her up, and he drove down to the Beacon. He circled the block a couple of times, but finally she came out and jumped into the car. They drove back to his place.

Wayne went back to doing his laundry. She grabbed a bowl and some Froot Loops, sat on the floor with the newspaper and started eating. When Wayne was finished with the laundry, he started playing around on the computer. They talked a little. She did a fix. Wayne asked what she was up to that night, and she said not much, but she needed some of her clothes.

She asked Wayne if she had any clean clothes. "Because I used to do her wash," he says. "She really had me trained!" Yes, Wayne told her, she had clean clothes. They were in her dresser drawers. The evening was ordinary, relaxed. Sarah didn't stay long. Eventually Wayne suggested that it might be time to go. He gave her some vitamins as he always did. She carried a glass of water over to her dresser and took vitamins in between putting a few of her clothes into a pillowcase.

Wayne took her back down to the Beacon and dropped her off. She had on the clothes that she is wearing in the photograph on the cover of this book.

A few weeks later, he looked over at the dresser in his apartment and the water glass was still sitting there. Sarah had stood there, swallowing vitamins, glass in hand. Then she set the glass down, went on her way, and never came back.

SARAH HAD BEEN IN THE HABIT OF CALLING WAYNE every two or three days. Occasionally a week would go by without his hearing from her, but never more than that. On April 21, he started wondering why he hadn't heard from Sarah and he drove to the Downtown Eastside to check on her. He didn't get worried until he discovered that no one had seen her in days. Charlie was worried. When Charlie said that he was thinking of putting in a missing persons report, Wayne knew that something was really wrong.

Wayne walked through the neighbourhood looking for Sarah and asking about her. When he got to the police station on Main Street, he stopped and phoned 911 on his cell phone. He tried to file a missing persons report, but was told that he couldn't because he wasn't family. That was when he called me.

I listened carefully, hung up and dialed 911 myself. I did not know then that twenty-nine women had already disappeared from the Downtown Eastside. But I did know that if Sarah hadn't been seen by anyone in a week, something was wrong.

1998   July 14   Sheila Catherine Egan last seen

nine

MISSING

FOR SOME TIME AFTER APRIL 21 we had no idea what had happened to Sarah. It was not like Sarah at that time in her life to go off like that. But we—her family and friends—came up with ideas about what might have happened. We hoped and we feared. Then Wayne ran into someone who seemed to know a lot more, although she didn't know that she did.

He was outside Charlie's house, talking to Mum on his cell phone about the possibility of offering a reward to help find Sarah. A woman who had been standing nearby drifted over to him. "She's wearing Sarah's clothes," blurted Charlie, who was standing nearby. And she was. The woman was Shauna*, the friend with whom Sarah had been sharing a hotel room when she disappeared. Shauna and Sarah traded clothes all the time, so it wasn't surprising that the woman would be wearing Sarah's clothes. But once Wayne and Shauna started talking, Wayne gradually realized that Shauna almost certainly had been with Sarah the night Sarah disappeared.

In the wee hours of April 14, 1998, Sarah stood in her usual spot, on the northwest corner of the Princess and Hastings intersection.

Shauna stood kitty-corner across from her. Shauna was picked up, but she arrived back at the corner again within minutes, unable to come to terms with the man. When she reached Princess and Hastings again, Sarah was gone. As far as we can tell, no one who knew Sarah saw her again after Shauna drove away in that car. We believe that Sarah was still wearing the same black stretchy pants, heels and frilly blouse that she had had on when Wayne dropped her off earlier that night. And she carried a tiny black purse.

By the time Wayne learned Shauna's story, I had already filed a missing persons report and had had a brief conversation with Detective Al Howlett, the only missing persons detective at the time. He phoned me on May 1. I have only vague memories of what he said to me or I to him. He did not ask me to come in for an interview, which made sense to me because I was not the one who had information to give. Wayne did. I told Detective Howlett about Wayne and he called Wayne not long after he spoke to me.

He called Wayne, but did not encourage him to come in quickly. "There's no hurry, but come in when you can," he said. Wayne went as soon as he could. "He seemed like a nice enough guy," Wayne says. But Detective Howlett brought up all the arguments that we would hear over and over: the reassurances that Sarah was probably just off somewhere, the claim that women like Sarah are transient. Wayne told him that that was not like Sarah. To my knowledge, Sarah had not left Vancouver since Mum ran into her in Calgary eleven years before. Detective Howlett told Wayne that he was working on five missing persons cases at that time.

Today, Sarah is at least number thirty in the list of missing women, but at the time they had not placed all the women together in a group. If one misconception is more responsible than any other for the slow action on these cases, it might be that women involved in survival sex are transient.

Yes, young women in sex work are sometimes transient, as are women who are not yet addicted. And women sometimes do go into treatment without telling their friends. In 1999, four of the women on the list were found, two of them dead and two of them alive. One of the women who was alive had started a new life and didn't want anyone to know where she was. On the day I'm writing this, another woman was found alive.

But as women get older and become addicted to drugs, they become less transient, to the point where they are more or less rooted in one spot. The chances that one woman who had not been heard from in a while had left town or gone into treatment might be high, but when the cases were taken together, it became highly unlikely that all or even most of the women had simply gone away. The Vancouver Police Department (VPD) had the information they needed to see that many women were disappearing from the Downtown Eastside, but I believe that it took far too long to consider a link among the missing.

WHEN SARAH DISAPPEARED, my energy was already depleted from fourteen years of worrying about her and trying to help. Sarah's disappearance came after she had been using drugs and involved in sex work for exactly half her life. My relationship with her, while important to me, was exhausting. I did not know how to help her, only how to stay in her life, at least a little bit. All I knew of her life was what I observed on my brief visits several times a year.

It was hard to face up to the possibility that someone I loved had been murdered, that Sarah had suffered as she must have and that she was gone, but, while I considered other possibilities, I did believe almost from the beginning that she had been killed. I also could not grasp that my life had become one of the stories that I barely glanced at in the papers, a sensationalistic story that feeds on people's misery to feed other people's insatiable appetite for that misery, especially when it involves sex and violence. Well, the story was now my life, the misery mine and my family's.

In my journal from that year, the first entry after I reported Sarah missing is made on May 2, ten days after I phoned 911. "Again, time has passed," I wrote. "I am sad. Sarah has been missing for almost three weeks. Where is she? Is she alive? Is she suffering? Or did she just take off on a whim?"

"What a stigma you live under," a woman said to me when I told her about what had happened. The more I thought about her words, the more angry I grew. I do not live under a stigma. I live with grief. There is no disgrace in Sarah's actions or her life, just struggle, sadness and love.

I wrote again on May 9: "Another week is gone. This has been a hard week—Sarah still missing, conversations with police, with Wayne, Dad, Mum, Aunt Georgi." I felt very alone. I finished up an entry four days later with "Sarah, I love you!" And on May 24, the simple acknowledgment, "The article was in *The Province* today."

That article was the first media coverage about Sarah's disappearance. Frank Luba, staff reporter, interviewed both Wayne and Mum for his piece, "Mother fears addicted daughter already dead," May 25, 1998. He tells about Sarah's children, about her journals, her poetry, her struggles, the many years that she spent working the streets, but the article does not acknowledge that anyone else might be missing, that Sarah's disappearance might be part of something larger.

I KNEW THAT I NEEDED TO TAKE ACTION, but found it almost beyond me. Wayne had the forward motion that I lacked. We talked about posters and he made them. Together, we went to Sarah's neighbourhood, from business to business, bar to bar, into corner stores and service providers, asking if we could put up the posters. As we were doing that, we talked about Sarah to the people in her community and I began to see what I had missed. I began to learn what a strong community the Downtown Eastside is and what an important part of it my sister was.

We needed the word of Sarah's disappearance to spread beyond the Downtown Eastside. One article was not enough. Wayne turned to Lindsay Kines at *The Vancouver Sun,* whom he had heard about from Constable Dave Dickson.

Lindsay's involvement with the cases started when Sandra Gagnon called him in 1997, after her sister, Janet Henry, disappeared. He wrote a story that ran on July 24, 1997. Sandra called him again around the anniversary of Janet's disappearance, and he wrote another story, which ran on May 11, 1998. At that time, nothing suggested to Lindsay that Janet's disappearance was anything other than an isolated incident.

Janet's life was filled with tragedy, with rape, murder, suicide and accidental death. She lived on the Downtown Eastside for seven years until she disappeared. Janet phoned Sandra almost every day, until a last phone call on June 25, 1997. The sisters had last seen each other a few weeks before that, when Janet was so skinny that her clothes were hanging off her body. Sandra and Janet's daughter, Deborah, still wait to learn what happened.

When Wayne went to see Lindsay with information about Sarah, he had no idea that other women were missing. He took Sarah's journals and some photos. "I was in rough shape," he says. "At times I was overcome, almost crying." He told Lindsay that Sarah wouldn't just take off, but that nobody would listen to him. Lindsay asked for contacts for Mum and for me, and began to investigate.

Lindsay knew about Janet, so for him there were two cases right away. He checked carefully into the information about Sarah. Then, on July 3, the Vancouver Police told *The Vancouver Sun* that they were concerned about the growing number of missing women who were involved in drugs and sex work. That must have spurred Lindsay on, because in July he interviewed me while he, Wayne and I walked around the Downtown Eastside. Lindsay struck me right away as a gentle, thoughtful, concerned person, easy to talk to.

Lindsay's article in *The Vancouver Sun* was the second to mention Sarah. "Police target big increase in missing women cases," July 3, 1998. "The police have outstanding files on 10 women who were reported missing in the past 2 years—including 5 already this year," he wrote. "By comparison, there is only one outstanding file from 1996, three from 1995 and one each from 1992 and 1986. In total,

Vancouver Police have 16 such cases of missing females dating back more than a decade." The police reported that they had assigned a second detective to the missing women cases. That detective was Lori Shenher, who did not actually take over files, including Sarah's, until July 28. She brought great ability and dedication to her work, but between them she and Al Howlett would not be able to solve the cases. It is also worth noting, I think, that the fact that it was Detective Shenher rather than Detective Howlett who interviewed Shauna meant that that interview did not take place until Sarah had been gone for at least three and a half months. Shauna's memory would have been more reliable, as would anyone's, if she had been interviewed sooner.

That headline, "big increase in missing women cases," was a turning point. With those words the women became a group. A link was being considered. Also, the term "missing women" was coined and it has stuck. The women would not be called "missing prostitutes" or "missing addicts"; they would be called what they were, "missing women." I am glad about that, even though that expression too has lost meaning over the years because no pair of words can contain sixty-three individual human beings or their deaths. Still, I think that they are the best words available to us. They stick even though more than fifteen of the women are no longer missing today. Their DNA has been found. In 15 cases charges have been laid.

BACK IN THE SUMMER of '98, I didn't want any of this to be happening. I didn't want to be out putting up posters. I didn't want to be doing anything. I loved my sister very much, but even thinking about that summer now brings the tension in my back, the humming in my skull as if a pop can with a pinhole in it were slowly decompressing in the back of my brain.

When Lindsay's article appeared in *The Vancouver Sun*, I was in the midst of preparing to teach two three-week courses on children's literature at UBC. I was visiting a dying friend almost every day as well. When I read the article I didn't feel much of anything, but later in the day I found myself crying uncontrollably. The fact that nine other women had disappeared in the previous year and a half made Sarah's disappearance seem that much more real and that much more sinister.

Nine days later, my friend died. I completed my teaching in a haze of grief.

That summer, Wayne set up a tip line: tips came to his pager number and the line ultimately proved useful to the police. He received two tips that seemed important at the time. The first came on a Saturday, July 25. A man called three times, speaking against a noisy background, perhaps a bar. "Sarah's dead," he said. "So there will be more girls like her dead. There will be more prostitutes killed. There will be one every Friday night. At the busiest time." In a second call, he continued, "So just stop looking for her, all right? She doesn't want to be seen and heard from again, all right? So, 'bye. She's dead." He called one more time: "This is in regard to Sarah. I just want to let you know that you'll never find her again alive because a friend of mine killed her and I was there." Wayne spoke to both the police and *The Province*, which led to an article two days later.

If the police had had their own tip line, they would have received calls such as this directly. They would have been able to act on them immediately, and they would have been able to keep them secret, which I would assume to be desirable.

The messages were horrifying, but somehow seemed like a hoax. Reading them now, they are more chilling than they were then because, even if they were a hoax, much of what they said turned out to be true. Sarah was dead. And many more women died after her. I remember those tips clearly. I remember thinking that Wayne should not have talked to the media about them. He agreed with me about that when I mentioned it later. The words and the voice from the tape floated around in my mind for some time afterward. I can hear it now if I try. But what could we do? Wayne turned the tape over and that was the end of it. As I say, we thought the calls were a hoax. But what if they weren't?

Sarah wrote a lot about dying, and at one time she wrote a list of her fears:

> I'm getting scared inside. Some nights I cry myself to sleep. I curl into the fetal position and wrap my arms around myself and rock myself to sleep.
>
> 1. I'm afraid of being alone.
> 2. I'm afraid of getting old with nothing.
> 3. I'm afraid of getting murdered by a trick.
> 4. I'm afraid of ODing.
> 5. I'm afraid of AIDS.
> 6. I'm afraid of withdrawal.
> 7. I'm afraid of being afraid.
> 8. I'm afraid of letting anybody too close.
> 9. I'm afraid of love. Given or taken.
>
> I'm afraid of death if I can't fight back.

Of everything in her journals, this last may be the line that haunts me the most. I wish for her that in the last hours of her life she was able to fight.

Detective Lori Shenher started working on the missing women cases the day after the story about those calls ran in the paper. Her work began with a bombardment of tips in response to those strange phone messages. Not long after that, another tip came in. This time the tip related directly to a farm in Port Coquitlam, the same property that police began searching three and a half years later in February 2002.

In response to that tip and other information, Detective Shenher tried to get enough information to justify seeking a warrant to search the Port Coquitlam site, but was unsuccessful. Finally, the Vancouver

Police turned all evidence relating to the property over to the Port Coquitlam RCMP. The farm was in RCMP jurisdiction; perhaps the RCMP would have access to leads that were unavailable to the VPD. The RCMP investigator with whom Lori worked was keen, Lori told me. But he was transferred off the case to do other things. The file bounced around a bit. Some serious efforts were made, but until other information came to light, the RCMP, like the VPD, was not successful in building a case or in getting onto the property to take a look around.

In the summer of 1998, I began writing letters to Sarah in an effort to express and work through my feelings.

Dear Sarah,

I have the idea in my head that I should write to you, but it is hard. I wrote to Amanda first (my friend who died) and now I think I know why, because I didn't want to face writing to you. I was with Amanda when she died—I got to talk to her, to tell her that I loved her. I don't even know how you died, Sarah, or if, for sure, you are dead. If I could have been there, I would have helped you if I could. That's ridiculous, isn't it? What could I do? I could have called the police at least. I could have borne witness/been a witness.

I'm not going to write a long letter to you today, Sarah, just a little one to tell you how monumental is my love for you and how sad I am that you are gone.

You are my one and only sister and very, very dear to me.

I was just thinking that for you I hope that there can be something beyond death—some peace, some joy. But maybe we just change form. Maybe your life force, which was substantial, is simply passing into all the growth around you, wherever you are.

Thus life begets life, not to mention the two lives you created—each substantial as well. I will see Jeanie and Ben on Thursday and I can't wait.

Rest, Sarah, rest. If there are flights of angels, I know they have sung you to a better place. If there are not, you still may rest now. Much, much love,

Maggie

ON MY BIRTHDAY in August, I flew to Ontario to visit Mum, Aunt Jean, Jeanie and Ben for a week and to bring Jeanie, then seven years old, back to Vancouver for a holiday. The first thing that Jeanie wanted to do once we were back in Vancouver was to see her father. I asked Roland to come along so that I could leave Jeanie in the car while I got Charlie to come out of the house. And Charlie emerged, a wide, shy grin on his face. Two women came out with him, women who were living in the house, who had been living in the house before Sarah disappeared. They gushed over Jeanie; so like her mother, they said. Charlie and Jeanie faced each other awkwardly, from a bit of a distance. Jeanie clung to me. Roland took a few pictures. It was awful for all of us, I think. Certainly it was for me. I don't know what Jeanie as a child could make of it, but she had insisted upon the reunion. At least here was something real, something true. This man was her father and this house was where he lived.

Jeanie also insisted that day on seeing the evidence that people were looking for her mother. At other points during her visit, she suggested that we go into the woods and look for Sarah's body ourselves. She had the idea that Sarah might be buried somewhere and that she might be able to find her. Anyway, she was willing to try. We did not go into the woods during that visit, but we did walk hand-in-hand along Hastings Street looking at posters of Sarah in windows, including the one on the cover of this book.

After Jeanie went home, I got bronchitis, which became pneumonia and plagued me through much of that fall. I continued writing letters to Sarah and tried to settle back into substitute teaching.

In mid-September, the police formed what they called a "working group" to review the missing women cases. At that time, they had put together a list of forty names of missing women, not all of them drug addicted or sex workers. The team included geographic profiler Detective Inspector Kim Rossmo. In an article in *The Vancouver Sun*, "Missing women cases probed," September 18, 1998, Lindsay Kines quotes me: "I think it's a very good thing that they're starting to put more people on to it and to try to find connections and to identify all of those cases," I said. "Maybe that will help them to figure out what's actually going on. It starts to seem more and more as if there's something happening. There's a pattern to this."

Kim Rossmo is now well known for his wrongful dismissal trial with the Vancouver Police and for his high-profile position as a geographic profiler in Washington, D.C., including involvement with the sniper case of 2002. He drafted a press release, when he was working with the VPD in September 1998, about a statistical analysis on the cases. His press release was dated September 30 and used the words "serial killer." The powers that be considered it inflammatory and premature. Maybe it was. Maybe it was not. They did not release it. Later on, though, public awareness of the possibility of a serial predator increased pressure on the police. Public pressure made it impossible for the police to let the matter drop. Had Rossmo's press release been made public in September 1998, perhaps that pressure would have built sooner.

I did not and do not know anything about police work. Nor do I wish I did. Nowhere in me was there a whisper of a desire to go out and discover for myself what had happened to my sister and the other women. I needed to know that the work was being done. I needed to trust the police. And I needed to find something that I could do in the face of the horror that I was gradually coming to understand. In response to that need, my mother came up with an idea: the memorial.

❧

1998   October   *Julie Louise Young last seen*

1998   November 10   *Angela Rebecca Jardine last seen*

1998   December 11   *Michele Gurney last seen*

1998   December 27   *Marcella Helen Creison last seen*

1998   *Ruby Anne Hardy last seen*

1999   January 16   *Jacquilene Michele McDonell last seen*

1999   February 1   *Brenda Ann Wolfe last seen*

1999   March 2   *Georgina Faith Papin last seen*

ten

REMEMBERING

IN PARTICIPATING IN AMANDA'S MEMORIAL during the summer of 1998 and in the memorial of another friend who died that June, I began to learn what death is, what it means, and how to mourn. I learned what we were missing in not having a ceremony associated with Sarah's passing. I felt so helpless. We all did. As I was talking with Mum about my grief one day that fall and weeping on the phone, she suddenly said, "Let's have a memorial for Sarah. Let's have it on May 12, her birthday."

"Yes!" I responded, immediately excited and grounded by the idea.

"No," Mum went on, "let's have it for all the women who are missing, not just for Sarah." It was such a relief to me to have something to focus on, something that I could do. I couldn't find Sarah. I couldn't bring her back to life. But together with others, I could honour her passing and the passing of all the other Downtown Eastside women who were missing.

At some point in the late summer or early fall, I talked with Val Hughes, Kerry Koski's sister, for the first time. Kerry Koski went missing three months before Sarah did. When I called Val in

August 2002 to tell her that Sarah's DNA had been found, she was shaken, because, in her mind, Sarah and Kerry were together. If one were found, the other would be as well. To date, she has had no news about Kerry. She waits as we all do.

Val and her family last saw Kerry on the same day we last saw Sarah, Christmas 1997. Unlike Sarah, however, Kerry had been downtown only for a couple of months when she disappeared in January 1998. She had survived an abusive relationship in her twenties and had brought her three daughters into a new relationship, this time with a good man, but one who suffered from manic depression. In 1996, he went off his medication and, in the depression that ensued, hanged himself. After that, Kerry struggled and began turning to alcohol and drugs for relief. She spiralled downward, and in the fall of 1997 left home and went downtown. Val had a feeling that she was going to say goodbye to her sister that Christmas. She was right.

Almost a year later, it was a great comfort for Val and me to discover one another and our shared experience.

IN ADDITION TO TALKING with other family members at that time, I met with Sarah's friend Ken so that he could give me some things of Sarah's: a cross on a chain and a few photos as well as some pieces of Sarah's writing. The meeting was difficult for me. I wasn't sure how to relate to this man. Meeting Wayne while Sarah was alive and in Sarah's company helped me to sort out his place in her life and through that his place in mine. In Ken's case, I had to feel my way with no guidance from Sarah herself. Although on some level I had known the other important man in Sarah's life, Charlie, for years, I never talked to him about her disappearance. In fact, I don't think that I ever had a conversation with him beyond civilities.

At that same time, in October, I dealt with a request from the police for Sarah's dental records, a step that I tried not to think about.

Mum suggested that we hold the memorial at First United Church at Hastings and Gore, since she is involved in the United Church in Guelph and knew that First United served the Downtown Eastside community. We decided to hold the memorial on May 12, 1999, because þy then more than a year would have passed since Sarah's disappearance and on that date Sarah would have turned thirty. If it turned out that by a miracle Sarah was alive, we believed that she would be pleased to see what we were preparing, evidence of her importance in our lives. But we knew that that would not happen.

That fall, in addition to writing several letters to Sarah, I wrote pages and pages of journal entries without a mention of the deep grief that I was carrying. I did start attending the Unitarian Church, where a flexible approach to spirituality made me feel included. I would slip into the church for the service and slip out again as soon as it ended to listen to Stuart McLean's *Vinyl Cafe* on CBC on the drive home. What a joy it was to lose myself in his stories of family life! I gained much strength through that winter and the next spring from that Sunday morning routine.

I CALLED RUTH WRIGHT, the interim minister at First United, in early November and met with her soon after. In early December, with Ruth's guidance, I started making calls, putting together a committee to plan the memorial. I created the start of a plan, a list of people who might be willing to make some food for the event and a list of foods and some tasks that would need to be accomplished. Mum wrote a letter to Pete Seeger, the folk singer, whom we had seen perform at an outdoor benefit in Vancouver when we were kids, asking if he would participate. He wrote back a kind letter pointing out that he was seventy-nine years old! He was not able to come.

Detective Shenher contacted as many families as she could on my behalf. Gradually, I began to form a partial list of who the missing women were. There were twenty, approximately, that were considered part of the "group" at the time. I started talking to family members, mothers and sisters in most cases, and discovering that many of their stories were similar to mine.

In addition to Val Hughes and Sandra Gagnon, I met Lynn and Rick Frey and others. As we all began to know one another, we drew strength and support from each other and discovered our commonality. As I grew closer to Val and Sandy and Lynn and Rick, I got to know their missing sisters and daughters as well, and, through their stories, to understand Sarah's world a little better.

The downfall of Lynn and Rick's daughter, Marnie, was drugs. She had been a happy, active girl, living in the Vancouver Island community of Campbell River. But at seventeen, she started experimenting with drugs, and soon after, began to run away from home. For several years, her family struggled to help her, but finally, in the spring of 1997, she ended up on the Downtown Eastside. She called home on her birthday that year, August 30, 1997, but after that Lynn and Rick never heard from her again. More than five years later, they would learn that her DNA had been discovered on the Port Coquitlam farm.

At the same time that we all drew strength from knowing one another and sharing our stories, I felt a growing horror as the enormity of all of our losses joined together began to sink in. I was overwhelmed, going through the motions of planning, putting up posters, talking to media, dealing with the police, and trying to understand what had happened, to make sense of what was essentially senseless.

Then, in mid-April 1999, I went out with Wayne and a friend to put up new posters informing people about the upcoming memorial. This time, instead of leaving Wayne to make the posters and following along in his wake as I had done the previous year, I worked on them with him and went with him to copy them. We walked up and down Hastings and to the Needle Exchange, Charlie's house and to the Mission. We entered every grocery store, bar and hotel, even one gas station and a few restaurants. In each case I approached the appropriate person with a poster and asked if we could put up a copy inside. Only one place said no. I came out each time feeling weak, almost as if my knees could buckle. But in another way I felt strong, able to speak to each person, to make those connections.

As May 12 drew closer, the memorial became my sole focus. Organizing eclipsed grief. I spent many hours on the phone soliciting food donations. In many instances, particularly when I approached big companies, I was turned down. It was the smaller businesses that were happy to support us. I was surprised by that at the time, because it seemed to me that large corporations could afford to help so much more easily. But now I understand that local businesses are more a part of their own communities, so they are more eager to participate.

My agenda is full of notes to myself in the weeks leading up to the May 12, 1999, event. I had to pay for the tents that a local company rented to us at half price. I had to pick up the replica of the plaque that would appear on the bench, so that we could at least use it in the ceremony (we wouldn't have the bench itself until the next year). I had to go to a board meeting at the Carnegie Centre so that they could make a contribution to our memorial. I was terrified, sure that I was doing the whole thing wrong, that I was going to be criticized, but they were kind to me and quickly agreed to support the event.

The Police Board meeting at which the investigation was discussed took place on Wednesday, April 28, and I did many media interviews both before and after that, which I will discuss more fully in the next chapter. Then, on April 30, I flew to Ontario to spend a week with Mum. I was in Guelph for Ben's third birthday on May 1. Jeanie sang in a concert on May 4 and I was there. We all flew back to Vancouver together on May 8, four days before the memorial.

A friend of my mother offered to take me on a Costco run to buy some of the food that we needed with money that had been donated. Another friend picked up the bread that Terra Breads had given us. We had a sandwich-making party that night. We must have made at least three hundred sandwiches.

On the morning of the memorial, I needed to be down in CRAB Park (CRAB stands for Create a Real Accessible Beach) in time to meet the people with the tents. Everything went smoothly, although the firefighters who had agreed to watch over the tents and food while we were in the church were called to a fire, so were unable to come.

My brother-in-law, Robbie, and his wife, Valerie, who is of the Salish Nation from the Katzie band, made pouches of herbs for us to give as thank-yous. I have one still and it is beautiful, a plastic pouch filled with lavender and sage, with one feather in the centre. The label reads:

Sacred mix of Sage:
Sagebrush & Lavender
Used to cleanse the soul and bring in the positive.
May 12, 1999

Over four hundred people filled the church. Hundreds of tulips that had been donated to Val Hughes were arranged in vases and water jugs all around us. People arrived gradually, over the hour before the ceremony, and as they entered, if they so wished, were smudged—a sacred Aboriginal cleansing ritual in which sage or sweetgrass is lit and individuals brush its smoke over their bodies. Everyone took a burgundy ribbon, made by Lynn Frey. The Downtown Eastside Women's Centre (DEWC), which had helped plan the event, hung their banner in the sanctuary. The memorial was shaped by many, many people whose visions varied, but all of whom cared deeply. We had encouraged all families who wished to bring a photo of their loved one and a special candle that could be lit in her memory. Early in the service each woman's name was read and a family member or friend came to the front to light their candle.

Then came a time for all who wished to do so to come to the front, light a taper, and speak or remain silent. A line of people snaked across the carpet waiting patiently.

Dad was one of them. He had written a short piece that he considered reading aloud that day, but realized once he got there that it was not suitable. His words are well worth recording here, though:

My name is Jan de Vries. I am the father of Sarah, one of the twenty women who have disappeared. Sarah was both a heroin addict and a prostitute.

Right now, as we are gathered to think about and mourn the disappeared women, just a few blocks from here women are active in the sex trade to get money to obtain heroin. We all know that the women are working in a highly dangerous environment.

I shall offer some ideas that I feel would mitigate both the heroin and the prostitution problem.

In other jurisdictions, including the city of Liverpool, U.K., heroin addicts are identified and are provided with heroin according to need. This approach decriminalizes heroin use. Also, and this is important, it removes the necessity for addicts to commit crime, or be involved in the sex trade to obtain money to buy heroin.

Three years ago, my wife and I, on our way to a flag store in the city of The Hague, walked through a combined small business–residential area: four-storey row houses with small businesses at street level. At one point we found ourselves in an unusual street. Prostitutes were sitting behind the storefront windows. We had entered a sex mall. It was an eerie, depressing place. The thing I remember most is the silence. Men were shopping for sex. Women were offering themselves.

Sadly, in every city live men who like prostitutes and women who for one reason or another work as prostitutes. This is a sad and unfortunate fact of life. So, why not follow the example of a progressive city like The Hague and provide safe places for prostitutes to work?

It is almost certain that Sarah is dead. We would very much prefer her to be working in such a mall than the present situation. It would be sad to see her there, but nowhere near as sad as we are feeling now.

So, federal government, provincial government and City of Vancouver, please follow the Liverpool and The Hague examples. These cities have the most promising policies I know of to prevent the deaths of both heroin addicts and sex workers.

I had bought more than a hundred tapers and every one was lit and stuck into a tray of sand by the end of the ceremony. Loved ones, friends, caring community members took turns saying a few words. I read a poem that I had written the previous June:

Thoughts Filled with Love, Loss and Sorrow

Sarah, my beloved sister, loved by many more as well,
May you know somehow and somewhere that you are loved
That you always were
That your face smiles at me from photos daily
    at four . . . at twenty.
And I smile back.
That your name is spoken and thought over and over again
As the people among whom you made your life
Worry and wonder.
I treasure each moment we have had together in all our years.
Twenty-eight, I guess. Years.
I'm so glad that you came and ate my blueberry pancakes last
    Christmas.
That you danced your son Benjamin in your arms so many
    months ago.
That you have a daughter named Jeanie.
That once you sent me an e-mail.
That last year I ate a bean from your garden.
That a few days ago I saw Charlie,
Drenched in sunlight and pain,
Stirring the soil,
Breathing life and beauty into that same garden.
That you have friends who love you.
That I have had you in my life.
And that I love you and you love me.

Oh, Sarah, this is only the beginning.

Beautiful songs were sung. Women drummed. And an Anglican minister gave a sermon. The words to the hymns were included in the Order of Service so that all could sing along. We had predicted that the service would be about an hour and a half long, but it was an hour longer than that, lasting until about 4:30 p.m. As we left, each of us picked up a tulip to carry on the walk to the park.

Media had not been permitted in the church, but when we emerged the sidewalk was lined with TV cameras all the way down the block. Philip Owen, our then-mayor, was waiting impatiently to join us on the walk. He had agreed to say a few words in the park, but we went so far overtime that he wasn't able to stay long enough for that. How empowering it is to step right out into the street with no regard for cars, to take over the space in a large peaceful group! The DEWC led with their banner and eight-and-a-half-year-old Jeanie immediately moved away from us to the front of the procession. She led the march, walking right through the Downtown Eastside where her mother once lived and worked, where her mother once sped down the street on Rollerblades and from which her mother disappeared. Jeanie led the march, walking among people who knew and cared for Sarah, people from all parts of Sarah's life— her family, her childhood friends and her community. Jeanie looked wonderful in a soft leather vest with fringes. She remembers that day and I know that it meant a great deal to her.

Many of us carried flowers, others carried placards. I had not wanted it to be a walk of protest, but a walk of remembrance. So that is what it was for me. For others, I think, it was both. It was an opportunity to speak out.

In the park things took their own shape too. The sound system that we had arranged did not work well. We had planned not to serve the food until a little later, after the outdoor portion of the ceremony concluded. But, "People are hungry," Jamie Lee Hamilton, one of our committee members, said to my friend who was valiantly trying to follow my instructions and keep the covers on the food. Jamie was right, of course. People needed to participate as they chose rather than as I had decreed. And people *were* hungry. The minister from the Unitarian Church, Sydney Craig, had agreed to MC that part of the day and she quickly figured out that she had to turn herself over to the pattern that evolved. First Nations women circled the display that stood in place of the memorial bench that would come later and drummed; the member of Parliament for the Downtown Eastside, Libby Davies, spoke; the then British Columbian member of the Legislative Assembly Jenny Kwan spoke as well. My mother, with Ben perched on her shoulders, talked about Sarah. My friend Clea had made the beautiful display with driftwood for the plaque. The plaque reads:

In memory of L. Coombes, S. de Vries, M. Frey,
H. Hallmark, J. Henry, A. Jardine, K. Koski, S. Lane, J. Murdock,
D. Spence & all other women who are missing.
With our love. May 12, 1999.

It includes only ten names because I would include only names of those women whose families wanted me to, which limited me as well to those families with whom I was in contact.

The bench is there still, in CRAB Park at the foot of Main Street over the viaduct, Portside Park to the uninitiated. I have sat on the bench many times looking out at Burrard Inlet and the mountains and the gangly, brilliant orange, giraffe-like structures that grace the harbour.

On May 12, 1999, people laid their tulips on the table with the display and on the ground by the rock in memory of those murdered. A painting by a local artist was displayed under plastic to keep it safe from the rain; it depicted more than twenty women—pink, brown and black—standing before a backdrop of downtown buildings below a sky in which the gods lament.

At the end, everyone stood in a circle, held hands and sang a song of my mother's choosing, "We Shall Overcome."

In late June 1999, I attended a meeting of a group of private investigators who had offered to help us. I didn't know what to make of their offer. I was exhausted by the effort that it took to attend the meeting and listen to these people—whose motives I did not understand—talk about a process that I knew little about. Investigating murders, discovering what has happened to a group of people who have vanished, searching in the bush, using cadaver dogs—I didn't want to be a part of it. But my sister had been missing for more than a year. I was a part of it whether I liked it or not. Their involvement did not end up going very far, however, perhaps because the police did not co-operate with them, or perhaps because they realized that they did not have the resources to find the answers, or perhaps for some other set of reasons.

Not long after that draining experience, I received a call from a woman who had had my phone number since February but had not been able to bring herself to attend the memorial. I had made copies of a video of the memorial to distribute to family members, but she didn't want to see that either. She was just beginning to consider connecting, acknowledging her place among the family members of the missing women. She was Laurel Windover, sister of Inga Hall, whose DNA has now been found on the Port Coquitlam site. Speaking with her touched me, brought my own grief back to the surface.

While I was growing increasingly exhausted, and more and more desperate to put the whole investigation behind me, others were unflagging. Some members of other families remained active and vigilant through 1999 and 2000, and so did Wayne. My mother and I were encouraging him to move on. To us, he seemed overly invested in the missing women, but I think that is because unlike us, he believed the cases might be solved. We did not have his faith. Wayne did not turn away. He has been living in California for several years now, but he continues to maintain the missing women website, to circulate articles about the case and to facilitate connections between people where appropriate. He has helped me to meet a number of people who knew Sarah.

By the fall of 1999, I had retreated into my own grief and my own life, making the decision to stop talking to the media and to move from the public into the private realm. In March of 2000, when the park bench was finally in place, I did surface enough to hold a dedication ceremony in CRAB Park. The group included family members of several missing women; Constable Dave Dickson; Detective Lori Shenher; Bob Stall, the reporter from *The Province*, who came not to report but to honour the women, propped up by his daughter and a cane, in recovery from a heart attack; Peter; Troy; Mum and me. We stood in a circle in the rain, spoke the names of all the missing women, passed from hand to hand a five-foot talking stick—a First Nations ritual that requires that the person holding the stick speak from the heart and have the floor until ready to pass the stick on to another—and remembered.

At that point, I did not believe that I would ever learn what had happened to Sarah. Still, if I passed a bundle by the highway, I would wonder if that might be her body; if I drove along behind a window-less van, I would wonder if she might be held inside or might have been held inside a similar van in the past. If I drove by a farmer's field, or a small wood, I would wonder if she might be buried there. Such thoughts came to me regularly until February of 2002, when the search on the farm in Port Coquitlam began. Now I don't wonder so much. I've been too close to the truth and it's uglier than anything I imagined.

1999   November 27   Wendy Crawford last seen

1999   December 27   Jennifer Lynn Furminger last seen

1999   December 31   Tiffany Louise Drew last seen

2000   November 1   Dawn Teresa Crey last seen

2000   December 21   Debra Lynne Jones last seen

2001   March 3   Patricia Rose Johnson last seen

2001   March 16   Yvonne Marie Boen last seen

2001   April 1   Heather Gabrielle Chinnock last seen

2001   April 17   Heather Kathleen Bottomley last seen

2001   June 6   Andrea Joesbury last seen

2001   August 1   Sereena Abotsway last seen

2001   October 19   Dianne Rosemary Rock last seen

2001   November 23   Mona Lee Wilson last seen

eleven

FIRST PHASE OF THE INVESTIGATION

Two important topics need their own chapter, the investigation and the media, but I must go back in time a few months to address them.

On March 30, 1999, six weeks before the memorial, I wrote the following letter, slightly shortened here, to the mayor of Vancouver and the chair of the Vancouver Police Board, Philip Owen, and a similar letter to the Attorney General at the time, Ujjal Dosanjh.

Dear Mayor Owen:

Re: Steps to Solving the Cases of the 20 Missing Women

I am writing to you in your role as chair of the Police Board. My sister, Sarah de Vries, disappeared from the Downtown Eastside last April. . . .

About ten days ago, I saw you on Community Television speaking about the issue of prostitution in Vancouver. You responded to two calls about the twenty women who are missing from the Downtown Eastside by saying that you would take the issue to the Police Board. I was pleased to hear that and would like to know what the results of that meeting were.

On Saturday, March 27, I again saw you on television. This time you were speaking about the reward being offered in the case of the garage robberies. In your comments you acknowledged that "nobody's been injured." Then you went on to say, "think of the trauma that's experienced; think of the families. So that might be just the husband in the garage, but think what happens to the rest of the family, maybe children that are in their home worried about going to school or coming back at night from a family outing and they're all in the car. How are they going to deal with that? It's very traumatic; it's very destructive; it's very harmful to family life. We want to put a stop to this quickly before it spreads throughout the city."

I agree with you. I am sure these families *are* traumatized. It *is* important to stop these robberies before they spread. But my family is traumatized too. And so is every other family that I have talked to, nine in all. We are suffering. We do not know what has happened to our sisters, daughters, mothers. We imagine all kinds of scenarios. We imagine what they may have suffered, or even, be suffering.

My nephew, Ben, only met his mother once after she gave birth to him. He was about five months old. He is now almost three. Luckily we have photographs of that encounter, but now he will almost certainly never see her again, never be able to ask her questions, to figure out where he came from and why.

We need to know what happened, to find her body, so that at least we can grieve properly, lay her to rest. My sister had a hard life; she did some things that I struggle to understand. She was addicted to heroin and cocaine and she worked the streets to support her habit. But she was my baby sister, eight years younger than I am. I loved her very much. And she loved me. I visited her regularly and she kept in touch.

I am calling for the police to go after new information aggressively by:

1. publicly acknowledging the possibility that the disappearances may be related and may involve abduction and murder;
2. offering a reward that matches the other two rewards currently before the public;
3. setting up a task force to deal with whatever information comes in and to bring more points of view to the cases;
4. offering police protection to anyone who may be afraid to come forward, a girlfriend, for example. . . .

Thank you for your consideration of my points and my invitation. I will call your office late next week to follow up.

Sincerely yours,

Maggie de Vries

This letter and the whole process that followed were precipitated by a conversation that I had with Detective Shenher. In contrast with the official position of the police department, she felt that a reward might generate useful tips. More important, she felt that the case should be more heavily resourced, that a task force was needed in order to move forward. I was spurred to action by her recommendations. I had the word from the person who knew more about the investigation than anyone else did, so I was not dissuaded by arguments against a reward or against the need for a task force. Without her help, I would not have been able to follow through as forcefully as I did.

Other people wrote to all the levels of government as well. Michelle Pineault, the mother of Stephanie Lane, and a friend of Michelle's started a petition, which they presented at the Police Board meeting. Media began to cover the struggle. I wrote a letter to *The Vancouver Sun* that ran as a "Voices" column. One of the most illuminating media events was a two-hour radio interview on *The David Berner Show* on CKNW. David Berner is a local radio personality who, coincidentally, knew Janet Henry, one of the missing. She and her sister, Sandra, had lived with him as foster children decades earlier.

His show was the one place where a police officer who was actively involved with the case was able to speak out. Soon after that, the job of communicating with the media was turned over to Ann Drennan, the VPD liaison officer at the time. The guests on the show were Detective Shenher, Detective Don Smith, Sandy Gagnon, her sister, Dot, and me.

Detective Shenher repeated what we had heard so many times— that the police had very little information to work with and that just because family members are convinced that something terrible has happened to their missing loved one does not make it so. Then Berner asked her if she had an instinct about the case.

"I'm starting to get one, I think," she said. "I don't see this as having a positive outcome. It's interesting because as a police officer you learn through talking to people that very few people really know the people in their lives. You learn to take the things that family tells you with a bit of a grain of salt. However, when you have families that are in contact with their loved ones the way Sandy and Dot were, the way Maggie was . . . and all of a sudden that contact stops . . . And as Maggie said, you're not talking about women who can jump on a plane and you're not talking about women that are going to be recruited, if you will, to work in different areas. Many of these women were very sick either through their addictions or through HIV, some had AIDS. They were at points in their lives where they really needed the support systems that they had built here. To have them disappear, I find that extremely strange. You or I have the freedom to get up and go somewhere, but they're not only imprisoned by their poverty and their social situation; they're imprisoned by their addictions, they're imprisoned by illness. That makes it highly unlikely that they would just up and go."

Berner then brought up the fact that two of the women had been found alive, one in a mental institution and another alive and well but not wanting her whereabouts known. He went on to say that "the fact that two out of twenty-four people have been located does not obviate that the others could be dead, murdered, victims of unhappy circumstance." Those two women being found seemed to make it easier for the police to dismiss the need for a more intensive investigation. It is not the job of the police to find adults who have simply relocated and chosen not to tell their family. Within the previous month or two, Philip Owen had said to the media, "We are not running a locating service." He was right in a literal sense but wrong in that his comment implied that no foul play had taken place.

Detective Shenher did not believe that finding two women alive meant that the same outcome could be expected for the other twenty. "I'm not sitting here saying I believe they're all victims of murder. I believe that there are probably going to be a mixture of outcomes here. But my gut feeling is that some of them have met with foul play."

Detective Shenher confirmed that all the information about the women had been entered into ViCLAS, the Violent Crime Linkage and Analysis System (a computer database), but again pointed out the sketchiness of the information she had on some of the cases. In many instances, she had to leave whole sections blank.

A caller asked, "What have the police done about flooding that area and check, check, check?" Detective Smith responded to that question. He said that many people on the Downtown Eastside have several aliases, that it is difficult to keep track of people down there. He said that his officers did go out and talk to the women and that efforts were being made to collect and keep information about johns.

I'm sure that what he says is true, but at the same time I wonder if it couldn't have been done better. The struggle that so many families had in just getting their loved one listed as missing created delays. When the police refer to being thwarted in their investigation because many of the women were not listed as missing until months after they disappeared, they need to realize that in some cases, the women were not listed as missing because the police were refusing to accept missing persons reports from family. This is certainly the case for Leigh Miner, Kerry Koski and Tanya Holyk. I do not know for how many others. Further, in many cases, after a woman had been listed as missing, it did not seem from the outside that the police were doing very much to find her. In my case, I did not hear back from Detective Howlett for ten days. Then, when he spoke to Wayne, he said that Wayne did not need to rush in to see him.

In addition, a major obstacle for the police must have been lack of trust. While Dave Dickson, the constable who was supportive of many women on the Downtown Eastside, had told me that Sarah was always polite to him, I know that her feelings toward the police were not warm. The relationship would have had an adversarial component considering that the main activities of Sarah's day— injecting and dealing heroin and cocaine and communicating for the purposes of prostitution—were illegal. Individual police officers helped Sarah at times, but certain other officers treated her badly. On the Downtown Eastside, women in sex work are at the bottom of a complex hierarchy; both society at large and the microcosm of the Downtown Eastside place them there. We as a society stand behind a set of laws—the laws relating to prostitution and to drugs—that victimize the weakest people among us. We cannot expect those people to trust us enough to tell us what they know. They then have to trust us not to further endanger them or to interfere with what they need to do to earn the money they require to feed their habit.

It seems to me impossible that more than sixty women could vanish from a small area of Vancouver without anyone seeing or knowing anything. Yet, at least in the early years, the police did not seem to be able to come up with much useful information, although the court case will probably show that they had much more information than any civilians, including me, are aware of. The frequent lack of communication between police and people on the margins of society is not solely the fault of the police department. Both our laws and societal attitudes play a part as well. In addition, the fact that serial predator cases do not come along very often makes it difficult for police to recognize the signs that such a criminal is at work. In April 1999, a reward seemed to be one way of bringing forward information that had not been forthcoming so far. I said to host David Berner, "Somebody has to know something out there, and we need to find that out." That led to a discussion of how many men there are out there who are capable of and even guilty of violence against sex workers. At that time, the list was already long. In the fall of 2001, we were all shocked when we were told at the meeting with the review team that their list of suspects, local men whom they considered capable of murdering many women, topped six hundred.

Many of these men are living apparently "normal" lives with jobs and wives and children. They act out their violent impulses against sex workers because they can. They can drive downtown, invite a woman into their car, drive her to an isolated spot, rape her, beat her, even kill her, without consequences. In Vancouver alone, there are hundreds of such men, whose names are known to police. Sex workers need, like the rest of us, to be able to do their job without risking their lives.

When the police talked about how many potential suspects there were, they were pointing out as well that, given the number of violent men, we had no reason to think that a serial predator was responsible for all the disappearances. In a way, they had a point. Jumping to the conclusion that a serial predator was responsible changed the conversation from one about societal problems to one about catching one bad man. Still, I had to listen to my gut. "It seems to me unlikely that we're talking about a serial killer who has killed all twenty-two of the women, but it seems equally unlikely to me that we're talking about twenty-two different circumstances," I said to David Berner. "It seems to me that some of them must be linked. Common sense tells me that."

It turned out that the DNA of close to twenty of the missing women would be found on one property. As the search continues, that number may grow substantially. We err, though, if we believe that the problem stops with whatever occurred on a single farm in Port Coquitlam. It was reassuring to me to see the police at *The David Berner Show* nod their heads when I said that I thought some of the cases must be linked. However, it would be the fall of 2001 before the VPD would even publicly consider the possibility of links among the cases.

When I had followed up on my letter to the mayor by calling his office, I learned that the matter was to be discussed at the Police Board meeting on April 28, a few days after that panel discussion on CKNW. I asked to be included in the delegation to address the issue. In the weeks leading up to that meeting, it seemed that the mayor was resisting offering the reward. The Attorney General, Ujjal Dosanjh, said that he would support the decision of the Police Board; thus it came down to the mayor, but he did not seem to understand the seriousness of the situation. He was quoted in a community paper, *The Westender*, on April 22: "You generally put up a reward when you say, 'I think there's a particular person here and they live in Vancouver and we've got the description and a composite drawing of them.' There's people missing all over the place. It's not as though it was some world issue that's unique."

If the chair of the Police Board still believed after months of investigating that many of the missing women had just gone off somewhere and might call home at any time, no wonder the case was not getting the resources that it needed! It was a unique situation, but either Philip Owen had not yet realized that or he was not yet prepared to say so publicly. The message that was being sent to the public from the police and local government was this: There's nothing to worry about.

Then Bob Stall from *The Province* interviewed Philip Owen. He phoned me soon afterwards to say that he had persuaded Owen to argue at the meeting in favour of the reward. The next day the front page of the paper was taken up with the headline "$100,000 to find out: Vancouver's mayor bends to public pressure and will fight this week to put up a reward to discover whether their disappearance is the work of a serial killer." Above were photos of twenty missing women. Below, photos of Owen and Stall.

It was done. The meeting would be a formality. I wrote a short speech about what a wonderful decision the mayor had made. I focused on reinforcing the other demands, in many ways much more important than the reward: the establishment of a task force and the acknowledgment of the possibility of crime and of a pattern.

As it turned out, I did not hear the police use the word "homicide" publicly until the fall of 2001, and they did not formally call a task force with regard to this case until 2002—four years after Sarah disappeared.

Even the reward seemed to be slipping away on the morning of the Police Board meeting, when I was informed that the mayor was now suggesting offering $5,000 rewards for each woman who called home instead of the larger sum for information leading to a conviction. When I approached the podium in the packed boardroom, I was angry. The room was lined with TV cameras, the eighty or so chairs were full, and more people stood against the wall at the back. This was my speech:

My name is Maggie de Vries. My sister, Sarah de Vries, is one of the twenty-three women currently missing from the Downtown Eastside of this city. I am very glad to be here today. I and many others have been bolstered and encouraged by the events of the last few days.

When I speak here today, I speak for others as well as myself. Many family members of the missing women are right here in this room and several who could not be here have asked that I represent them. I also would like to draw your attention to the petition that has been submitted by Michelle Pineault, Stephanie Lane's mother, and her friend. People from across the city have signed, well over 500 in all. And Michelle has spoken to me of people's eagerness to sign all over the city, to express their support, and of the lack of people who did not want to sign. Everyone wanted to sign.

Mayor Owen, when you agreed to recommend the offering of a reward you made a powerful statement. That's the $100,000 reward. You acknowledged the possibility of crime in the disappearances of the twenty-three women. And that's something that hasn't happened publicly, yet that I feel is very, very important, that there is public acknowledgment that crimes may and probably have been committed in at least some of these cases.

You showed us your own compassion and your recognition that these women could be anybody's sister, anybody's daughter and anybody's mother. And you stated that these women's lives are important, just as important as anyone else's.

In recommending the reward, the $100,000 reward, you also take a critical step in the investigation. I have been told many times that in crimes like these someone other than the perpetrator always knows something. The $100,000 reward will stand behind an appeal to the public for information. It adds an incentive for those who would not come forward otherwise.

The detectives on the missing persons cases, Lori Shenher

and Al Howlett, have been and continue to be dedicated and creative. However, in addition to the reward and the appeal for information, the Police Board now needs to establish a task force: a group of people to consider incoming information and to bring different perspectives to the investigation.

Finally, it has been pointed out to me that someone out there may know something but be terrified to come forward—a girl-friend of a murderer, for example. If someone fears for her life, the offer of money will not be an incentive. She needs to know she will be safe. I do not know what forms of protection the police are able to offer, but I believe that some sort of assurance is necessary.

Alone, then, the reward stands as a powerful symbol. In combination with other equally important steps, it may be instrumental in uncovering information that will lead to our finding out what has happened to our sisters, our daughters and our mothers. The reward is not the only thing that needs to be done here.

Over the last month I have been hearing concerns from the police and from the mayor about the wording of the reward and possible dangers involved in offering a reward under these circumstances.

I understand these concerns and am encouraged that the police do not want to do anything that could jeopardize lives or safety. At the same time, I remain confident that appropriate wording can be found.

I am not a legal expert, but it seems to me that if the reward were tied to a criminal conviction related to foul play in the disappearances of the women, then it would not be in anyone's interest to commit further crimes or to commit murder in the hopes of claiming the money. In my mind, the reward is not to aid only in finding the women, it is to aid in finding out what has happened to them and to aid in convict-ing the perpetrator or perpetrators. Offering only $5,000 for women who come forward does not serve the above purposes. We need to find out what has happened to the women and to convict the perpetrator or perpetrators. That is the purpose of the $100,000 reward.

In closing, I would like to invite all of you to attend the memorial for the missing women. It will take place two weeks from today, on Wednesday, May 12, which would have been my sister's thirtieth birthday. The service begins at 2:00 at First United Church at East Hastings and Gore. Afterwards we will walk together to CRAB Park at the foot of Main over the overpass. There, at approximately 3:30, a number of public figures will speak and we will dedicate a memorial park bench.

Mayor Owen, I would like to repeat my personal invitation to you to say a few words at the park. It would mean a great deal to all of us to hear your voice as Police Board chair on May 12.

Thank you.

Mayor Owen responded by explaining why he had come up with the idea of smaller rewards for each woman. "About the $5,000 figure—police have said there is no indication of crimes. Why don't we start with that until we find out that somebody is killing these women? . . . Until the police find out there's an organized effort to take these lives, we'd see if we could identify or find some of them— a third of them, half of them—maybe with $5,000 for any one of them that we could locate. Start with that." I do believe that he was genuine in his suggestion. He believed that it might bring more results than the bigger reward that assumed criminal activity.

To me, his idea demonstrates one of the key problems with the investigation. The police kept saying that there was no indication of crimes. The chair of the Police Board, the leader of the police, was unwilling to take a stand against the police position. More simply put, he believed them. The Attorney General was not willing to act without the support of the Vancouver Police Board and the Vancouver Police Board was unwilling to act without a clear indication from the police that crimes had been committed. The police repeatedly stated that they had no evidence of crimes (which was true). No one was taking leadership; no one was willing to say, in the face of that lack of evidence, that more than twenty missing women was sufficient evidence in and of itself that something was wrong. They were willing to let that number continue to climb, to take the chance that someone was murdering women and hiding all evidence. The police were not going to take real action until they found concrete evidence to justify that action, and the Police Board and the Attorney General were not going to challenge that approach.

So women continued to disappear through the rest of 1999, 2000 and 2001; even when the VPD and the RCMP joined forces to review the files, women continued to disappear, many of them women whose DNA has since been found on the Port Coquitlam property. Women could continue to disappear without much public awareness or public outcry because the women were considered lost to begin with. Their disappearances did not create fear in the rest of us. Most women in our society have never knowingly met a prostitute; the dangers that threaten women in sex work have nothing to do with them! The disappearance of my own sister and my certainty that she had been murdered did not make me fear for my own safety. I even felt safe walking around in her neighbourhood. I knew that whoever had killed her would not hurt me. Thus there was no public hysteria with the accompanying pressure on the police to make an arrest.

For the average person, I think, the dangers that threaten women in sex work are the stuff of drama and comedy, of movies, cop shows, jokes, even sitcoms. Several weeks ago, Roland and I watched an episode of *Frasier*, a show that I have loved for the quality of the writing and for the strong characters and performances. In this episode, Frasier's dad is trying to relax by studying an old case in which a "hooker" was killed and her body stuffed into some kind of bag. Memory tells me it was a golf bag, but I'm not sure. The dead woman provided a running gag throughout the show. It would never occur to the writers of *Frasier* to replace "hooker" with a derogatory term for a black or Asian person or for a woman and to derive humour from an account of her murder. That would make too many people flinch. A dead "hooker" does not. I hope that with time, that changes. Fifty years ago, those writers could have taken their pick of racist or sexist slurs; now their options are more limited. Many times in my life, people who knew that my sister worked in the sex trade have made jokes about prostitutes in front of me. Even since my sister disappeared and now that we are almost certain that she was murdered, people continue to say things that I wish they would not.

Not long after the search began on the Port Coquitlam property, a man approached my brother at work and asked him if he would like to join the poll. What poll? Peter asked. The poll to guess how many dead hookers they're going to dig up out there, the man replied. Peter walked away in horror, and someone else had to tell that man who Peter was and why he had been offended. But such a joke should be offensive to everyone, not only to people whose family members are buried out there. I think that the fact that most people are not offended by such jokes has a direct bearing on investigations into crimes against sex workers, in particular this investigation.

The police don't want predators killing women in any profession in any part of any city. They take their jobs seriously. Many of them work with women in the sex trade every day. Unlike most of us, they see how people on the Downtown Eastside struggle. But the police are part of society; each police department is a system within a large network of systems. Their priorities reflect society's priorities. It is dangerous for us to sit back, feel self-righteous and go on about how we hope an inquiry gets to the bottom of what went wrong. An inquiry is necessary, but so is a good deal of soul-searching and an evaluation of what is wrong with the whole network, not just with one system within it.

I have learned in the past few years that the Vancouver Police Department is rife with problems, probably most of them systemic, and that the whole system of policing in British Columbia needs attention. I have also learned that the VPD and RCMP are made up of human beings with minds and hearts and souls. Many of them come into regular contact with women in sex work and women who are addicted to drugs. Some police officers are worn out, jaded, even hateful and violent toward the people they are supposed to serve. Others care deeply and go on caring despite the abuse that is hurled at them and the hopelessness that they see every day. The police are a mix of people like any other, good and bad together, except that their jobs are tougher than many, their responsibilities greater. I don't think that we can slough off responsibility for what happened to Sarah and the other women onto the police. We need to take part of that responsibility onto our own shoulders.

In my response to Mayor Owen's comments, I said, "I am worried by the assumption that there are twenty-three completely unrelated circumstances and many of them have probably just gone off some-where and they would love to phone home to get $5,000 when they won't phone home to put all of our terrible pain to rest. My sister would not do that. And I've talked to thirteen of the twenty-three families. In most cases, I've talked to them many times. And the stories that I hear are all the same. At least ten or eleven of the fami-lies that I've spoken to feel exactly the same way that I do. They feel that their daughter or their sister is dead."

My sister would not have walked away. Most of the women would not have done that. Sarah's silence was scary for us. The silence of each woman was horrifying for her family. Taken together, the silence was deafening. I'm surprised that I didn't have to go around with my hands clamped over my ears. Women were dying. We knew it. We cried out for help.

The deputy police chief spoke at length after that, outlining what the police had done over the years to solve the missing women cases. He referred to an in-depth investigation that took place in 1991, but then went on to refer to outstanding homicides, making clear that that investigation was really into unsolved murder cases. He referred to delays in reporting women missing that interfered with investigation, not addressing the fact that, in several cases, family members had difficulty in getting the police to accept that their loved ones were missing, sometimes having to wait weeks or even months before the police would take their report.

He expressed concern that a reward would bring forth false tips. "In most situations where a reward is offered," he said, "a known describable crime has been committed, specific information and hold-back information is contained within the police files that assists them in filtering out tips that may come through as a result of the reward offered. Proper leads can then be followed up. In the cases of the missing women, there is nothing with which to measure this. There is no crime scene, suspect description, forensics or any other lead with which to filter out false information or misleading information. There are not enough specifics to test against. There's been an extensive amount of media coverage surrounding this issue to date. Neither the police department nor Crime Stoppers have received a single tip."

In fact, the police *had* received the tips that Wayne had passed on to them the previous summer. And Crime Stoppers had refused to run a piece on the missing women for exactly the reasons outlined by the deputy police chief for not offering a reward. Certainly I can see that it would be more difficult to deal with tips when the police had nothing to measure them against, but the attitude that they couldn't deal with new information without information already in hand seemed to me dangerously circular reasoning, especially in an investigation in which so little information had been forthcoming. While the police waited for a break that would prove to them that crimes had taken place, the list of the missing was growing longer.

One of the concerns that the deputy police chief raised about offering a reward was that it would bring forth misleading tips. "We may expend valuable investigation time looking at misleading information or following down the wrong path in that regard," he said. He then pointed to police officers all around the room and continued, "The missing persons section falls within the homicide unit of the VPD. In the homicide unit, we have twenty detectives that are available at any given time to the investigators in the missing persons section. We also have two strike-force teams that have been assisting in some of the investigative techniques that we've been using to date. It's important for the community to know and the families to know that those resources are available to Lori and Al and Dave at any time should they need them."

The challenge in this case was coming up with leads, with evidence in the absence of a crime scene. Rather than saying that all these people were available if and when they were needed, it would have been much more useful to make them available then and there, to devote people and resources to the case immediately to find that evidence. Instead, only very limited resources were applied to the case until the big break in early February 2002, at which point, suddenly, millions of dollars and more than a hundred officers did become available.

Detectives Shenher and Howlett needed help and support bringing information forward and developing it, not just following up once they had it. That support was not there, even after the Police Board meeting, except that Dave Dickson then joined their team.

After the deputy chief finished, the police chief said a few words. They were the words that I had been hoping to hear, but somehow, they did not make it fully into the public consciousness. "Some may indeed have been the victims of homicide." The police should have called a press conference, I think, and stated that publicly—something that did finally happen in July 1999, when the poster and reward were made public.

The discussion over, the chair put the motion to a vote, which was carried unanimously in favour of offering the reward. It felt like a triumph. I watch myself in CBC coverage of the meeting, and see myself break into a grin. Success! I did not take in, though, that none of our other demands was being addressed adequately.

After the Police Board meeting, I was invited to appear on CBC Television's *Midday*. The show was to be filmed live at Oppenheimer Park the following morning. Oppenheimer Park is a green space right at the centre of the Downtown Eastside. It covers a full city block and is lined with trees that were just leafing out that day. I had to be there early, at about 7:45 a.m. It was a glorious day: across Burrard Inlet mountaintops gleamed white, and the streets were lively for so early in the morning.

I waited in my car for a few minutes when I arrived, to collect myself and because I was a little early. The Broadcast One truck was parked opposite, and a couple of camera operators were waiting just the way I was. Farther down the street, at the corner of the park, a small group had gathered, men and women, around a bench. They appeared to be enjoying themselves, socializing. They were also clearly aware of an alien presence: the media.

I was particularly nervous about being interviewed because my interviewers were in Toronto. They were going to speak into a mini-speaker in my ear and I was going to speak into a microphone pinned to my sweater. They could see me, but I couldn't see them.

Finally, it was time to get out of the car. As soon as I did so, one of the camera operators approached. He ushered me over to a bench near their truck and they did their best to put me at ease. The minutes dragged by. The group on the corner grew louder, then quieter. They did not approach us. I sat down on a bench that faces the chain-link fence surrounding the park. A man wandering by stopped to chat. He told us that he had been "a good boy last night." He had been home early and had had a good night's sleep. His words explained the nearby gathering. The day before had been "Welfare Wednesday." The people at the corner were high, most likely on rice wine. The ground along the chain-link fence was littered with empty rice wine bottles. Rice wine is a cooking wine, sold in grocery stores, that is loaded with salt to make it undrinkable and therefore exempt from liquor laws. It is widely available on the Downtown Eastside and it is widely drunk, salt or no salt. It is poisonous as a beverage, destroying the kidneys and eventually killing the imbiber.

Seeing those bottles and their immediate effect on people on this glorious spring morning, while I waited in my flowing dress to appear on national television to talk about my sister's disappearance/murder and what we were pressuring the police to do about it, was incongruous, horrifying and perfectly appropriate.

I was right there, but I was so far away from there.

A man passed by on the other side of the fence and stopped to talk, friendly, high on something. Behind me a woman and a little girl walked past on the sidewalk, the girl, about six years old, dressed for school, sporting a pink backpack. How awful, I thought, that they have to pass the bottles from the night before and the people still carousing or already carousing again. But the woman and the girl reminded me as well that the area is home to many ordinary people who simply go about their lives. It is the Downtown Eastside community—diverse and, in many ways, vibrant.

The interview time drew near. The other woman to be interviewed arrived. We were stationed side by side, standing, angled unfortunately into the sun. Various wires were attached to us. A camera was aimed at us and we were instructed to look right into it. A man with a big white board stood to our right to reflect the light. A man in a Toronto studio spoke into my ear and told me what the first question would be. The next six minutes are something of a blur, trying to answer questions while squinting into the sun. I do remember that they asked questions that seemed to require me to criticize the police; several questions were leading, and I wasn't that pleased with how I handled them.

When I saw the show later I felt that it wasn't that bad. I appreciated the publicity. I was unsettled by what followed, though. There the hosts were in their Toronto studio, and, as required, they had to chat about what had just transpired. They talked about how dreadful it was that all these women had vanished without a trace, and how hard it must be for the families. Then the female host said that all you had to do was watch *Da Vinci's Inquest* and there was the story.

And she is right, in a way. That is why I have never watched *Da Vinci's Inquest*. Not because I don't want to watch shows about crime or about human misery, but because I don't want to watch entertainment that so closely mirrors my own experience. Still, I thought that it was inappropriate to compare these real events to a television show. Her comment made light of the disappearances, although that was not her intent.

Another experience with television media that spring and summer stands out for me. I was invited to appear on a national daytime talk show, one that I had never heard of. I would have forty minutes, though, which I thought would be good. It would be live, which meant that nothing I said would be edited away. I agreed. I had to go to a local studio for the interview, although, again, the host was in Ontario. When I got there, I told the receptionist who I was and she started chatting away about how dreadful it all was. There was a certain prurience to her tone that I didn't like, but that is very common. I think people assume that because I'm being public about this I don't have feelings about it, that my personal connection has lessened. They are wrong, but since good, kind people make that mistake all the time, I try to accept it, to answer questions as briefly as possible and just let it all slide on by.

Finally, the person who was responsible for me arrived and shepherded me into the newsroom, a huge room bustling with all the activity of getting the news out to the public several times each day. I assumed that we were going to pass through the newsroom to a small studio where I would have privacy. We did not. He led me to the back corner of the room where stood a platform, little bigger than a metre square. On the platform was a chair behind a low podium facing a monitor and camera. The man wired me up with a microphone and headphones, gave me a glass of water, told me to wait to hear the host's voice in my ear, and left. On the monitor I could see the show before mine wrapping up. Behind me was the bustle of the newsroom in high gear: phones ringing, people moving about and talking to one another. It dawned on me rapidly that I was going to have to stare into the camera, listen to a stranger's voice in my ear and carry on a focused and thoughtful conversation about my sister's murder for forty minutes while several dozen people went about their business in the same room.

Eventually the show began. I focused. I did it. I even found an opportunity to read aloud my sister's poem—a poem that resonates with particular force now that she is gone:

> *Woman's body found beaten beyond recognition.*
> *You sip your coffee*
> *Taking a drag of your smoke*
> *Turning the page*
> *Taking a bite of your toast*
> *Just another day*
> *Just another death*
> *Just one more thing you so easily forget*
> *You and your soft, sheltered life*
> *Just go on and on*
> *For nobody special from your world is gone*
> *Just another day*
> *Just another death*
> *Just another Hastings Street whore*
> *Sentenced to death*
> *The judge's gavel already fallen*
> *Sentence already passed*
> *But you*
> *You just sip your coffee*
> *Washing down your toast.*

> *She was a broken-down angel*
> *A child lost with no place*
> *A human being in disguise*
> *She touched my life*
> *She was somebody*
> *She was no whore*
> *She was somebody special*
> *Who just lost her way*
> *She was somebody fighting for life*
> *Trying to survive*
> *A lonely lost child who died*
> *In the night, all alone, scared*
> *Gasping for air.*

I was glad to have the chance to read Sarah's words, and I sensed that the room behind me grew a little quieter as I did so, but then the show continued.

Whenever there were breaks for ads, I was on my own. The host stopped speaking to me. The man who had gotten me set up seemed to be gone forever. And then the host would start in again. At last it was over. The set-up man reappeared as if by magic. I was unwired. The next guest, criminologist John Lowman from Simon Fraser University, mounted the platform, taking my hand as he passed me to express his sympathy. That was the only warm moment of the afternoon. With hardly a word, the set-up man led me back across the newsroom to a door onto the street. He opened the door and stood aside so I could step out. I stepped. He said goodbye. The door closed. I was done.

I walked to the car—which I had had to park several blocks away since the station had no guest parking that I could find—got in, and sat and wept for a solid ten minutes. It had been an inhuman experience. To them I had been a product, something to be used and then discarded.

One of the great challenges of the past five years has been managing the media, learning when to say yes and when to say no, and which criteria are important in choosing whom to speak to and when. I have tried not to let my emotional response to Sarah's disappearance, to her death, and to the sometimes thoughtless or cruel questions that are posed to me interfere. That day of the talk show taught me that I needed to make room in the process for me too, that my feelings do matter.

After that, it became a little easier to say no.

2002 February 7   Police start search of Port Coquitlam
property

February 22   Two murder charges; no names released

February 25   Names released; Sereena Abotsway
and Mona Wilson

April 2   Three murder charges: Jacquilene Michele McDonell,
Dianne Rock and Heather Bottomley

April 9   One murder charge: Andrea Joesbury

May 22   One murder charge: Brenda Wolfe

June 25   Helen Hallmark and Patricia Johnson identified
through DNA

July 25   The list grows from fifty-four to sixty-three

August 6   Sarah de Vries identified through DNA

September 29   Four murder charges: Helen Hallmark,
Georgina Papin, Jennifer Furminger
and Patricia Johnson

October 3   Four murder charges: Heather Chinnock,
Tanya Holyk, Sherry Irving
and Inga Hall

October 3   Angela Jardine identified through DNA

November 13   Marnie Frey identified through DNA

June 2003   Tiffany Louise Drew's DNA found

twelve

SEARCH AND ACCEPTANCE

March 2003

IT IS HARD to summon the energy to write about the past two years.

Since the spring of 2002, I have been writing as I go along: on the one hand, working on this book, and on the other, writing about my life as I am experiencing it. In this chapter those two hands come together. It has been a strange, layered process, writing about and learning about my sister's life while living through the weekly, even daily, developments in the case against Robert Pickton and the search on the Port Coquitlam property. At the same time, I have joined the board of PACE Society (Prostitution, Alternatives, Counselling and Education).

The current phase began in the spring of 2001, although I did not know it at the time. Detective Jim McNight of the Vancouver Police called to tell me that a review team had been formed made up of both VPD officers and members of the RCMP and that they were going to look at all the information again. I listened, responded politely, hung up and went on with my life. I've heard that before, I thought. I know just how much it means.

Early that summer, Lindsay Kines, Kim Bolan and Lori Culbert were sent out to look into the story for a series to run in *The Vancouver Sun*. For several months they investigated the missing women cases exclusively. The new review team and the addition of three more names to the list of missing women were the impetus behind that assignment. For six weeks they came up with nothing. Then they began to find police officers who would talk to them.

The new review team consisted of four officers, two each from the VPD and the RCMP. One of their tasks was to consider unsolved cases everywhere in B.C., trying to cast as wide a net as possible to be sure that they didn't miss the right suspect or other important information. They also went back methodically through all the files, all the information that had been gathered during all the years of the investigation. At the same time, women on the Downtown Eastside began to note more of a police presence and more interest from police.

What it seems they did not do was actively investigate new cases. While they were going back through old files, women continued to disappear: Andrea Joesbury in June, Sereena Abotsway in August, Dianne Rock in October and Mona Wilson in November. Robert Pickton is now charged with the murders of all four of those women. It seems like a serious oversight to put extra effort into going through old information but to continue to use exactly the same system—two investigators in the missing persons department— to investigate new cases.

The Vancouver Sun series ran daily from September 21 until September 27, 2001, followed by several more in-depth pieces over the next two months. And the paper gave the series prominence. Even though the *Sun* was devoting a great deal of space to the events of September 11, most of the missing women stories began on page 1, many of them above the fold. Each story was headed with the words "Special Report: Missing Women" in red ink. I could not read them at the time, but I was glad to see them. The articles explored the imminent adding of more names to the list of missing women, flaws in the investigation, parallels with the Bernardo investigation in Ontario, and other issues. Not much had been said in the media for the previous two full years. It is impossible to say what role, if any, that *Sun* series played in what transpired, but things did happen quickly from then on.

The Fifth Estate decided that they wanted to do a story on the missing women. Diane Ngui-Yen, the producer-director, came to my apartment on the morning of September 24. We spent four hours together. I pulled down all my dusty old stuff that had been sitting on the top of the bookshelf in the bedroom since we moved into this apartment at the end of July 1999. The episode was filmed in early November and aired on December 5, 2001. It was strange and confusing once more to go through everything that had happened, but, given what was to come, it was a good thing.

Police liaison workers called all family members to tell us that there was going to be a meeting on Sunday, October 14. Victims' Services, I thought. I don't need services. Sarah's the victim, not me. I went to the meeting, though, because I thought someone from Sarah's family needed to be there; Sarah needed to be represented. The meeting was hard. People had great anger to express and I didn't want to hear it. I sat, silent and hunched over, waiting for it to end. The next meeting was on November 25, 2001, at the RCMP head-quarters in Surrey (just outside of Vancouver), where all subsequent meetings have been held. Four more hours, also hard. I had no hope, so for me the meeting was just hashing over old pain—to no purpose, as far as I could tell.

On February 6, 2002, everything changed.

The police called family members. In my case the police officer spoke to Roland, who then phoned me in Victoria where I work three days every week. A search warrant had been issued against an unspecified property, he told me, and the police wanted the families to hear from them before we heard from the media. Again, I didn't take it too seriously. It's sure to be nothing, I thought, proceeding with my evening plans and going to sleep with no trouble.

As I was getting ready in the morning, I turned the radio on to CBC. A press conference had been called and they were going to interrupt regular programming to air it. I continued preparing for work, half an ear on the radio. The press conference started. It pre-empted the news. The police were searching a property in Port Coquitlam. What could this mean? Probably nothing, I told myself once again, and set out to walk the few blocks to the Orca Book Publishers offices where I work. When I got there my co-workers had heard the news. I stood in the doorway to their downstairs office. "We're worried about you," Maureen said. Yes well, I was sure it was nothing. Time would tell. I strung a few clichés together and turned to climb the stairs. "No!" Christine said emphatically, "come here." And I walked into their arms and burst into tears. I don't know how she knew how to do that, to break through my careful reserve, or how she knew how important it was that I have a moment of connection, of deep feeling, to acknowledge what was taking place. She did, though, and I thank her for it. I was able to get on with my day after that, although I was not all there.

I returned home to Vancouver early on Friday with Maureen, who had to come over for work. We went into the cafeteria at the ferry terminal. I hadn't seen the local papers yet. As we returned to the car, I had to walk between two rows of newspaper boxes. It was like walking a gauntlet. Every paper featured either Robert Pickton's face or the Port Coquitlam property with its heaps of debris, wrecked cars and a surfeit of signs warning people off. On the ferry, papers were strewn everywhere. All around me were people devouring the story while they sipped their coffee. It felt surreal.

I arrived home to a dozen or so messages from the press. I called CBC Television, and a reporter and cameraperson were at my apartment within an hour. I did an interview, still floating in an indefinable space. Afterward, I regretted talking with the media so quickly. I had not defined what I wanted to say or determined if I had anything of value to say in the first place. But talking in front of a camera was something that I could do and I think that I felt better while I was

doing it—more focused, less surreal. The next day, Roland drove me
to the site. The police had cordoned off Dominion Avenue, but they
directed us to the parking lot behind Home Depot, from which we
could walk down a muddy slope to the gate to the farm. I tried
unsuccessfully to fight back tears. Seeing those officers approach our
car, the road blocked, their solicitousness—it all pointed to something
actual, something true. We parked, made our way among the trucks
with various TV station names splashed across their sides, past the
media tent, among the gatherings of bored reporters waiting for
the next press conference, set for 3:00. No one bothered us as we
picked our way down the hill and stood and looked at what was
before us. I couldn't make meaning out of what I was looking at. I still
can't. I've been there a number of times now, but it's the media and
the police who make it as real as it can be for me. I could not make a
link between Sarah and those heaps of dirt, a car perched atop one of
them with an enormous boulder nested inside it. Even now, knowing
that her DNA has been found there, that link eludes me.

Roland and I went back up to the tent just in time for the press
conference, which I had decided to attend. I wanted to hear what the
liaison officers had to say. Their main sentiment stays with me from
that day, words that brought it all crashing home and gave me hope at
the same time. Whatever resources we need are being made available to
us, one officer said. And we will be here for as long as it takes and those
resources will continue to be available for as long as we need them.

Four years earlier, Jeanie had wanted to see the evidence that
people were looking for her mother. Well, we have the evidence now.
They are digging in the dirt, just like she wanted to do. And now
they know where to dig.

For me, and I suspect for many other families, the search that is
going on in Port Coquitlam makes a powerful statement. I cried when
I first saw the big wire fence around the property and the crowds of
media. I have cried at the sight of the officers in white coveralls searching; I cried when I heard that DNA from that site is being tested
across the country. The tears are shed because with each of these steps

forward Sarah's death becomes more tangible to me, but they are also shed because it moves me to see that hundreds of people across Canada are working day in and day out to find the remains of my sister and more than sixty other women who until recently hardly seemed to be worth the effort of mounting a search at all.

At the same time it is discouraging to see the vast mobilization of such resources to dig up dead women while the funds to help living women working in the sex trade have been cut. I believe that the police do need to keep digging on the property in Port Coquitlam and that the money needs to be available to allow them to do their job thoroughly and completely. It should be clear to everyone, however, that helping the living is more important than digging up the dead.

Still, I do not agree with those who say that enough charges have been laid, so the digging should stop. People see the great expense and they reason that fifteen murder charges are enough. And fifteen murder charges may well be enough to convict the perpetrator or perpetrators and to send him or them to jail for life. Then again, the police may find evidence as they continue searching that is more compelling or that links someone else to the murders. That is one reason to continue the search, but it is not the main reason.

If an elementary school burned down with sixty children inside, parents would want the search to continue until every child's body had been identified, regardless of whether any crime had been committed. In the case of the September 11, 2001, terrorist attacks on the World Trade Center towers, the search of the rubble continued until it was done. I think that people find it easier to say that the search should be abandoned in these cases because the women were sex workers. They don't realize that the fact that the police have found the remains of more than fifteen women provides little in the way of answers for the other forty-five families, all of whom wait every day for the fateful phone call or knock on the door.

BY THE TIME ROLAND AND I DROVE HOME from Port Coquitlam that day, I was overwhelmed. After the earlier press conference, I had walked out of the media tent and a reporter had approached me and asked if she could ask me a few questions. I agreed and was quickly swarmed. I stood in the midst of a crowd, many microphones held close, and answered the questions as best I could. When I was done, it turned out that several people had missed out, so I did it again. Then someone from Radio Canada asked me if he could interview me. I walked meekly with him to a more private spot and did a third interview.

One prominent TV reporter from Ontario told me that she regretted that her station had not done more on the story earlier. "We asked," she said. "We called the VPD and asked and they said there was no story. We believed them." The Vancouver Police Department stifled media coverage that might have helped to pressure them into doing a better job. And the media allowed itself to be stifled. However sensationalistic some of the coverage may be now, and however prurient many readers' and viewers' interest may be, I believe that that coverage is essential to the progress on this case, past, present and future.

In my journal on May 11, 2002, I wrote, "In the paper this morning a report about getting archaeology students involved along with retired police officers. In particular those who know about human bones and forensics. They are going to set up conveyor belts. Soil and debris will move along the belts and be examined by these employees." So matter-of-fact. I wrote down the facts with no comment. And little comment is needed. They were looking for bits of bone. All the speculation about how bones would end up in bits still does not play itself out fully in my mind. I keep telling myself that I will wait until I know for sure what happened. Then I will have only that one scenario to deal with rather than all the grisly possibilities.

I finished my writing that day with "Tomorrow would have been Sarah's thirty-third birthday. Mum put flowers in the church for Grandma and Sarah and they will all be wearing flowers. I like that." Three years had already passed since the memorial and more than four since Sarah disappeared.

That night I attended the Amnesty International banquet that concluded their AGM. A friend of mine was on the executive. After dinner Bryan Stephenson, a charismatic man from the Equal Justice Initiative of Alabama, spoke about capital punishment and about the state of American prisons. He said that the numbers in prison in the United States has climbed from 200,000 to 2 million in recent years. A large proportion of those people are there because of American drug laws. He said that once prisons are in place, whole systems grow up around them to support them. If they are not full, those systems suffer. It becomes in the best interest of a segment of society for the prisons to remain full. I was fascinated by what he had to say. I believe that putting people in jail for possession of small amounts of any kind of drug is wrong-headed, and that the "war on drugs" and its Canadian counterpart have made things worse, not better. I believe that drug addiction is a sickness, not a crime, and that people need choices about how to treat their own addictions. I also remain strongly opposed to capital punishment.

But at the banquet I could not help but reflect on the complexity of my position vis-à-vis the speaker, because when he was talking about people in prison for drug-related offences, he could have been talking about Sarah, but when he was talking about people on death row, he could have been talking about Sarah's murderer. Still, I am reassured when I contemplate that complexity and learn that my convictions regarding the death penalty hold true despite my personal experience. Were Sarah's murderer to be convicted, I think that I would feel relief along with a host of other emotions as yet unknown to me. Were he to be sentenced to die, I would feel sick. I feel sick at the thought of it. If the state killed the man who killed my sister, I would become party to killing. I want no part of that.

I would rather see the energy and resources that would be put into setting up the state to kill instead go into finding a way for women to work in the sex trade safely. For every murderer in a cell, dozens of violent men regularly seek out vulnerable women to beat, rape and even murder.

Two weeks after the Amnesty International dinner, Roland and I flew to Holland, our bicycles in tow. We got off the plane in Amsterdam, unpacked the bikes, put the pedals and handlebars back on, got into our rain gear and headed out. It was pouring rain and windy on the way into the city and, even though my father had given us excellent instructions, it took us a while to find our way. Nevertheless, it was healing. It was Roland's first trip back since his family moved to Canada when he was three, in 1957. As we cycled, we stopped periodically and asked passersby, "Amsterdam?" And they would point and we would carry on. Finally, we arrived at our hotel. The trip was begun.

AS OUR NINE-DAY CYCLING TRIP IN HOLLAND PROGRESSED, I thought less and less about the missing women, about Sarah or about my book. I rode along dikes, looking out at the ocean, through endless sand dunes, on narrow bike paths through farmers' fields, past calves and foals and lambs. We camped at night in campsites that were more like mini resorts than the North American clearings in the forest with firepits and outhouses a five-minute walk away. We cycled by the house where my father grew up, and by the apartment building where Roland's mother grew up, and we took pictures of the house where Roland lived as a baby. It was wonderful to have a real break like that.

Then, we returned to Amsterdam and spent an afternoon in the Red Light District. I had wanted to see what it was like and to see if it seemed to offer up any solutions that could be viable here in Canada. It was much less gaudy than I had expected. The windows where the women sit or stand are plain, identified by red lights above them. Women rent a window for a set amount and then are free to choose whom they do business with. They are safe from predators, and help is available if needed. Clear guidelines are set for potential customers. In the sex museum, a display about prostitution in Amsterdam explains how the system works.

Roland and I walked through the area again after dark, when the red lights were turned on and women were in many of the windows. The area was crowded then, men in the street actively trying to lure tourists into sex shows. "It's for couples, for couples," a man shouted after us as we walked by. I saw one man making a deal with a woman through the glass. He was writing a phantom figure on the window with his finger. That seemed straightforward enough. I was more uncomfortable with the prurient gawking of the crowds of tourists, of which, in a sense, I was one. I had the impression that Dutch men who visit prostitutes are probably more low-key about it than tourists for whom a visit to a prostitute is part of the whole foreign experience. And if those tourists are North American, they most likely bring the North American disgusted fascination to the whole thing. That was what I believed that I was seeing in their faces.

I found myself reflecting on an episode of *Oprah* that I had seen a few weeks earlier. Phil McGraw, the psychologist who now has his own talk show, was her guest. The topic was teen sexuality and the rise in oral sex among young teens, particularly girls performing oral sex on boys. I agreed with much of what Phil McGraw said, but I was disturbed when he voiced the opinion that it was not realistic to expect boys to turn down oral sex from girls, that it's got to be up to the girls to refuse. When he spoke to boys on the show, he used them to demonstrate to the girls what boys' attitudes really are, that they don't respect girls who perform oral sex on many different boys.

I thought that he passed up a good opportunity to talk about what men and boys can do to contribute to change. He could have talked about boys' responsibility to treat others with respect. Why not suggest that men teach boys that women, all women, deserve pleasure and respect and that women are dimensioned human beings? Why not suggest that men model those attitudes with their wives, mothers, sisters, daughters and co-workers? Phil is right that girls cannot wait around for boys to change their behaviour, that girls have to take responsibility for their own sexuality, but he seemed to me to let boys off the hook entirely.

I think that that is a very dangerous thing to do. It perpetuates the notion of girls and women as gatekeepers. Those girls and women who open the gate, so to speak, lose men's respect and become fair game in many men's minds for violence. Sex workers end up at the far end of that spectrum. Everybody, it seems, is allowed to disrespect sex workers.

Arguments have been made that prostitutes are women who take control of sex, who use it for their own gain. They trade sex for money and walk away without ties or responsibilities to the men who pay them. There is room for real power there for those women who are comfortable making that trade. But we do all we can to take that power away. We are uncomfortable setting things up in such a way that women can truly control their own bodies. The right to abortion has been hard won in Canada and is still being fought for in many other places. I think that the right to choice needs to extend to sex work. We've done away with back-street abortions by making it possible for all women to obtain safe abortions in hospitals or clinics. Dangerous street prostitution could be reduced by making the selling of sex indoors a legal and viable choice.

One of the things that needs to happen to bring that about, I think, is to start teaching boys and men that a woman who sells sex (or, equally, a girl who performs oral sex on boys) is no less worthy of respect than a woman who "saves herself" for her husband. And we need to create a system in which women in the sex trade are better able to choose to do business with those men who do view them with respect.

An interesting corollary here: criminologist John Lowman told me that studies on attitudes to prostitutes have shown that women as a group are the most prejudiced against sex workers, while the group with the most healthy, open-minded attitude toward women in the sex trade are men who buy sex.

John Lowman also told me that after the Berlin Wall fell, Holland saw an increase in prostitution as women came from Eastern Europe and then turned in desperation to prostitution. Amsterdam started having prostitutes on the street again. The city did not try to get those women out, as might have happened here in Canada. It did not try to drive those women into industrial areas where they would be out of sight, out of mind, as has happened here. Instead, it decided to look at both the short term and the long term. To keep the women safe and to contain prostitution in designated areas, Amsterdam created a parking lot for the purposes of prostitution. Men could drive in, park and buy sex from women. They could not drive the women away. Others were always around in case of trouble. It was not ideal, but it worked. Apparently such parking lots are still in operation.

I don't know whether that would be a viable option here, but it bears thinking about. It bears asking women who are currently selling sex on street corners whether that would work for them. It bears asking them what other alternatives they would like to see.

We flew home from Holland on June 10. The day before we left, Penguin Canada had agreed to publish this book. Now, I had to write it. Seven months I had. Anguish set in. On July 10, I wrote, "I'm into writing right now; the first chapter is begun. But I had no idea how hard it was going to be. Draining. Keeping me on the verge of tears. Invading my dreams."

At around the same time, I talked to Erin McGrath and Lynn Frey. Both were caught up in fundraising plans. Lynn was planning a Bingo Night and a forty-kilometre walk from Campbell River to Courtenay to raise money for treatment for drug-addicted women; the walk took place in early October.

Every small community has seen girls and women, boys and men too, drawn away to the big city, to drugs, to prostitution. The missing women come from all over British Columbia and beyond. Thousands upon thousands of us were their neighbours, friends, schoolmates. And right now, thousands upon thousands of us are looking for a way to give something back, to help the living in memory of the dead and in hope for the future.

I find that I am more motivated to make a difference now that Sarah is gone, without the complications of worrying about and trying to help an actual human being. I was not motivated when she was alive the way I am now. And I think that's true for many of us. It's much harder to help a flesh-and-blood family member than it is to write about memories, to theorize about possibilities, to raise money and to raise hope. It is easier to help strangers. It's more generic. If it doesn't work with one, perhaps it will with another, and in a brutal way it won't matter which. It seems to me that after a death people often have energy to give that they didn't have before. I try to tell myself that it doesn't matter. If I have energy to give, I'll give it. All that energy flowing out of sixty murders seems obscene—a link between evil and good.

THE MODEL THAT IS CURRENTLY BEING ADOPTED by the City of Vancouver for dealing with drug addiction is the four-pillar approach: prevention, harm reduction, enforcement and treatment. Of the four pillars, enforcement is the one that I am the least sure of. It has been the dominant pillar for so many years, to such limited effect, that I am leery of it. PACE emphasizes harm reduction, but one of the ways of reducing harm is to have good detox and follow-up treatment centres available on demand. The new municipal government is committed to having a safe injection site in place soon and also plans to try giving free heroin to those who are deeply entrenched in their addictions.

I'm not sure that a safe injection site would have been of use to Sarah, but free heroin might have helped. It would have freed her immediately from the cycle of drugs and survival sex. She would have been able to contemplate her choices without having to go out every two hours to get her next fix. And, given that she had to get into cars with strangers to make money for drugs and that it was almost certainly getting into a car with a stranger that led to her death, free heroin might well have saved her life.

The best option for one person is not always going to be the best option for the next person. And the best option for one person today may not be the best option for that same person next week or next month. It seems to me that whatever maximizes people's choices will give them the most opportunities to take control of their own lives and thus will give them ways to feel good about themselves and to create a future.

Prevention is important, of course; there is no better way to help people than to discourage them from running away from home or getting into drugs in the first place. Education is critical to that end. But, as I will discuss at greater length later, I am not convinced that fear tactics are effective.

ON JULY 20, 2002, several families of the missing women held the first fundraiser for treatment for addicted women—a dinner, dance and auction in an Italian restaurant right down the road from the Port Coquitlam property. Seventy-six people came. The place was packed. The mood was celebratory. I thought it strange at first to hold an event so close to the place where many of the women are known to have died, but it was wonderful to see the community response. It seems to me that people in the Port Coquitlam community were glad that we, the families, were willing to spend time there, that they had a chance to let us know how much they cared.

I went shoe shopping with a friend that afternoon and then we got extravagant and went for pedicures, bright pink for me. The pale-green nubuck sandals that I had bought set off the pink perfectly, especially with the grey silk-linen-blend summer pants I planned to wear. There I was, giving care and attention to myself right down to my toes in order to get together with other grieving families and have fun. It felt strange. I was a little unsure, but at the same time, I loved it. We were raising money for something good, something that might save other women from hardship and violence, and we were going to eat good food together and listen to Elvis tunes. Given the slightest opportunity, I planned to dance. And dance I did.

Later in the evening, I walked down Dominion Avenue to the Healing Tent pitched on a corner of a man's property opposite the property where the women's DNA has been found. Laurel Windover had attended the evening, and she and her husband and I walked down together. They had not been to the property before. They were shaken, I think. But as we entered the tent itself, the sense of peace overwhelmed us. It was a creative, loving, healing place. Every one of the missing women was represented there with a candle and a little tag bearing her name. Sewing machines and fabric for quilting covered one table. We all felt the calm, almost a spiritual presence, even as dark fell. The shrine outside the property gates was a moving sight as well: photos of many women, candles, a boxed-in bit of earth so that plants can grow. All of that has been created in order to remember the women with love in the face of such evil. I was struck also on that day by the police presence. A trailer right inside the gate glowed with light. Two officers were inside going about their business. For me they made the place seem less sinister.

As we walked back to the restaurant we ran into my brother Peter and his wife, Troy. They had never been to the property before either. Laurel and her husband went on their way and I turned around and walked back to the tent once more. It was good to spend a few moments there with my family. Until then, only Mum and I had visited the site. Both Peter and Troy wept.

Several days later, on July 25, the police announced that they were adding nine more names to the list of missing. That brought the list from fifty-four to sixty-three. Ten days after that, they told me that they had found Sarah's DNA at the site, an experience that I relate at the beginning of this book. It seemed as if I couldn't take a breath without a new development taking place. It still feels that way sometimes.

I finished teaching my course, worked on this book, went to work in Victoria for a week, and then Jeanie, then nearing twelve years old, came for her yearly visit. We had a wonderful time, especially the four days that we spent on Hornby Island with Uli, the husband of Amanda who died the same summer that Sarah disappeared, and her children. Three of them are adults now and the youngest is well into his teens. They are brown like Jeanie and their mother is dead like Jeanie's is. Jeanie remembers them a little from when she was small and she thinks they are wonderful. (She is right.) We spent our days on the beach in Big Tribune Bay, hours in the water, digging in the sand, finding sand dollars, eating ice cream cones, enjoying ourselves. It was good to be together.

WHILE JEANIE WAS IN VANCOUVER, she brought up a difficult topic. Mum did not want Jeanie or Ben to hear for the first time about the ways in which Sarah's body may have been disposed of, about pigs or wood-chippers or dismemberment, from other children, so she addressed the subject honestly with them when they asked her what had happened to Sarah's body. She believes, and I do too, that when children ask questions, they want true answers and will let the adult know through further questions how much they are able to absorb. She also believes, and she told them this, that our bodies are like our clothes; once we die, they become extraneous, so in a sense what happens to them is unimportant. She did not go on to say that the true horror lies in what happened to Sarah before she died.

Jeanie's words to me were "Grammy says that Sarah's body was chopped up and fed to pigs." The statement left me reeling. "No, she didn't," I replied. "She said that that was a possibility." We talked about it a little more, but since I couldn't assimilate that information myself, I don't think that I was as much help to Jeanie as I would want to be.

On Jeanie's last full day in Vancouver, I interviewed her for this book. It was hard to talk in such a formal way, with a tape deck running and me asking questions, rather than Jeanie bringing up what she wanted to. She buried her face in couch cushions and some of her answers seemed different from what she had said earlier. But she did bring up the pigs again and the machine that cuts up wood. She put both those in context, explaining that that's why they have to sift through the soil. And that's why Mum told her and Ben those things. Because they asked. Because they want to know why there are no bodies, why the police are turning over the soil looking for small things rather than for whole bodies.

Apparently Ben also asked why Sarah was out on the street in the middle of the night. I don't know what Mum said to that. She did not try to explain sex work to a six-year-old.

THAT FALL, a reporter from Radio Canada called me, Frédéric Zalac. He was making a documentary, he said, about the missing women. He reminded me that he had introduced himself to me three years ago at the Police Board meeting about the reward. Recently, while working on a documentary about AIDS on the Downtown Eastside, he had found some old footage shot late in 1997. He thought that Sarah was on the tape. Would I mind coming in and identifying her?

I was tense going there.

He came out to the CBC entrance and ushered me into his office. He was tall, gangly, solicitous. I vaguely remembered him from before. He asked me a few questions and rolled the tape. I watched anxiously. I wanted it to be her. I wanted to see her. But I was afraid of what I might see.

"Might that be her?" he asked as we both caught a glimpse of a woman in a cream-coloured jacket and a hat. I was too busy staring at the screen to answer. On the tape it was Christmastime and a group was performing seasonal music and giving out hot drinks. Sarah was walking along the street. There was no question.

It was her.

She was wearing strappy high heels and skin-tight pants with a zipper up the side, a fluffy light-coloured waist-length jacket and a hat like the police wear. The camera focused on her feet at one point. I'm not sure to what end, but I didn't like it. Then it focused on her face. Her hair and makeup looked great, but her jaw was slack, her eyes unfocused. She was high.

I don't know that much about heroin, and I do know that for someone as addicted as Sarah was, there are two states: high or sick. In other words, whenever I saw her, she was high; she hadn't gone into withdrawal yet. But she would seem like herself, more or less, slipping occasionally but present. It felt to me as if the woman on the screen, my sister, wasn't there. If I had gone up to speak to her, her words would have tripped over each other. I can hear her voice as I type. It would be distinctive and clear, articulate, but it would slur, tangle itself, from the drugs.

I did not like seeing her that way. I did not like sitting there with that man, witnessing for the first time the last recorded image of my sister weaving around in the street, dressed for work, slack-faced. That is not my last image of my sister. I saw her a few days after that footage was taken, on Christmas morning. And she went on living for another three and a half months after that, fully herself.

Ironically, that last moving image freezes her. I knew that CBC was going to include it in their documentary. They were going to call it the last image of Sarah de Vries, and I thought that viewers would think, oh, that's how she was before she died. She was out of it. They weren't going to see the time she spent preparing that day—bathing, selecting an outfit that stood out and worked together, getting her makeup just right. They weren't going to hear the conversations she had that day, animated, connected. They weren't going to feel the sorrow in her heart, the despair. They weren't going to read what she wrote in her journal during that time, her struggle and her ability to define it for herself and others.

I cried in Mr. Zalac's office when I asked him for a copy of the tape. That *was* Sarah—Sarah moving and breathing, caught behind glass, caught on strips of tape. Yet Sarah is gone. Her body, I presume, has been dismembered, taken apart. Even her bones may be ground to dust. When she is included in a documentary or a newspaper article, she is re-membered. Remembrance is a powerful act, but it must be done right.

When the documentary was aired I was relieved. It is concise and human. Sarah comes across as much more than the swaying, out-of-it woman I glimpsed on the bit of tape. I am glad for that.

ONE IMAGE OF SARAH REMAINS on the Downtown Eastside after all these years. A block west of Main Street in the window of a corner store, Wayne and I put up a poster in the summer of 1998. We went into the store and asked if we could tape it up in the window, facing out. Later, they moved a fridge in front of the poster, kindly leaving it in place. Now it is a permanent fixture, growing more faded as time passes. The barred window grows more begrimed as well. But I like it that the poster is still there. Whenever I drive by, I glance in its direction, still seeking the white rectangle. I don't know why it comforts me, but it does.

To me, it seemed like the perfect cover image for this book. On a September day, I drove my cousin, who is studying photography in her native England, downtown so that she could take the shot. The weather was perfect, but it was exhausting as always being down there. People spoke to us, wanting to know what we were photographing. In some cases I think that they wanted to be sure we weren't photographing them or other people, that we weren't doing something exploitative. In other cases they wanted to warn us about the danger of theft. I didn't feel in real danger, though. We were careful. My cousin's cameras are valuable. But I felt more protected by the people on the street than threatened by them.

Also while I was there I noticed many people walking by with cameras of their own, some of them tourists, I suspect, out to capture the gritty side of Vancouver. Others were journalists of various kinds, a constant stream of people translating a place where people live into images to share with the rest of the world—exactly what my cousin and I were doing. How tiresome, I thought, being treated like animals in a zoo, but worse. Most people who are subjected to the cameras are living in some degree of misery; it is that very misery that makes them interesting to others.

ON SATURDAY, OCTOBER 5, I walked the whole thirty-eight kilometres, all the way from Campbell River to Courtenay, on the walk organized by Lynn Frey to raise money for treatment. I had planned to walk only partway, but as I went farther and farther I realized that I could actually do it, or . . . maybe I could. It would mean so much more if I completed the walk, I thought, and kept taking step after step after step.

At 5:05 that morning Lynn had knocked on my door. Coffee was brewed, carrot muffins ready. I drank. I ate. And climbed into the back of the pickup truck to drive the few blocks to our departure location, where we were meeting the mayor.

The media were there at the starting point. We tied a ribbon between street signs on either side of the road leading out of the parking lot and lined up behind it. The mayor snipped the ribbon and we were off, headed for Courtenay along the Old Island Highway in the pitch dark.

We made good time and it felt great. The scenery was beautiful; by the ocean at first with the occasional heron, then through farm country and a series of small towns. We spotted horses, cows, sheep, geese, turkeys, llamas. We lost our accompanying pickup truck for an hour or so as the occupants went on a rescue mission with two Rottweiler puppies that had narrowly missed being hit by a car.

As the day progressed, more and more people honked and waved, or stopped to give us money or to ask us about ourselves and congratulate us on our efforts. Two reporters from local TV stations met us at several points to interview the increasingly exhausted Lynn. She, it turned out, had stayed up talking all night. Sleep had been out of the question. Her love for her daughter was driving her—that and her anger at the system that let her daughter die and allowed her daughter's fate to go undiscovered for five years. At one point she was weaving back and forth. I was afraid that she would step out in front of a car, but instead she led us to the finish line.

RECENTLY, I WATCHED A LOCAL TALK SHOW about restorative justice. I was not familiar with the term, although the concept is not new to me. Restorative justice, as I understand it, involves bringing together a criminal and his or her victim (where both parties are willing and thoroughly prepared), and having them talk to one another in a structured setting with a view to their understanding one another and arriving at a set of ideas for what the perpetrator could do to restore justice. One person in the discussion suggested using the term "transformative justice" as an alternative because, while it may be impossible to restore the status quo, both parties can be transformed.

That adjustment of language interests me. Charlotte Kasl, in *Many Roads, One Journey,* advocates the use of the word "uncover" rather than "recover" because recover implies returning to a prior state, which in many cases is not desirable.

The thing that I find most interesting about the idea of restorative justice is the way in which it acknowledges the connection between a person who commits a crime and the victim. When a crime is committed today, the law swoops in and separates the parties. In most instances they never speak a word to one another again. I think about the crime in my life. Sarah committed crimes. Yet she was a compassionate, thinking person. If she had had the opportunity to meet with her victim and hear from him or her about the effect of the crime, I could imagine that having had an impact. It would have been a much more meaningful exchange than the endless string of court appearances and stints in jail or prison. It is easy, I think, during the court and prison process, and through all the talk that goes on with fellow inmates and others who commit crimes, to convince oneself that certain types of crimes are victimless even when there was an identifiable victim. The person she mugged was wealthy or not a nice person or so stupid that he deserved it or . . . I am making these descriptions up, but I think that people tend to think that way, to convince themselves either that no one was hurt or that any hurt was deserved.

That is harder to do during a session where one has the opportunity to listen, to really listen, and where that is followed with concrete ways of healing the hurt.

But Sarah is not the only criminal in my life. The other one is the person who killed her. Restorative justice cannot be achieved between Sarah and her murderer because Sarah is dead. Someone asked me the other day if I had anything I would like to say to

Sarah's murderer. I said, no. And I cannot imagine anything I could say that would not somehow fail to encompass the enormity of what the murderer or murderers of Sarah and the other women have done. Yet Sarah's murderer's life is bonded to mine permanently. Much of what I have done and felt for the past five years is a direct result of his actions. I feel remote from him, yet watching the show made me question that remoteness, just a little.

Dad drew a parallel recently between what happened in the Auschwitz concentration camp in Germany and what he imagines took place on the Port Coquitlam property. And the person or people who perpetrated the suffering on that Dominion Avenue property are out there living and breathing, sitting in a cell or going on with their lives. My brain reaches out for the truth of that one small fact and cannot encompass it. I wonder if, when I finally attend the hearing or the trial, I will be able to make it any more true for myself. If I could speak words to Sarah's murderer, what would I say? I would have questions, I think, but he would not speak the truth to me— and where would the purpose lie in that?

IN LATE NOVEMBER 2002, I went on a retreat of sorts. Andrea Spalding, a writer I work with, offered me the use of a cabin on her property on Pender Island. The whole cabin was smaller than my office at home, perhaps two and a half metres square, with a sleeping loft above a desk, surrounded by trees overlooking the water. It was utterly peaceful. I worked there for two full days, the most productive, I think, of the whole project.

While I was there, I went to visit a woman who makes documentaries, Sharon Jinkerson. She showed me two films that she has made about adoption, one a forty-minute piece, not quite finished, about adoption out of First Nations communities, the other about a healing circle that took place after an adopted man committed suicide. I wept throughout both, wanting to sob openly but keeping myself under some sort of control. Here, I thought, was someone who knew so much from so many angles: a First Nations woman who was herself adopted by white parents, who sought out her birth mother when she was grown up, who is open emotionally, non-judgemental, not bitter. A woman who is filled with love and pain. I responded so powerfully to her that the afternoon became about my healing, not about my interviewing her about her work around adoption or in film. She did a smudging circle for me. She asked me questions, and she listened to me and mirrored what I said back so that I could consider and reconsider. I left Pender Island strengthened, centred and substantially further along in my work.

As I moved closer to my early January 2003 deadline, my emotions ran higher. And with the depth of feeling came opportunities for depth of insight. On November 30, I wrote, "I wonder how many of us are only one or two steps away from sticking a needle in our arms. More, perhaps, than we realize."

Those words were written because of an argument between Roland and me. Roland made a comment in passing, a mild one, he thought, but one that felt critical to me. I spun almost instantly into a rage. He was devaluing me, I thought, implying that everything that I do is worthless. I had to protect myself at all costs. I wanted either to annihilate him or isolate myself. The emotion was consuming and instantaneous. I do not know, even now, what I could have done to prevent it. I did realize within a few minutes that I was over-reacting. We talked about it and reached some sort of peace with each other. Still, those were a dangerous few minutes. I had spoken words that should never be said. I had been angry enough (almost) to walk out. And Roland was angry in response to my rage, of course.

He went out for the evening as planned, and I sank into some sort of despair, a place in which it was hard to live with myself, a place where I wanted to contemplate death, to contemplate deliberately sabotaging all the good things in my life. Somehow, after all these years, all the accomplishments of my life, all the love and friendship, the solid confidence in my work, the brisk efficiency at times, all the things that I have pieced together into an identity for myself can be peeled away in an instant, in one casual comment.

In the stark guilt- and grief-ridden world that I inhabited while I pieced together my sister's life, that sense of worthlessness had grown. It now lurked closer to the surface. The Maggie who earned her right to life through her accomplishments was paper thin, the Maggie who barely has the right to inhabit her body's worth of space threatened to take over.

Few words have become more trite in the past decade or two than "self-esteem." It pains me to write them, but I was coming to the place where I realized that I would not make progress in my life unless I got some. And I think that many of us are in that exact same place. Self-esteem is exactly what Sarah lacked too. Her problem, my problem, the key problem in so many lives, whether those of prostitutes or executives . . .

Generally speaking, my life is good. I am blessed with a loving husband, a comfortable home, a supportive family, a good education, a job that I love, friends and co-workers who are a joy to know, but I have some foundation building to do. It may be hard for most of us to look at a heroin addict and see ourselves, but if we look at our own addictive behaviour and honestly examine its source, many of us, I think, will find that the gap is narrow indeed. It is for me.

A GREAT GIFT I RECEIVED THROUGH WRITING this book has been the women who have come forward and shared stories with me about my sister. They knew her when I did not and they gave that knowledge to me. They shared their love for her with me.

Two weeks before Christmas 2002, I met Alex. She was a friend of Sarah's downtown in the eighties. Alex did not become a drug addict until the early nineties, many years after she had started working in the sex trade. She got off drugs and left sex work in 1999 when she went through rapid opiate detox.

I arrived at Alex's home a little early. Alex was in the shower, so I met her children first and was charmed by them. Then Alex swept out of the bathroom in an ankle-length white terry-cloth robe, her thick, dark hair twisted up into a bun. It took her only a minute or two to dress and she was back, sitting beside me on the couch, taking her baby, whom I had been holding, into her arms and turning her attention full to me.

I was deeply affected by her beauty, her radiance. We talked for three hours, the conversation meandering. I turned into a sponge, soaking up all she had to say about Sarah and about her own life and her journey away from the Downtown Eastside.

It was dark when I left to make my way onto the freeway and drive home. Christmas lights were up. Almost immediately, I found myself in tears, trying to make sense of the depth of my emotions. Then it hit me. Alex could have been Sarah. Alex worked the streets for sixteen years, two years longer than Sarah did; her drug habit when she detoxed was roughly equivalent to Sarah's. She was adopted at six months, Sarah at eleven. And Alex is beautiful and bright and warm and is living the life she chooses.

What if I could drive to a little house far from the Downtown Eastside and visit my sister and find her happy, living the life she chose for herself? If Alex could do it, Sarah could have too. Who can say when the right moment might have come?

So many of the women that I have interviewed are the same in that they have made it out, and they are gifted and beautiful and generous and intelligent. But that day, on the way home from a little house not entirely unlike Sarah's house except surrounded by green and all fixed up, the loss was particularly keen. I could imagine Sarah sweeping out of that bathroom in an ankle-length terry-cloth robe, her thick hair wound up into a bun. I could imagine her throwing on some clothes and sinking onto the couch next to me. The more I learn, the greater my loss. With what I've learned I could relate to my sister so much more deeply today, even if she didn't change a thing about her life, but irony is a terrible thing: I've learned what I have only because she is gone.

It feels as if we are on parallel journeys, Sarah and I, but her journey (which of course isn't really her journey, because it's happening inside my head) is happening too late for her. I can't tell her how much better I understand her life. I can't tell her how proud I am of her, how much

I admire her. I can't ask her questions or read what she is writing in her journal today (if she would allow me to) because she is not writing in a journal today. She is (I think) chopped up into little pieces in the dirt.

But as I journey, I want to talk with her about it. I want to ask her the questions that I'm asking everyone else. Why am I interviewing them and not her? Why am I coming to this only when she's dead? If only I could have really, truly opened my heart to her when she was alive, so much could have happened, for both of us.

I could have accepted her as she was and opened up to her more about who I was. I am learning just how much we had in common. I know that we all learn things in our own way, in our own time, and often too late. That is the way life works. In my experience, the deaths of loved ones hold out enormous opportunities for growth in those who survive, but always, of course, too late for that growth to inform the relationship with the loved one who is gone. All we can do is move on and apply what we have learned to the living.

But how can I let writing this book (and learning what I have in the process) move me forward in my life, when it all comes at the expense of my sister's death? When I raise that question, people try to brush it aside, but it is fundamental for me and unanswerable. I will let writing this book and learning what I'm learning move me forward in my life—I will have more to offer others if I do—but I wish that it all could have been different.

On January 13, 2003, Robert Pickton's preliminary hearing began. My brother Peter and I attended the first morning. We had agreed ahead of time that we would leave at lunchtime unless one of us had a strong desire to stay. The front two rows in the courtroom were filled with reporters, many of whom will attend the whole hearing faithfully even though a publication ban prohibits them from printing anything substantial about what goes on in that court. I'm glad they are there, that all that information is being collected, even though I dread reading and hearing it in the future when the ban is lifted.

Robert Pickton sat in a glassed-in area in the front corner of the room. I felt nothing when I looked at him. He seemed like such a small, insignificant person, sitting silent behind glass while the morning wore on. Part of my reason for attending was to be in the same room with him, to see what my feelings would be, but I had no feelings. I was relieved that nothing was said that morning that will disturb my dreams. Peter and I left at noon. We had done what we set out to do.

SARAH AND CHARLIE'S HOUSE was all boarded up the last time I stopped by. Charlie doesn't live there any more, although I hear that he still lives on the Downtown Eastside. Jeanie hasn't seen him since that visit back in '98. The roof of the house sags. The garden is all but gone. A few straggly vines grow up the wire fencing between the house and its matching neighbour. A rose bush still grows there and a small plant nestles in the dirty corner between the house and the front step. It bore a single yellow flower the day I was there. I am thankful for that house because it brought me closer to my sister, it gave her a room of her own, and it gave Charlie a bit of earth.

THE OTHER DAY, Ben asked Mum why Sarah didn't have a grave.

Someday, when we are ready, we will gather in Guelph, in Chalmers Church where members of my family have worshipped for more than a hundred years, and we will remember Sarah together. We will place something of Sarah's in the family plot at the Guelph cemetery, where Mum and Aunt Jean will eventually join her. There, Sarah will rest, away from murderers, investigations, media hype and gruesome stories.

In my heart, she rests already.

EPILOGUE

April 2008

It is almost five years since *Missing Sarah* was first published, and now I have been asked to write a new Epilogue to bring it up to date.

Much of the time since this book was first published has been taken up with the court case. The preliminary hearing filled the first half of 2003. The search of the Pickton property on Dominion Road lasted until November 2003, and the testing of thousands of exhibits seized from the property continued long after that, through 2004. In 2005, twelve new murder charges were added against Robert Pickton, including a charge in Sarah's case. Two thousand and six was taken up with the voir dire, during which decisions were made about what evidence would be allowed during the trial. At the conclusion of the voir dire, the judge split the charges, and Robert Pickton went to trial on only six charges, reserving the other twenty (including Sarah's) for a second trial. That first trial lasted through almost all of 2007.

Wally Oppel, the attorney general of British Columbia, has now informed us that there will be no second trial unless Pickton wins his appeal, which is scheduled to begin on March 30, 2009. So we wait. As soon as all appeals and trials are over, I hope that a public inquiry will be held to determine what went wrong with the investigation into the disappearances leading to such terrible delays and so many unnecessary deaths. For me, the trial was necessary, but the inquiry almost more so, as it holds within it the potential for real change.

After attending that first half-day of the preliminary hearing with my brother in January 2003, I did not set foot in a courtroom again until November 2007. All the preparation for the trial and most of the trial itself took place on the periphery of my life. I continued my work as a children's book editor and a writer for children, and wrote several pieces for adults as well. Last year, I stepped back from editing, and now I am writing and speaking full-time with a little teaching thrown in for good measure.

From 2002 on, I grew more and more involved in my sister's community. My work on the PACE board became a central part of my life. Not long after this book came out in the summer of 2003, I dropped by the PACE offices with a copy. Several members were present, one in particular whom I had met a few times. I will call her Diane. She's strong and outspoken, and I confess that at first I was a little frightened of her, although she never gave me a reason to be. She asked to look at *Missing Sarah*, and that was the last I saw of the book for a while. I needed it back as it was still my only copy. Each time I approached her, she looked up and grinned. "I'm on page twelve," she said. And a little later, "I'm on page thirty." Then she disappeared entirely, and I found her on the roof of the adjoining building reading her way more and more deeply into my sister's story. I gathered my nerve and asked for the book back. She handed it to me gamely enough, but I could tell that she was frustrated at having to wait to read the rest.

That experience made me more deeply determined to find a way to get copies of *Missing Sarah* into the hands of women from Sarah's community. A book club turned out to be the perfect vehicle. A group of us started Beyond Words, a book club for Downtown Eastside women that ran for three and a half years.

Our first book was *Missing Sarah*, and Penguin generously donated 140 copies, which were absorbed into the community in no time at all. About thirty women gathered for our first meeting, and almost all of them carried the book. When I entered, women were snacking on donated food, drinking coffee and talking, settling into the space, but they paused to welcome me. I recognized many of the faces, but far from all. My hands shook as I took my seat and pulled my battered copy of *Missing Sarah* from my bag.

I was struck by the generosity of the women in the room, their care for others' comfort as woman after woman shared a bit of her story with me, with all of us. Some of them had known Sarah. They shared their memories. Some told about what parts of Sarah's story they found most compelling, most like their own. Some responded to me, to my story, to my connection, however difficult, with my sister. They thought about their own family members, wondered if they should call. One woman gave me a bookmark made from beads. I tried to respond openly and honestly to each woman, to keep my heart wide and to take in what all of this meant, the connectedness that I was experiencing that I had never felt when Sarah was alive.

During a lull, the woman beside me, who had not spoken in front of the group, leaned over and whispered that this was the first whole book that she had ever read. She just kept going, she said, reading and reading. I smiled and met her eyes and listened; I didn't know any other way to let her know what that meant to me.

To me, the book club was important because it put books in the hands of women who wanted them, something like two thousand volumes and twenty-five titles, and it created the opportunity for women to come together around literature, to build a common ground apart from the content of their daily lives. In the end, it turned out that our meetings, while important, were the least significant part of Beyond Words. Its greatest impact was felt out in the community in each woman's experience with each book and in the interaction among women around the books. Often the books we read for Beyond Words were the same titles that I read in my other book club. We read *A Fine Balance* by Rohinton Mistry, *Fall on Your*

Knees by Anne Marie MacDonald and *Breath, Eyes, Memory* by Edwidge Danticat, among many others.

For years now, I have spoken about Sarah at book clubs and conferences, at high schools and women's clubs. I've talked about Sarah's life and how we can change our thinking, our behaviour and our laws to allow women like my sister to live with dignity. When I talk about her, I keep Sarah's spirit close—I wear the earrings she gave me. I read her poems, her letters and her journal entries aloud to audiences; it is almost as if she speaks through my mouth. I bring a large photo, my favourite, in which she grins broadly, glowing with beauty and love of life, and I ask people to look at her instead of me while I read her writing. Some do. Others close their eyes.

Despite the fact that I feel as if Sarah speaks through me when I read her words, I recognize that it is I, not she, who is actually present. I have felt guilt, I think, for being me, not her. I used to think that I was standing in for Sarah, that I was doing the work that she could have done (better than I) if she had lived. I no longer believe that. If Sarah had lived, she would have done her own work. I don't know what she would have done, but whatever it would have been, it would have been her journey. I am on my own journey. I am not standing in for my sister. I am living my own life in the way that means the most to me.

Missing Sarah is a collaboration between two sisters, one living and one dead. I am starting to see that it is helping women (and men) bridge the chasms between themselves and others. Women are recognizing that perhaps the connection matters despite the pain, despite the messiness of relationships, despite all our many imperfections. My sister wanted to see me even though it hurt. And I wanted to see her, even though I didn't, even though I put it off, even though I sat in her living room mute, and many of the words that I managed to speak felt hollow, untrue.

When I speak publicly, I am able to inhabit my relationship with Sarah fully, to honour her with each word, and reach deep inside myself to ensure that what I say is true. Each time I am drained, but

I receive something precious all the same. I receive Sarah back again, Sarah at her strongest and most loving.

UNTIL RECENTLY, even though I talked about Sarah extensively and embraced every opportunity to meet someone who knew her or to hear another anecdote about her life, I kept myself as far away as I could from the circumstances of her death. I can see now that right from the beginning I was trying instinctively to protect myself. When Victims Services first contacted me several years ago, I was mortified. I didn't want to hear from them. I was not a victim, I thought. Sarah was the victim. I still feel a twist in my stomach if someone uses the word "victim" in reference to me.

When I speak to an audience, someone often asks me about my anger. Where is it? they want to know. Over and over again, I have told groups calmly that I cannot feel it, that I think it's too big to feel, that I would not be able to bear it. I also used to say that I did not plan to attend Robert Pickton's trial, read the reports in the newspapers or watch the clips on TV that would describe what was discovered on the Port Coquitlam property. "I don't want those images in my head," I would say. And I would move on, calm and cool and in control.

Or I would try to.

Then, in the fall of 2004, I spoke to a group at the library in Port Coquitlam, just a short walk from where my sister died. As I addressed the audience, I was calm enough, but an elderly woman with a long braid wrapped around her head was not. She was seething with her own rage when she asked me about mine. When I said that I didn't want to know the horrors of my sister's death, she cried out, "The truth will set you free!" and glared at me. She went on to say that we need to face up to the fact that the world is a sewer. I did not take her seriously, not at the time. I had seen her before at another event, witnessed her anger, her seeming irrationality. She was a person to be "dealt with," not listened to. And to me the world is not a sewer.

In the weeks that followed my encounter with the braided lady, though, her words rang inside my head and whispered in my ears. The trial is coming, I thought to myself, and suddenly the idea of keeping at bay all the gruesome details that would be revealed in that courtroom made me tired. I wasn't going to be able to do it, I realized. I was going to try really, really hard, and I was going to fail. I remember the Bernardo case, when I tried not to know, not to take in what was being reported. I didn't succeed then, and I wasn't going to succeed now.

I decided I could not bear the prospect of waiting for the trial to learn along with the rest of the world how my sister died. I began to realize that such deliberate ignorance was exacting a cost. I was using enormous energy trying to keep at bay knowledge related to her death, but really I did know. I was not keeping it at bay; I was keeping it buried. I now understand that I had taken the bits of news that had been reported over the years, along with all the thoughts and feelings they evoked, and packed them away in a deep, dark place within me. Along with that was my anger at Sarah's murderer or murderers, any anger I might feel toward Sarah herself and all my grief about the manner of her death, all the horror of not having her body, of not knowing for more than four years what had happened to her.

I decided that I needed to lift the lid and look inside. I wanted to feel my anger and my grief. I went to see my therapist, who told me that the only way to the other side of all that pain was through it. There was no other way past. I could either live my whole life on the one side, using much of my energy to keep pain locked in and locked out, contorting and hardening myself to avoid feelings and thoughts that I didn't want to have, or I could let myself learn and feel in a supported way.

That was the key. The support. The talk.

My therapist, who is trained in helping people deal with vicarious trauma, led me to an understanding of how to approach what I had kept at bay for so long. She told me that I needed to speak the terrible thoughts in my head, to speak them to someone who could reflect back to me what I was saying, someone who would not try to take away my pain, to diminish what I was saying, but who would be able to stay with me. That someone has been Roland, my husband.

I decided that I wanted to learn ahead of time what was going to be revealed at the trial, to prepare myself, and I approached a journalist to help me. He had attended the preliminary hearing. I asked him to share with me what he had learned. At first, I thought I would ask him to give me written material, but my therapist warned against it. The learning needed to be shared, she cautioned: spoken and heard in the same moment, talked about. So I arranged to meet with him. We were both afraid. He didn't want to hurt me, and I didn't know what he would say, how it would feel. But I trusted him, and I trusted the process. Piece by piece he told me what he knew. Piece by piece I repeated it back to him and recorded it in my journal. I asked him questions, hypothesized about what the bits of information might mean. They were gruesome, explicit, and the implications were monstrous, but the two of us kept on going together until we were done.

After our meeting, I had a few hours to myself before Roland came home. I took a break, as my therapist had suggested, and then wrote about what had happened. I also wrote a letter to my sister—not recognizing that, once again, I was bringing her to life for me. I felt relief, exhilaration. I had done what I had feared for so long and survived. And really, hadn't I known all along most of what the journalist had told me? Hadn't I, at some level, been working on assimilating this information for seven years? Now I had taken the last step—I thought.

When Roland came home, I told him all that had happened, told him of my sense of relief, of completion. And really, I said, whatever happened to Sarah's body after she was dead has more to do with her murderer than with her or with us. I went to bed and slept soundly that night, no nightmares lurking anywhere near.

The next day I went to see my therapist. I still felt jubilant. I opened my journal and told her everything, explaining why I felt it would not be that difficult for me to move on. It took her all of three minutes to return me to reality, to have me sobbing in my chair. And I realized that I had been trying to protect myself, to do once again what I had been doing for seven years—pack away the horror of Sarah's death, keep from facing it fully by focusing on her life.

That night Roland rented the movie *Troy*. It is not the best movie that I have ever seen, but we both found the story compelling. Toward the end, Achilles, in an act of grand vengeance, comes to the gates of Troy to engage Hector in single combat. Achilles triumphs, killing Hector. He then ties a rope around Hector's ankles and drags Hector's body behind his chariot back to the Greek camp. Under cover of darkness, the Trojan king slips into Achilles' tent. "Please," he begs, "return my son's body to me." At that moment I began to weep. By the time the movie was over, half an hour later, I was sobbing openly.

When I saw the Trojan king beg for his son's body, I recognized for the first time the extent of my own loss. I understood that when Sarah's murderer killed her, he committed a heinous act against us, against everyone who loved her. And when he disposed of her body in such a way that we would never see it, never be able to confirm her death through her body, and never be able to bury her or scatter her ashes or place an urn containing her ashes in our family plot, he committed another heinous act. He dishonoured her *and* took something infinitely precious from us.

For seven years, I had tried to convince myself that what happens to a body after a person is dead does not matter. Now I know that it does. Now I can no longer separate Sarah's murder or her murderer from myself.

EVEN AFTER ALL THAT WORK, I did not attend the trial, at least not at first. As planned, I read all the newspaper reports at the beginning, but eventually I stopped doing that as well. It wasn't that I didn't want to know what the articles said, it was that I didn't like the casual nature of reading them. I didn't like sitting on my couch with my coffee, turning the page of the paper and finding myself face to face with a headline, or driving somewhere, listening to the CBC, and hearing something on the news. It didn't feel like the correct way to learn what was happening in the trial. So Roland started clipping all the articles and putting them in a file so I would not happen upon them when I came to read the paper. And, though I had not planned to, I decided to attend the closing arguments and the judge's instructions to the jury. A courtroom, I realized, was the appropriate place to hear what I had avoided all those months. The setting had the necessary formality, and being there with others who also cared deeply was good. My mother, my niece, Jeanie, then almost seventeen, and my brothers attended parts of the ten-day procedure.

Those were hard days. I told myself that I was going there to bear witness, simply to see what this trial was. I did not go to see the truth spoken, because I had no faith that the truth would be spoken. I did not go to see justice done, because I knew I could not count on that. But I could see and I could hear. I could be present with the other family members and friends who were there.

The defense gave their closing arguments first, and for several days everything unravelled around me as they pulled apart any case against the accused. They were doing their job, and they were doing it well. But to me it felt like an attempt to disperse responsibility rather than to discover where responsibility lay. And it began to feel as if the case against Robert Pickton had no substance, none at all. At the same time, their closing arguments contained information I did not yet know about the remains, about guns and other things that had been found on the property, things that pointed to depravity that, despite my preparations, I was ill-equipped to contemplate.

Then the Crown began its closing arguments, and things swung into some sort of balance. And on the first Friday afternoon, everything changed for me when they played clips of the interrogation of the accused. The defense had said that the interrogation went on for too long, that Pickton was exhausted, that he was just parroting back to the police officers what had been said to him. They had gone to great lengths to establish his intellectual weakness to support this position. But there he was on the tape. He did not appear tired or frightened or particularly lacking in intelligence. He looked relaxed. He put his feet up on the table. He bragged. And he implied that he only needed to kill one more woman to reach his goal of fifty victims.

My intention had been to bear witness. I had not expected truth. And I had felt that they might be trying a scapegoat, that while Robert Pickton surely bore some responsibility, he might be only an accomplice, not the mastermind. I came away that Friday with a completely different point of view. I don't know whether or not that man acted alone. I don't know who else knew of the murders, who else bears responsibility along with him. But I now feel sure that he is guilty of multiple murders and that he is guilty of the murder of my sister, even though he may never go to trial for that crime.

Though some questions remain, I now believe that one murderer is in prison, and I came away from the trial with the surprising feeling that, yes, I had seen some measure of justice done.

The other part of those two weeks was the bombardment with horror. I mentioned depravity. Despite all the work that I have done, it seems to me that hearing what I heard should have some effect, some effect that shows. Viewers should start blithering or bleeding, speaking in tongues. In the middle of one particularly difficult morning, a poem wrote itself in my head. It is a harsh poem. Dreadful. But I share it with you here:

A Sane Woman Imagines Madness

Sanity is elastic.
It stretches,
Contains jawbones;
Bisected skulls;
Blowflies.

A sister long dead,
Her death and its aftermath
Rising before me:
A bullet to the skull;
Sawblades;
A twist of a wrist,
An ankle,
And bones:
Where are her bones?

All of her gone.
But ghosted
In other women's remains.
In this courtroom
On that screen
From a judge, word by word.

I should be screaming
Wailing
Crawling into a corner
Rocking back and forth
Knees to forehead.

Instead I gaze at my own hands
My feet
I stroke my jawbone.
I am here.
Whole.
Sane.

IT IS STRANGE to think that the very devastation Robert Pickton has wrought, the horrors that I learned about in that courtroom, connect him to me forever. He is guilty of acts that I cannot comprehend, and he has changed my family in indescribable ways. Yet, weeks after the trial was over, with the sentence handed down, I had my first glimmer of Robert Pickton as a human being, which, of course, he is, despite all that he has done.

The shift came about because of kittens.

I read about men in an American prison—murderers, rapists, predators—receiving kittens and falling in love with them. The small creatures brought out a tenderness in those hardened criminals, a humanness. I was moved by that.

Immediately I thought about the murderer in my life. I wondered how I would feel about his being given a kitten and I found that I liked the idea, assuming he would not harm the animal. Part of me was horrified at myself, but another part was glad to feel that moment of warmth, of willingness for Robert Pickton to experience a connection to another living being.

It doesn't mean that I believe that he can be rehabilitated, or that I would ever want him released from prison. But for years I felt cold and empty when I thought about him. More recently, when I sat in the courtroom, only an arm's length and two layers of bulletproof glass separating him from me, I felt nothing. Then, when I saw him on the interrogation tape I felt stirrings of a kind of anger, and the dawning of certainty in terms of his guilt.

The image of the kitten in his arms has helped to return me to myself, to the person who believes that all humans, all living things, are connected and that if we deny the humanity in others, however evil their actions, we deny the humanity in ourselves and cripple ourselves spiritually.

CHARLIE IS DEAD NOW. And so is Char. The house on Princess Avenue has been torn down. The poster of Sarah you see on this book's cover is gone from the shop window on Hastings Street. The healing tent has long gone from Dominion Road in Port Coquitlam. I have resigned from the PACE board. The book club is no more. And while I was writing this Epilogue, the tenth anniversary of Sarah's death came and went.

But the bonds that I formed over the years, many of those are still in place. Women call or send me emails. Jacquie and I meet for tea when she is in town. I still hear about what PACE is up to and support them in small ways.

And Jeanie and Ben are growing up. Jeanie is seventeen now. She will play Puck in an upcoming production of *A Midsummer Night's Dream*. She swims and she sings and she searches, as all seventeen-year-olds must, for her direction in life, or at least the next bit of it. Ben is twelve. He loves his new skateboard and goes to dances on Saturday nights and spends a lot of time on the trampoline. He is fascinated by science and a master at friendship.

Twice, first in Prince George, then in Kamloops, I have attended the opening of an art show called *A Roomful of Missing Women* by Betty Kovacic. Several years ago, Betty felt called to paint portraits of all the missing women. At that time there were fifty on the list. The portraits are beautiful and each is unique. They are framed in elaborate gold frames. And they hang together around the walls of each gallery, gazing out into the room at viewers and at fifty figures shrouded in black fabric that float above the floor wearing banners that proclaim in gold letters, "When I grow up I...," spelling out the dreams of girls in many languages.

I have faced Sarah's death, yet I still feel her with me when I read her words. She is present in my life in so many ways. But I know what happened to her and I am not afraid. How powerful it is in the face of such knowledge to enter a room where Sarah stands with forty-nine other women, also lost to us! The extent of our loss hits home in that room full of missing women, but paradoxically, our pain is lightened by their presence.

They are together there. They are beautiful. And we are with them.

(Parts of this Epilogue have previously appeared in *Chatelaine, Readers' Digest* and *Dropped Threads 3: Beyond the Small Circle*.)

ACKNOWLEDGMENTS

MANY PEOPLE'S GENEROSITY played a part in creating this book.

When I decided to write about Sarah, I had no idea that, in the process, I was going to learn so much about her life. Every memory that someone has shared has been a gift to me and to my family as well as a contribution to these pages.

Angela*, a woman who lived with Sarah in a series of hotels and apartments downtown, invited me into her life and shared her memories despite the pain that those raised for her.

Jackie, who last saw Sarah in March 1998, approached me in a park during a fundraiser, said, "Are you the one who's writing a book about Sarah?" and shared her memories with me.

Mindy, Sarah's childhood friend, shared memories that helped to explain the pull that Sarah felt toward downtown.

Char Lafontaine, outreach worker at PACE Society, www.pace-society.ca, worked in the Hastings Street sex trade and was a heroin addict through the seventies and eighties. She took me with her on an outreach shift, shared her own story with me and read the manuscript when it was done. Char battled cancer of the esophagus and died in December 2007.

Char introduced me to Alex, who knew Sarah when they were both teenagers, both runaways, and who gave me a glimpse of what Sarah's life might have been had she survived.

Susan sent a card to me by way of the Downtown Eastside Women's Centre, telling me that she had known and been touched by Sarah. She was so affected by Sarah's disappearance that she took a job as a chambermaid in a small town, scraped together bus fare and detoxed cold turkey while keeping her addiction a secret. She spoke to me several times, sharing stories about my sister. She has now been clean for four years.

Wayne Leng took the time to travel to Vancouver from California to spend several days with me, driving to key sites and sharing his memories.

Ken Craig shared his memories of Sarah with me and has passed on several keepsakes to Sarah's children. I learned recently that Ken has died.

Mum reread twenty years' worth of her own journals, highlighted every passage relating to Sarah and read them all onto tape for me.

Dad revisited years' worth of notebooks and put together fifty pages of notes that related to family history and to Sarah in particular.

Joan, Aunt Jean, Peter, Mark, Troy, Aunt Georgi and Jeanie shared their memories.

Jeanie and Ben allowed me to tell their mother's story and thus, by extension, parts of their own.

It is hard, I think, for a family when one member decides to write about family history. I have told Sarah's story as it seemed to me, but the result is very different, I'm sure, from the way anyone else in my family would tell her story. I appreciate the understanding that I have received about the subjective nature of this project.

While I was working on revisions, a friend from high school, Nancy Horsman, e-mailed me to say that she had been vacationing on Isla Mujeres in Mexico and talking with her travelling companion about the missing women. A man at the next table overheard the conversation. That man, photojournalist Daniel Gautreau, had known Sarah in 1986, he told my friend, when he was working on a photo essay about street kids in Vancouver. Daniel interviewed Sarah on October 2, 1986, and seventeen years later, two days before my final revision was due, he shared with me the tape of that interview and some of Sarah's poems, along with his own memories.

Diane Ngui-Yen encouraged me to write a book and then supported me as I got going.

In addition to cooking me dinners while I worked on revisions in Victoria, Sarah Harvey introduced me to Kathryn Mulders at just the right moment.

Kathryn Mulders, agent for Transatlantic Literary Agency, took me on, showed me how to write a book proposal and then found the best possible publisher for my sister's story, Penguin Canada.

Cynthia Good, my editor, believed in the book on the basis of one chapter and an outline and then let it evolve, gave expert feedback and managed to suggest cuts and changes in this sensitive material without devastating me.

Everyone at Penguin—Joe Zingrone, senior production editor; Susan Folkins, senior editor; Allyson Latta, copy editor; Sarah Weber, proofreader; Debby de Groot, publicity manager; Martin Gould, dust jacket designer; Martin Litkowski, who shares a birthday with my sister, and many others—approached this project and me with support, care and attention to detail.

Ryder Gilliland of Blake, Cassels & Graydon lent his time and invaluable legal expertise to the book. His efforts are much appreciated.

Lindsay Kines of *The Vancouver Sun* wrote about the missing women before anyone else did and continued to write about them, always with sensitivity and integrity, when everyone else had stopped.

In addition to working hard to find out what happened to my sister, Lori Shenher has been a great support to me over the years.

Bob Tyrrell, my boss at Orca Book Publishers, gave me time off at critical points during the writing and was supportive throughout the process. My co-workers, Maureen and Christine, helped me through two of the toughest days, February 7 and 8, 2002.

Alice Pennefather, my cousin, took the cover photograph along with other photos of important sites in Sarah's life.

Clea Parfitt and John Masters gave me the run of their house when they were away, so that I could write in solitude.

Andrea and David Spalding invited me to write in the tiny cabin on their Pender Island property and wined and dined me while I was there.

Sharon Jinkerson created a circle of care around me on a day when I could hardly bear to go on.

Ria Orr and Laurel Johannsen shared memories and photographs, and Bo Myers revisited with me an important day in 1983.

John Lowman, criminologist and PACE board member, shared his knowledge and read and gave feedback on the chapter about sex work.

Patrice Keats, Marv Westwood, Clea, Kathryn, Tanis and seven others helped me find a way to say goodbye through enactment.

To everyone named above and to all who helped in the process of creating this book, my heartfelt thanks. Whatever weaknesses or errors that remain within these pages are, of course, my responsibility alone.

And, thank you, Roland, for reading and commenting when asked, transcribing hours of tapes, holding me when I cried, and, most of all, for standing by me as I find my path.

I HAD PLANNED TO INCLUDE THE STORIES of other missing women in this book and so I interviewed their family members, whom I have come to know over the years. Lynn and Rick Frey, Sandra Gagnon, Val Hughes, Erin McGrath, Patricia Young and others gave me their time and trusted me with memories of their sisters and daughters. As the book took shape, I was able to tell Sarah's story so fully that I was not able to do justice to those of the other women. In the end, only one paragraph remains of Marnie's, Janet's and Kerry's stories, and Leigh's and Frances's do not appear at all. It was painful to shorten or cut the pieces that I had written about each of those women, but this book didn't turn out to be the right place to tell about their lives at greater length.

I hope that in the years to come all their stories will be told.